汉语言专业本科系列教材

编写委员会

主　编　郭　鹏
副主编　崔　健　许　皓　赵　菁
编　委　（按姓氏音序排列）
　　　　崔　健　郭　鹏　金海月　刘谦功　刘苏乔　沈庶英　舒　燕
　　　　王　锐　魏新红　许　皓　张亚茹　赵　菁　赵　雷　朱　彤
汉语言技能与知识序列执行主编　　赵　菁

编辑委员会

主　任　张　健
副主任　王亚莉　陈维昌
各序列负责人（按姓氏音序排列）
　　　　陈维昌　付彦白　刘艳芬　王　轩　王亚莉

"十二五"国家重点出版物出版规划项目

汉语言专业本科系列教材·综合类

BASIC CHINESE: COMPREHENSIVE COURSE (Ⅰ)
基础汉语综合教程

上

本册主编：全　军
编　者：全　军　徐京梅　柯润兰　李靖华
翻　译：何　洁

ERYA CHINESE　尔雅中文

北京语言大学出版社
BEIJING LANGUAGE AND CULTURE
UNIVERSITY PRESS

图书在版编目(CIP)数据

基础汉语综合教程.上/全军主编.—北京：
北京语言大学出版社，2013.8（2019.8 重印）
（尔雅中文）
ISBN 978-7-5619-3617-7

Ⅰ.①基… Ⅱ.①全… Ⅲ.①汉语－对外汉语教学－教材 Ⅳ.①H195.4

中国版本图书馆 CIP 数据核字（2013）第 188150 号

"十二五"国家重点出版物出版规划项目

书　　名：	尔雅中文　基础汉语综合教程（上）
	ERYA ZHONGWEN JICHU HANYU ZONGHE JIAOCHENG (SHANG)
责任印制：	周　燚
出版发行：	北京语言大学出版社
社　　址：	北京市海淀区学院路 15 号　　邮政编码：100083
网　　址：	www.blcup.com
电　　话：	发行部　010-82303650/3591/3648
	编辑部　010-82303647/3592/3395
	读者服务部　010-82303653/3908
	网上订购　010-82303668　service@blcup.com
印　　刷：	北京虎彩文化传播有限公司
经　　销：	全国新华书店
版　　次：	2013 年 8 月第 1 版　　2019 年 8 月第 2 次印刷
开　　本：	889 毫米×1194 毫米　　1/16
印　　张：	课本 16.75　练习活页 6.75
字　　数：	446 千字
书　　号：	ISBN 978-7-5619-3617-7 / H·13201
定　　价：	79.00 元

凡有印装质量问题，本社负责调换。电话：010-82303590

总　序

《尔雅中文——汉语言专业本科系列教材》（以下简称《尔雅中文》）是面向以汉语作为第二语言的学习者的汉语言专业本科学历教育教材，是继上世纪90年代至本世纪初出版的《对外汉语本科系列教材》之后推出的新一代大型系列教材。

近年来，国际职场对复合型汉语人才的需求猛增，对专业建设、教学改革、课程建设以及教材编写都提出了新的要求。我们顺应这一发展趋势，将汉语言专业的人才培养目标由以往单纯强调语言技能的"汉语专门型人才"调整为目前的具备"语言＋专业"复合能力的"汉语通用型人才"，在汉语言专业陆续增设一些新的方向，凸显出汉语言专业课程体系的时代特色。但是，我们充分认识到，对于汉语言专业的学生而言，核心问题仍是如何更有利于自身语言能力的提高，特别是语言交际能力、认知能力、跨文化交流能力等综合性、复合型能力的提升。因此，虽在语言技能、语言知识课程外增设了较为系统的历史文化、国情社会、经济商务等方向课程，但是，这些课程不是仅用来灌输知识的，而是为更好地扩展语言能力而服务，以语言能力培养为核心的理念并未改变。

《尔雅中文》教材体系与专业课程体系紧密相连，包含了横向和纵向两个序列：横向上，在不断完善语言技能、语言知识、文化系列教材的基础上，增设了较为系统的商务、翻译、教学等专业方向的专业语言技能和专业知识教材；纵向上，建立起更为缜密的综合课与听、说、读、写、译各分技能课的一至四年级的梯度等级，平衡了一般技能课跟各序列的专业技能课、知识课的比例。横向与纵向协调发展，形成了汉语言专业本科大型教材的网状系统，最大程度地体现出专业教学的系统性、关联性、层级性和针对性，也为以汉语言专业为依托、面向汉语作为第二语言学习者的本科专业群的建设奠定了坚实的基础。《尔雅中文》教材相对应的课程序列与梯度等级如图所示：

课程序列与梯度等级示意图

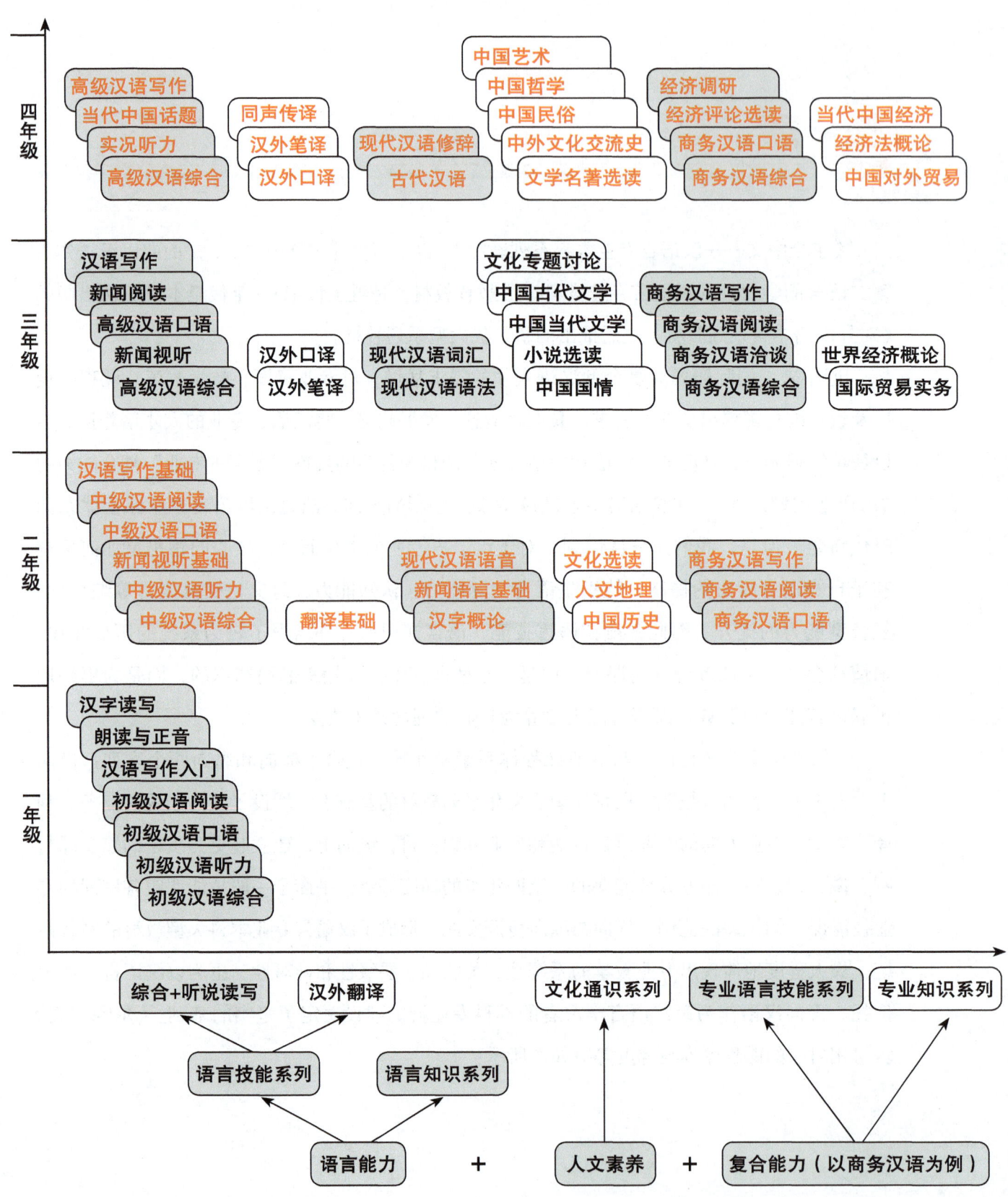

《尔雅中文》系列教材在继承上一代《对外汉语本科系列教材》长处的同时，更加贴近现实社会需要和学习者的需求，也融入了近些年汉语言专业课程建设与教学改革的多方面成果，从而呈现出崭新的面貌，形成了自己的特点。概括起来有以下四点：

一、总体设计更具系统性和前瞻性，最大程度地反映出专业人才培养的新目标

语言技能、语言知识、文化知识、专业语言技能、专业知识五大板块既相互关联，又各自独立。语言技能课程贯穿始终，凸显以养成语言能力为主的专业发展理念；文化知识序列不断丰富，体现出对汉语国际教育本质的全面认识，自觉地将提升人文素质、培养全面发展的人作为汉语言专业本科教育的最终目标。专业技能和知识课程在中高级阶段逐步增加，循序渐进，实现由初级的"语言技能＋语言知识"基础能力向中高级的"语言＋专业"综合能力的自然过渡。同时，各专业方向的教材都具有自身特色，自成体系，体现了统一中的多样性，也体现了专业人才培养模式向厚基础、宽口径、复合型的转变。

二、语言技能序列的设计更具延展性，结构更加合理

作为面向汉语作为第二语言学习者的汉语言专业本科系列教材，由汉语综合技能与以"听、说、读、写"分立形成的各分技能训练无疑是其主干部分。这套教材的设计与编写，不仅填补了中高级阶段"听、说、读、写"分技能教材的诸多空白，而且增强"译"这一重要的技能，形成了"听、说、读、写、译"各自独立并相互关联的完整的分技能序列。与此同时，初、中、高各教学阶段逐层递进，且横向延伸，使得语言技能教材序列更加协调和完整。由于汉语综合课以及听、说、读、写、译各技能课都自成体系，具备面向初、中、高三个阶段、四个年级的多层级和覆盖面广的特点，因此，教材的使用范围、对象就不限于本科学历教育，而是对各种层次和需求的中文学习者都具有不同程度的适用性，可以各取所需。

三、强化以学习者为中心的教材编写意识，跨文化视角更加突出

编写者大都为多年从事汉语作为第二语言教学工作的资深教师，基本上都具有海外汉语教学的经历，对不同课型的教学原则和实践策略有着较为深入的了解和体会，对大量的同类汉语教材的编写理念以及教学法、跨文化交际理论等做过前期研究。从教师规划学习内容、层级、知识点，到编排教材中的练习及设计课堂活动，尽量从学生学习的视角和跨文化的视角去安排、镕裁，换言之，更加重视教材编排跟教学过程、习得过程与效果的关联程度，使语言及文化、商务的教材内容丰富而生动，以提高学生主动学习的兴趣以及课堂活动的参与度。

四、通过调查统计、大纲设计和试用试验等环节，使教材编写有章可循，科学实用

新一代汉语言专业本科系列教材的编写工作启动于2007年，首先对原有教材、国内外市场同类教材的使用情况进行调研。编写者均为相应课型的任课教师，且大多参与过上一代教材的编写工作，对任务轻重和努力方向都有较深的体会。同时，组织资深的教学研究专家以及语言、文化、商务、翻译等领域专家，与教材编写小组共同研讨，确立各部教材的基调，审阅推敲文稿，斟酌取舍。教材编写过程较长，各位作者付出了大量心血，已编成的教材提交出版前大多试用过几个学期，对象涉及来自世界上80多个国家和地区的上千名留学生，每学期试用后，教师都会汇总情况，分析研究，做出适当的修订、更新。

大纲是教材编写的重要前提，并贯彻于整个编写过程。教材与大纲处于动态关系之中，大纲统摄教材，但并非一成不变，教材编写促使大纲趋于完善。本系列教材主要参照《高等学校外国留学生汉语言专业教学大纲》（2002）和《新汉语水平考试大纲（1-6级）》（2009、2010），同时参酌各类语言大纲、框架、标准、词表、调查报告等研究成果，其中的各个序列、各部教材都按照自身性质与类型，研制了便于操作的词汇、语法、功能及话题大纲，既自成一体，又相互照应。对此，各部教材都有自己的编写前言，会做更详细的说明。大纲编订与教材编写相辅相成，教材一面世，大纲也随即推出，如商务汉语方向的教材编写者同时研制出版了《经贸汉语本科教学词汇大纲》（2012），文化大纲的编订也与教材编写协调配合，这些使得教材编写的科学性和内在系统性得以保障。

根据不同的课程性质和专业方向，《尔雅中文》系列教材划分为四大序列：汉语言技能与知识；汉外翻译；文化通识；商务汉语。翻译往往被视为一种语言技能，原本可归入语言技能与知识序列，但鉴于翻译能力是一种复合能力，翻译类课程及教材在一至四年级自成一统，翻译综合课、口译课、笔译课等体系完备，且涉及多个国别，所以这里单列出来。

北京语言大学面向留学生开办汉语言专业的本科学历教育，始于上世纪70年代末，其成长过程历史地见证了中国改革开放以来汉语国际教育的发展。历经几代人的辛勤努力，2008年9月，汉语言专业被批准为国家级高等学校特色专业；2010年7月，汉语言专业教学团队被评为国家级教学团队。这套教材的大部分编著者均出自这一专业团队。汉语言专业的每一步改革与创新，都离不开北语几代对外汉语教育工作者的关心与鼓励，离不开学校领导及海内外专家的大力支持。这里要特别感谢北京语言大学出版社董事长戚德祥、总编辑张健和各位责任编辑，这套教材历经数年终于得以问世，跟他们的严谨态度、耐心督促和细致工作密不可分，而教材得以入选新闻出版总署"十二五"国家重点出版物出版规划项目，正是教材编写规划团队与编辑出版团队精诚合作的结果。

系列教材取名"尔雅"，众所周知，《尔雅》是中国古代汇集分类专门词语以供人学习的经典，这里取其字面义，"尔"通"迩"，"尔雅"指趋于雅正、得体。语言学习不可一蹴而就，而是一个不断接近目标语和目标文化的累积过程，或许正因如此，英人威妥玛（Thomas Francis Wade）将其所编的汉语口语和书面语教材命名为《语言自迩集》和《文件自迩集》。我们编写新一代汉语言专业本科系列教材，同样是希望学生通过系统的学习，逐渐接近目标语言与文化，获得较强的跨文化交流能力，最终不仅要达到较高的汉语水平，而且要更加深入地了解中国社会政治经济和历史文化。

是为总序。

郭　鹏

于北京语言大学

编写说明

一、适用范围

本教材为零起点教材，具体的适用对象为：准备学习汉语言专业本科但无 HSK 三级证书者，短期汉语进修（半年到一年）者，海外专修及选修汉语的学习者。本教材为基础汉语综合教材，分上下册，共 32 课，另配有练习活页以及相关教学资源。

二、总体结构

本教材从第 1 课到第 8 课为语音阶段，旨在使学生掌握汉语语音的基础知识。第 9 课以后为语法阶段，每 4 课配有一个复习，供教师对学生进行平时成绩考查或学生自评使用。本教材总体结构编排如下：

语音阶段（第 1～8 课），该阶段的特点是即讲即练，呈现语音新内容之后，立即进行相关练习。编者结合每课的语音新内容设计了短小的对话，在训练学生语音的同时，满足学生开口说话的要求。

语法阶段（第 9～32 课），其中第 9～16 课是语音巩固阶段，承上启下，仍配有多种语音练习，进行语音重点巩固训练，同时开始进入语法阶段的学习。第 9～32 课所设板块为：学习提示、课文、生词、注释、语法、情景交际、写作、语音、汉字、实践活动、文化点滴、学习后记。汉字知识切分成若干单元，贯穿全书（上下册）。从第 17 课开始，增加了由对话内容改写的叙述性文字，目的是为了进一步培养学生的语篇意识，增强其篇章理解和表达能力。语法阶段每 4 课有一个单元总结，为该单元内的注释和语法汇总。

三、编写原则

在教学内容的编写上本着"循序渐进，螺旋式提高，加强重现"的原则，由浅入深，由实到虚，以旧带新，不断重现，反复强化，加强记忆。以新 HSK 二级语法点为主线，以功能和场景为辅线来设计全书。严格遵循第二语言教材编写的通用性原则：针对性、实用性、系统性和趣味性。教材选取了反映社会时代特点和贴近学生生活的真实语言材料；课文场景的选取从解决学生基本生存需要入手，逐步扩大到校园内外的交际生活；课文语言选取日常生活中常用的规范口语，便于学生即学即用；语法安排上由实到虚，由易到难；语料的编排上符合青年的认知心理特点，富有启发和益智作用。注重幽默感的引入、文化内容的适度穿插和练习形式的图文并茂。

四、特色

1. 与从声韵母入手处理语音阶段的传统思路不同，本教材遵循汉语语音的最大特点，从声调入手，以声调带动声韵母和语音知识学习，即讲即练，在训练中强调音义结合，帮助学生建立声调意识。强调听说，强化训练口耳功能。考虑到初级阶段语音的重要性，本书除重点词、练习、注释、语法、情景交际、写作、实践活动之外的其他汉字下方均标注拼音。语音练习以不同方式贯穿全书。

2. 汉字学习分为三个阶段。第1课到第4课为第一阶段，不讲汉字知识，不要求学生书写汉字，只要求学生大致认读课文中的汉字。第5课到第8课为第二阶段，开始涉及汉字知识，要求学生按照所学知识书写简单汉字，课文中的汉字仍然只要求认读，不要求书写。第9课到第32课为第三阶段，汉字知识在该阶段贯穿始终，要求学生书写、记忆课文中出现的全部汉字。

3. 语法点严格按照新HSK二级大纲选取，每课语法点数量适中，难易穿插，层次分明。本书词汇85%以上为新HSK二级大纲词汇。

4. 课文语言极其贴近实际生活，使用频率高，时效性强。话轮衔接自然紧密，便于学生记忆和使用。强调在课文中穿插幽默语句，点滴渗透文化知识。

5. 练习体现先易后难、先短后长、先框架后活用的原则，在练习中注重学生语言生成能力的训练，注重设计交际性、实用性、可操作性强的题型。

五、教学安排及建议

本教材可在两到三个月内完成学习，之后过渡到《初级汉语综合教程》。教学安排建议如下：

1. 第1～16课，每课2-4课时。
2. 第17～32课，每课4课时。
3. 六次单元复习，每次可用2课时完成。

具体安排也可由教师根据教学进度灵活把握。

六、鸣谢

本教材为北京语言大学汉语学院本科系列教材项目的一部分。感谢汉语学院院长郭鹏教授，感谢赵菁老师、沈庶英老师，他们为本书的策划和组织付出了很多辛苦和努力，使得教材编写工作得以顺利进行。同时也感谢陈田顺老师、倪明亮老师对本书的编写工作所给予的全面关注和大力支持。在此还要特别感谢崔永华先生对全书的修改提出了诸多宝贵意见，使得本教材得到了非常大的突破。

最后，要感谢北京语言大学出版社总编辑张健女士对本书的出版所给予的有力支持。

在编写本教材的过程中，尽管我们付出了很多的努力，但仍难免存在不足和疏漏。我们期待各位教材使用者和同行提出批评、建议，我们将视之为最大的鞭策和支持，并将针对您的意见深入思考和总结，以期对本教材进行不断的修改和完善。

编 者

2013年3月

A Guide to the Use of This Series

1. Scope of Application

This series is designed for total beginners. It is specifically targeted at the following people: those who plan to pursue an undergraduate program of Chinese but without the certificate of HSK Level 3; short-term (i.e., 0.5 ~ 1 year) Chinese program takers; and learners taking Chinese as a selective or major course in countries other than China. Being the elementary Chinese comprehensive teaching material, this series consists of altogether 32 lessons in two volumes, with the loose-leaf worksheets and pertinent teaching resources in addition.

2. Overall Structure

Lesson 1 ~ Lesson 8 of this book aim at equipping students with the basics of Chinese phonetics. Starting from Lesson 9, it teaches grammar, with every four lessons followed by a review for teachers to evaluate students' progress or for students to make self-evaluations. Its overall structure is as follows:

The Stage of Pronunciation (Lesson 1 ~ Lesson 8)

The characteristic of this part is that the instructions are immediately followed by exercises, i.e., the pertinent exercises are carried out right after the presentation of phonetic knowledge. Combined with the phonetic knowledge presented in each lesson, short conversations are designed to meet students' needs to make oral communication while practicing their pronunciation.

The Stage of Grammar (Lesson 9 ~ Lesson 32)

Lesson 9 ~ Lesson 16 are at this stage designed to consolidate the phonetic knowledge students have learned. It follows the preceding part and is supplemented by a great variety of pronunciation drills to help students consolidate their learning at the stage of pronunciation and move on to that of grammar. Lesson 9 ~ Lesson 32 includes such units as the Learning Tips, Text, New Words, Note(s), Grammar, Communication, Writing, Pronunciation, Characters, Activity, Cultural Note, Summary, etc. Knowledge about Chinese characters is presented in several units of the books (Book 1 & Book 2). Starting from Lesson 17, narrations based on conversations are included to further develop students' discourse awareness and improve their discourse comprehension and expression skills. At this stage, every four lessons are followed by a unit review, in which the grammar notes and grammar rules of the units are summarized.

3. Compilation Ideas

In terms of its compilation ideas, this series follows the principle of being spirally progressive, with what is taught in it reappearing many times. Mainly based on the grammar points of the new HSK Level 2 and also on language functions and scenes of conversation in its design, this series strictly observes the general principles in the compilation of second language textbooks: pertinence, practicability, systematicness and interestingness. Authentic language data are selected to reflect the contemporary social characteristics and students' lives, with the scenes in it firstly selected to meet students' basic daily needs, and then gradually move on to daily communication inside and outside campus. The language materials of the texts are selected from frequently-used standard spoken Chinese in daily life, which facilitate students' learning and use. Grammar is arranged from real to virtual and from easy to difficult. The arrangement of language materials conforms to cognitive and psychological characteristics of young people, thus is inspiring and has educational functions. Importance is attached to using humorous language, with cultural tips and well-designed illustrations for the exercises provided.

4. Features

(1) In contrast to the traditional approach of teaching pronunciation starting from initials and finals, this textbook abides by the Chinese phonetic characteristics and teaches tones before initials, finals and knowledge about phonetics. Instructions are immediately followed by exercises, in which the combination of pronunciation and meaning is stressed to help students establish their sensitivity of tones. Listening and speaking skills are emphasized. The importance of phonetics at the elementary stage being considered, *pinyin* is provided under all the Chinese characters except the Key Words, Exercises, Note(s), Grammar, Communication, Writing and Activity. Pronunciation drills of various forms are supplied throughout the book.

(2) The learning of Chinese characters is divided into three stages. Lesson 1 ~ Lesson 4 are at the first stage. Neither are students taught the knowledge about Chinese characters, nor are they required to write characters. They are just required to have a general recognition of the characters in the texts. Lesson 5 ~ Lesson 8 are at the second stage. Students are taught the knowledge about Chinese characters and required to write simple characters. They are still just required to have a general recognition of the characters in the texts rather than writing them. Lesson 9 ~ Lesson 32 are at the third stage. Students are taught Chinese characters and required to write and memorize all the Chinese characters in the texts.

(3) The grammar points are selected strictly in accordance with the syllabus of the new HSK Level 2. The number of grammar points is well-proportioned, with the difficult ones combining with the easy ones in each lesson. More than 85% of new words in this series of books are of the new HSK Level 2.

(4) The language in the texts is quite practical, frequently-used and close to real life. One conversation is naturally connected to another, which facilitates students' memorization and use. Humorous language is used and cultural notes are provided.

(5) The exercises are designed by following the principles of "presenting the easy ones before the difficult ones, the short ones before the long ones, and the framed ones before the ones that students could do in creative ways". Importance is attached to developing students' language output and designing communicative, practical and easy exercises.

5. Teaching Arrangements and Suggestions

This set of teaching materials is suggested to be taught in 2 ~ 3 months and followed by *Elementary Chinese: Comprehensive Course*. The teaching arrangements are as follows:

(1) Lesson 1 ~ Lesson 16 are suggested to be taught with 2 ~ 4 class hours per lesson;

(2) Lesson 17 ~ Lesson 32 are suggested to be taught with 4 class hours per lesson;

(3) Each of the six unit reviews is suggested to be taught in two class hours.

Teachers can also make their own teaching schedules based on the specific needs of teaching.

6. Acknowledgements

This is one of the teaching materials for undergraduates developed by College of Chinese Studies of Beijing Language and Culture University. We'd like to extend our gratitude to the following people: Prof. Guo Peng, Dean of the College of Chinese Studies, Prof. Zhao Jing and Prof. Shen Shuying, for their hard work and efforts to plan and organize the compilation of the series. Our thanks also go to Prof. Chen Tianshun and Ni Mingliang for their concern and support. Our special thanks go to Prof. Cui Yonghua for his revisions, without which, it would be impossible for the series to make a breakthrough.

Last but not least, we appreciate Ms. Zhang Jian, the Editor-in-Chief of Beijing Language and Culture University Press, for her support for the publication of the series.

Although we made great efforts in the compilation process, the series is still not perfect. We will cooperate with the learners and teachers using it, heed their suggestions and advice with an open mind and make constant efforts for its further improvement.

The authors
March, 2013

人物介绍
Introduction to the Main Characters

山口爱子
Shānkǒu Àizǐ

女，19岁，日本留学生，在北京语言大学学习汉语，性格内向，喜欢听音乐。

She is an introverted 18-year-old girl from Japan who takes a Chinese program at Beijing Language and Culture University and likes listening to music.

金大成
Jīn Dàchéng

男，18岁，韩国留学生，在北京语言大学学习汉语，喜欢踢足球、看篮球比赛，喜欢姚明，会一点儿太极拳。

He is a 19-year-old boy from the Republic of Korea who takes a Chinese program at Beijing Language and Culture University and has hobbies including playing football, watching basketball games and practicing *taiji*. He is a fan of Yao Ming.

金在元
Jīn Zàiyuán

男，20岁，韩国留学生，在北京语言大学学习汉语，是金大成的朋友。

He is a 20-year-old boy from the Republic of Korea who takes a Chinese program at Beijing Language and Culture University and is Jin Daesung's friend.

杰克
Jiékè

男，18岁，美国留学生，在北京语言大学学习汉语，喜欢旅游、打篮球，想学太极拳。性格外向，住校外。他有一个弟弟，也要来中国留学。

He is an outgoing 18-year-old boy from the United States who takes a Chinese program at Beijing Language and Culture University and lives off-campus. He has hobbies including travelling, playing basketball and is interested in learning *taiji*. He has a younger brother who also wants to study in China.

安娜
Ānnà

女，18岁，俄罗斯留学生，在北京语言大学学习汉语，性格外向。

She is an outgoing 18-year-old girl from Russia who takes a Chinese program at Beijing Language and Culture University.

伊凡
Yīfán

男，俄罗斯人，安娜的朋友，现在在俄罗斯。
He is a Russian and now lives in Russia. He is Anna's friend.

丽莎
Lìshā

女，俄罗斯人，安娜的妹妹，现在在俄罗斯。
She is a Russian girl. She is Anna's younger sister and now lives in Russia.

李明
Lǐ Míng

男，19岁，中国学生，在北京语言大学学习。是杰克、爱子、金大成的中国朋友。
He is a 19-year-old Chinese student of Beijing Language and Culture University. He is Jack, Aiko and Jin Daesung's friend.

张小英
Zhāng Xiǎoyīng

女，18岁，中国学生，在北京语言大学学习。
She is an 18-year-old Chinese student of Beijing Language and Culture University.

王一中 老师
Wáng Yīzhōng lǎoshī

男，50岁左右，教师，在北京语言大学工作，教汉语综合课，是杰克、爱子、金大成的老师。
He is a teacher aged around 50. He teaches Comprehensive Chinese at Beijing Language and Culture University to Jack, Aiko, Jin Daesung and other students.

语法术语缩略形式对照表
Abbreviations for Grammar Terms

Abbreviation	Grammar Term in English	Grammar Term in Chinese	Grammar Term in *Pinyin*
A	Adjective	形容词	xíngróngcí
Adv	Adverb	副词	fùcí
AP	Adjective Phrase	形容词短语	xíngróngcí duǎnyǔ
Conj	Conjunction	连词	liáncí
Int	Interjection	叹词	tàncí
M	Measure Word	量词	liàngcí
MdPt	Modal Particle	语气助词	yǔqì zhùcí
N	Noun	名词	míngcí
NP	Noun Phrase	名词短语	míngcí duǎnyǔ
Num	Numeral	数词	shùcí
O	Object	宾语	bīnyǔ
OpV	Optative Verb	能愿动词	néngyuàn dòngcí
P	Predicate	谓语	wèiyǔ
Ph	Phrase	短语	duǎnyǔ
PN	Proper Noun	专有名词	zhuānyǒu míngcí
Pr	Pronoun	代词	dàicí
Pref	Prefix	前缀	qiánzhuì
Prep	Preposition	介词	jiècí
Pt	Particle	助词	zhùcí
S	Subject	主语	zhǔyǔ
StPt	Structural Particle	结构助词	jiégòu zhùcí
Suf	Suffix	后缀	hòuzhuì
V	Verb	动词	dòngcí
VO	Seperable Verb Verb plus Object	离合动词 动宾式动词	líhé dòngcí dòngbīnshì dòngcí
VP	Verb Phrase	动词短语	dòngcí duǎnyǔ

目 录 Contents

第 1 课　你好 1
Hello

语音　Pronunciation　1. 声母、韵母和声调　Initials, finals and tones
　　　　　　　　　　　　声母：b p m f
　　　　　　　　　　　　　　　d t n l
　　　　　　　　　　　　　　　g k h
　　　　　　　　　　　　韵母：a ai ao an ang
　　　　　　　　　　　　　　　i ia iao ian iang
　　　　　　　　　　　　　　　u ua uai uan uang
　　　　　　　　　　　　　　　in ing uo ou
　　　　　　　　　　　　声调：一声 ˉ (First tone)　二声 ˊ (Second tone)
　　　　　　　　　　　　　　　三声 ˇ (Third tone)　四声 ˋ (Fourth tone)
　　　　　　　　　　　2. 三声变调　Third tone sandhi

第 2 课　早上好 16
Good Morning

语音　Pronunciation　1. 声母和韵母　Initials and finals
　　　　　　　　　　　　声母：zh ch sh r
　　　　　　　　　　　　　　　z c s
　　　　　　　　　　　　韵母：e en eng
　　　　　　　　　　　2. 轻声 ˚ (Neutral tone)

第 3 课　打电话 28
Making a Phone Call

语音　Pronunciation　1. 韵母　Finals
　　　　　　　　　　　　o ong ie iou iong ei uei uen ueng
　　　　　　　　　　　2. 拼音拼写规则（1）　Spelling rules of *pingyin* (1)

第 4 课　对不起 37
I'm Sorry

语音	Pronunciation	1. 声母和韵母　Initials and finals
		声母：j q x
		韵母：ü üe üan ün
		2. 拼音拼写规则（2）　Spelling rules of *pinyin* (2)

第 5 课　汉语不难 47
Chinese Is Not Difficult

语音	Pronunciation	1. 拼音拼写规则（3）　Spelling rules of *pinyin* (3)
		2. 声调符号的标注　Place the tonal marks
汉字	Characters	汉字的种类　The categories of Chinese characters

第 6 课　快点儿 57
Hurry up

语音	Pronunciation	1. 特殊韵母 er　The special final er
		2. 隔音符号　Syllable-dividing mark
汉字	Characters	1. 汉字的基本笔画　Basic strokes of Chinese characters
		2. 笔画之间的位置关系　The positions of strokes

第 7 课　你叫什么名字 69
What Is Your Name

语音	Pronunciation	1. 韵母 i 的不同读音　Different pronunciations of the final i
		2. 注意三声的发音　Pay attention to the pronunciations of the third tone

第 8 课　你的电话是多少 ……………………………………………………………… 79
What Is Your Telephone Number

语音	Pronunciation	1. 注意区别几组声母的发音
		Distinguish the pronunciations of several pairs of initials
		2. 注意几组韵母中相同部分的发音
		Pay attention to the pronunciations of the identical part of the finals in several groups
		3. 声母的实际发音及其字母名称
		The actual pronunciation of initials and their names
汉字	Characters	汉字的复杂笔画（1）　Complex strokes of Chinese characters (1)

第 9 课　你是留学生吗 ……………………………………………………………… 94
Are You an International Student

功能	Function	打招呼、问候、询问身份　Exchanging greetings and asking sb.'s identity
注释	Note	副词"也"　The adverb "也"
语法	Grammar	1. "是"字句（表示判断）　A sentence with "是" (to indicate making a judgement)
		2. 用"吗"的是非疑问句　A yes-or-no question using "吗"
		3. 汉语的语序及主要句子成分：主语、谓语、宾语
		Word order and the main sentence elements in Chinese: subject, predicate and object
语音	Pronunciation	1. "不"的变调　Tone sandhi of "不"
		2. 重点训练（b-p-f / d-t / ai-ei / an-en / 轻声）
		Focus of drills (b-p-f, d-t, ai-ei, an-en and the neutral tone)
汉字	Characters	汉字的复杂笔画（2）　Complex strokes of Chinese characters (2)
文化点滴	Cultural Note	甲骨文　Oracle Inscriptions

第 10 课　你是哪国人 ……………………………………………………………… 108
Which Country Are You from

功能	Function	询问姓名、国籍　Asking one's name and nationality
注释	Notes	1. 后缀"们"　The suffix "们"
		2. 副词"都"　The adverb "都"
		3. 动词"叫"　The verb "叫"
语法	Grammar	1. 动词谓语句　A sentence with a verbal predicate

III

		2. 形容词谓语句　A sentence with an adjectival predicate
		3. 疑问代词"哪"　The interrogative pronoun "哪"
		4. 疑问代词"什么"　The interrogative pronoun "什么"
语音	Pronunciation	重点训练（g-k-h / ua-uo / uai-ui / 儿化）
		Focus of drills (g-k-h, ua-uo, uai-ui and the retroflex ending)
汉字	Characters	汉字的笔顺　Stroke order of Chineses characters
文化点滴	Cultural Note	百家姓　The Book of Family Names

第 11 课　你住哪儿 127
Where Do You Live

功能	Function	询问住址、电话　Asking one's address and telephone number
注释	Note	"……号码是多少？"　"What's the number of...?"
语法	Grammar	1. 数字的读法（1）　How numbers are read (1)
		2. 疑问代词"哪儿"　The interrogative pronoun "哪儿"
		3. 疑问代词"几"　The interrogative pronoun "几"
		4. 结构助词"的"　The structural particle "的"
语音	Pronunciation	1. "一"的变调　Tone sandhi of "一"
		2. 重点训练（l-n / l-r / i-ü / uo-e-ou）　Focus of drills (l-n, l-r, i-ü and uo-e-ou)
文化点滴	Cultural Note	中国人常用的数字手势　Chinese People's Frequently-Used Gestures for Numbers

第 12 课　银行在哪儿 143
Where Is the Bank

功能	Function	询问处所　Asking the location
注释	Notes	1. "请问，……？"　"Excuse me, ...?"
		2. 副词"就"（表示强调）　The adverb "就" (to indicate emphasis)
语法	Grammar	1. 方位词"里"和"外"　The nouns of locality "里" and "外"
		2. 语气助词"吧"　The modal particle "吧"
语音	Pronunciation	1. 重点训练（zh-ch / sh-r / an-ang / en-eng / ang-eng）
		Focus of drills (zh-ch, sh-r, an-ang, en-eng and ang-eng)
		2. 双音节中的三声读音练习　Practice the third tone of the disyllables
汉字	Characters	1. 汉字的部件（1）　Components of Chinese characters (1)
		2. 汉字的结构（1）　Structures of Chinese characters (1)
文化点滴	Cultural Note	中国的银行　Banks in China

注释、语法：单元总结（一）（第9课～第12课） 158
Notes and Grammar: Unit Review 1 (Lesson 9 ~ Lesson 12)

第 13 课　明天你有课吗 159
Will You Have Classes Tomorrow

功能	Function	询问时间　Asking the time
注释	Notes	1. 用"呢"的省略式问句　An elliptical interrogative sentence using "呢"
		2. 用"……，好吗？"征求意见　Use "……，好吗？" to ask for sb.'s opinion
语法	Grammar	1. "有"字句（表示领有、具有）
		A sentence with "有" (to indicate "have" or "possess")
		2. 钟点表示法　Expressing the time
		3. 时间名词做状语　A noun of time used as an adverbial
		4. 汉语的主要句子成分：状语
		A main sentence element in Chinese: adverbial
语音	Pronunciation	重点训练（z-c-s / uan-uang / uan-uen）
		Focus of drills (z-c-s, uan-uang and uan-uen)
汉字	Characters	1. 汉字的部件（2）　Components of Chinese characters (2)
		2. 汉字的结构（2）　Structures of Chinese characters (2)
文化点滴	Cultural Note	汉语热　Chinese Fever

第 14 课　周末你做什么 175
What Do You Do on Weekends

功能	Function	表达日期（1）　Expressing the date (1)
		描述活动　Describing an activity
注释	Note	星期的表达方式　Expressing days of a week
语法	Grammar	1. 名词谓语句　A sentence with a nominal predicate
		2. 连动句（表示目的）　A sentence with serial verbal phrases (to indicate a purpose)
语音	Pronunciation	重点训练（sh-x-s / ch-q-c / in-ing / ian-iang）
		Focus of drills (sh-x-s, ch-q-c, in-ing and ian-iang)
汉字	Characters	汉字的结构（3）　Structures of Chinese characters (3)
文化点滴	Cultural Note	北京的名胜古迹　Scenic Spots and Historic Sites in Beijing

v

第 15 课　你的生日是几月几号 190
When Is Your Birthday

功能	Function	表达日期（2） Expressing the date (2)
注释	Note	"多大" "How old...?"
语法	Grammar	1. 年、月、日的表示方法 Expressions of "年" (meaning "year"), "月" (meaning "month") and "日" (meaning "date") 2. 数字的读法（2） How numbers are read (2) 3. 汉语的主要句子成分：定语　A main sentence element in Chinese: attribute
语音	Pronunciation	重点训练（j-zh / j-q / ian-üan / in-ün / ie-üe） Focus of drills (j-zh, j-q, ian-üan, in-ün and ie-üe)
汉字	Characters	1. 汉字的部件（3） Components of Chinese characters (3) 2. 汉字的结构（4） Structures of Chinese characters (4)
文化点滴	Cultural Note	十二属相　Animal Signs (Chinese Zodiac)

第 16 课　咖啡多少钱一杯 206
How Much Is a Cup of Coffee

功能	Function	购物（1）　Shopping (1) 询问价钱　Asking for the price
注释	Notes	1. "二"和"两" "二" and "两" 2. 副词"还"（表示增加或补充）The adverb "还" (to indicate "also" or "in addition") 3. 人称代词"您" The personal pronoun "您"
语法	Grammar	1. 人民币的单位及表述　The units of RMB and their Chinese expressions 2. 量词　Measure words
语音	Pronunciation	总复习　Review
汉字	Characters	汉字的部件（4） Components of Chinese characters (4)
文化点滴	Cultural Note	中国的民族　Ethnic Groups in China

注释、语法：单元总结（二）(第 13 课～第 16 课) 223
Notes and Grammar: Unit Review 2 (Lesson 13 ~ Lesson 16)

生词表 224
Vocabulary Index

生字表 231
Index of New Characters

本册单音节声调表 234
Tones of Monosyllables in This Book

本册双音节声调组合表 235
Tones of Disyllables in This Book

本册多音节声调组合表 236
Tones of Polysyllables in This Book

汉字常用部件表 237
Frequently-Used Components of Chinese Characters

本册注释、语法总结 242
Summary of Notes and Grammar in This Book

1 你好
Hello

学习提示 Learning Tips

声母 Initials	b [p]　　p [p']　　m [m]　　f [f] d [t]　　t [t']　　n [n]　　l [l] g [k]　　k [k']　　h [x]
韵母 Finals	a [A]　　ai [aɪ]　　ao [aʊ]　　an [an]　　ang [ɑŋ] i [i]　　ia [iA]　　iao [iaʊ]　　ian [iɛn]　　iang [iɑŋ] u [u]　　ua [uA]　　uai [uaɪ]　　uan [uan]　　uang [uɑŋ] in [in]　　ing [iŋ]　　uo [uo]　　ou [oʊ]
声调 Tones	基本声调　Basic tones (including four tones) bā　　　bá　　　bǎ　　　bà 一声　　二声　　三声*　　四声 Yīshēng　Èrshēng　Sānshēng　Sìshēng (First tone) (Second tone) (Third tone) (Fourth tone)

---

* 本书的三声声调图示标示的是实际语流中的三声读音，发音特征低而平。

The illustrations in this book demonstrate the pronunciation variations of the third-tone in the actual situations, with the pronunciation characteristics of being low and flat.

- 找到你最放松状态下的低音，然后试着按照下图的标示发音。注意，这就是你的汉语声调调域。汉语的声调就在这相对的高音和低音之间变换，这是发好其他几个声调的基础。

Find your most relaxed and lowest-pitched voice, and read the following syllables according to the diagram. Note: This is your range of the Chinese tones, within which tones vary from high to low. This is the prerequisite to pronouncing other tones.

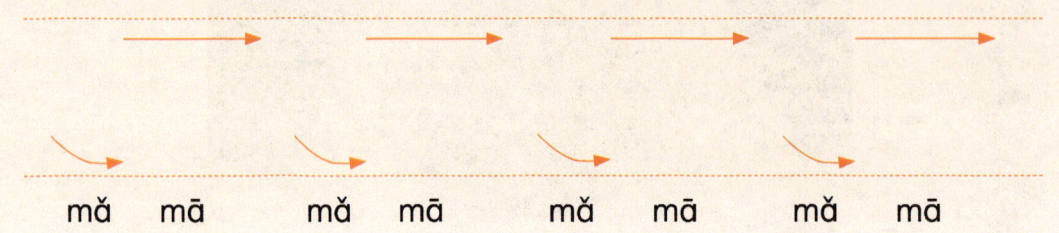

汉语的音—形—义关系示例
An Example Demonstrating the Relationship of Chinese Pronunciation, Form and Meaning

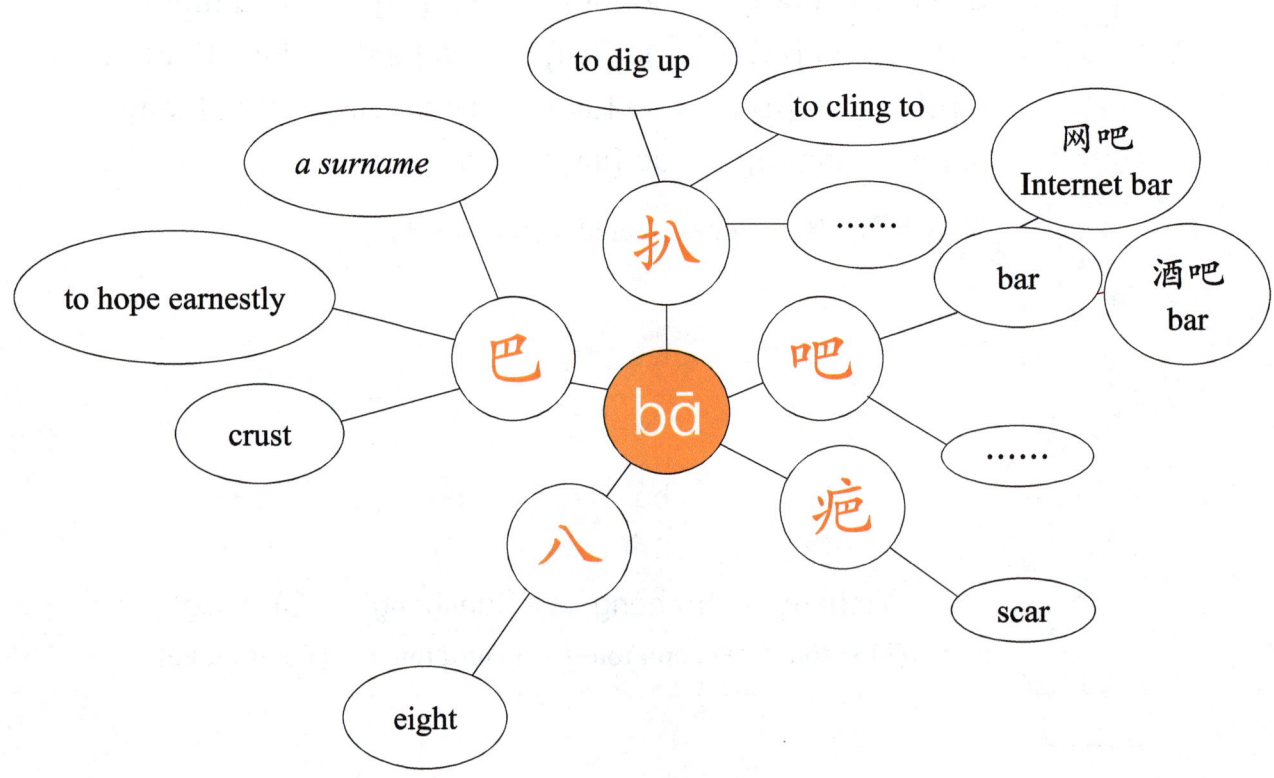

第 1 课 你好

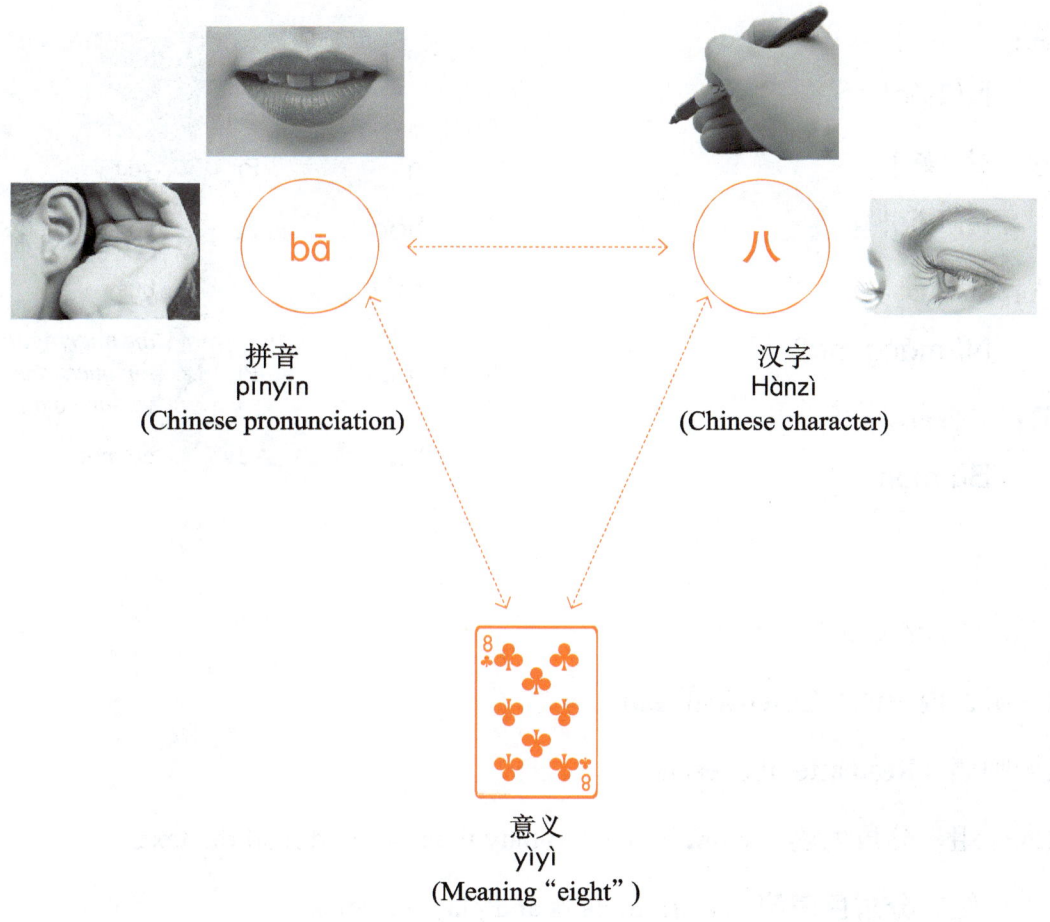

拼音
pīnyīn
(Chinese pronunciation)

汉字
Hànzì
(Chinese character)

意义
yìyì
(Meaning "eight")

听 说 学 拼音，读 写 靠 汉字。
Tīng shuō xué pīnyīn, dú xiě kào Hànzì.
Develop listening and speaking skills using *pinyin*;
and reading and writing skills using Chinese characters.

掌握 音 形 义，从 这里 开始。
Zhǎngwò yīn xíng yì, cóng zhèli kāishǐ.
This will be your first step to Chinese pronunciation, form and meaning.

课文　Text

A：你好！
　　Nǐ hǎo!

B：你好！
　　Nǐ hǎo!

A：你忙吗？
　　Nǐ máng ma?

B：不忙。
　　Bù máng.

生词　New words

01-01

词语 Word	拼音 *Pinyin*	词性 Word Class	英文释义 Meaning in English
你	nǐ	Pr	you
好	hǎo	A	good; fine; OK
忙	máng	A	busy
吗	ma	Pt	an interrogative particle for questions expecting a yes-or-no answer
不	bù	Adv	no; not

练一练　Exercises

1. 听一听，说一说　Listen and read.

2. 跟老师读　Read after the teacher.

3. 两人一组，分角色读　Work in pairs to play the roles and read the text.

4. 两人一组，分角色表演　Work in pairs and play the roles.

语音　Pronunciation

边学边练　Study and practice

① 声母、韵母和声调　Initials, finals and tones

汉语是有声调的语言。一个音节通常由声母、韵母和声调组成。音节的声调不同，意义就不同。

Chinese is a tonal language. A Chinese syllable usually consists of an initial, a final, and a tone. Syllables with different tones have different meanings.

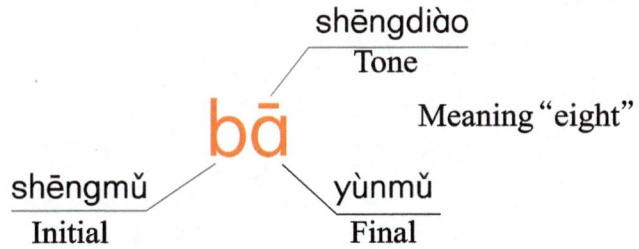

汉语的普通话一共有 21 个声母和 39 个韵母（本册学习其中最常用的 38 个韵母，其中 i 对应 3 种韵母读音）。本课学习 11 个声母、19 个韵母。

There are altogether 21 initials and 39 finals in Mandarin Chinese (the most frequently-used 38 finals are taught in this book and among them i has 3 different pronunciations). 11 initials and 19 finals are taught in this lesson.

看一看，读一读　Read and pronounce　🔊 01-02

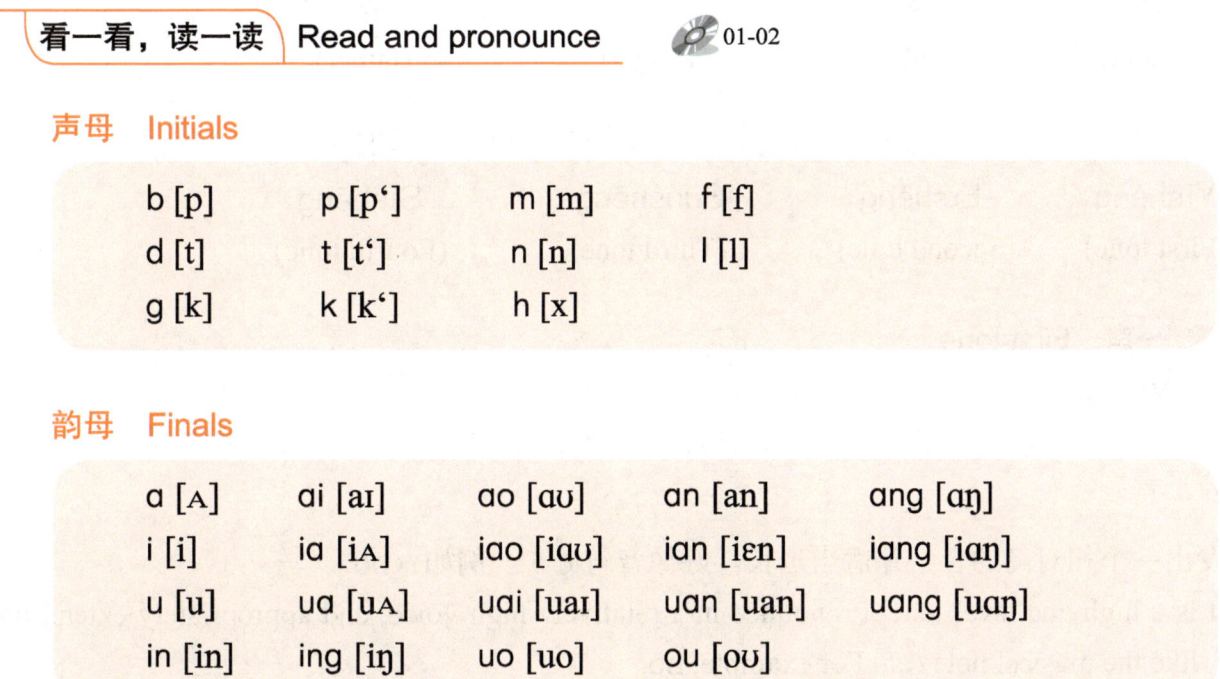

汉语的普通话有四个基本声调，分别是"第一声、第二声、第三声、第四声"，简称"一声、二声、三声、四声"，分别用"‾ ˊ ˇ ˋ"来表示。下图显示出它们各自的模拟调型和相对音高。

Mandarin Chinese has four basic tones, namely, first tone, second tone, third tone and fourth tone, which is respectively indicated as "‾", "ˊ", "ˇ" and "ˋ". The following diagram shows their respective simulated sound patterns and pitches.

跟我说 Read after me 🔘 01-03

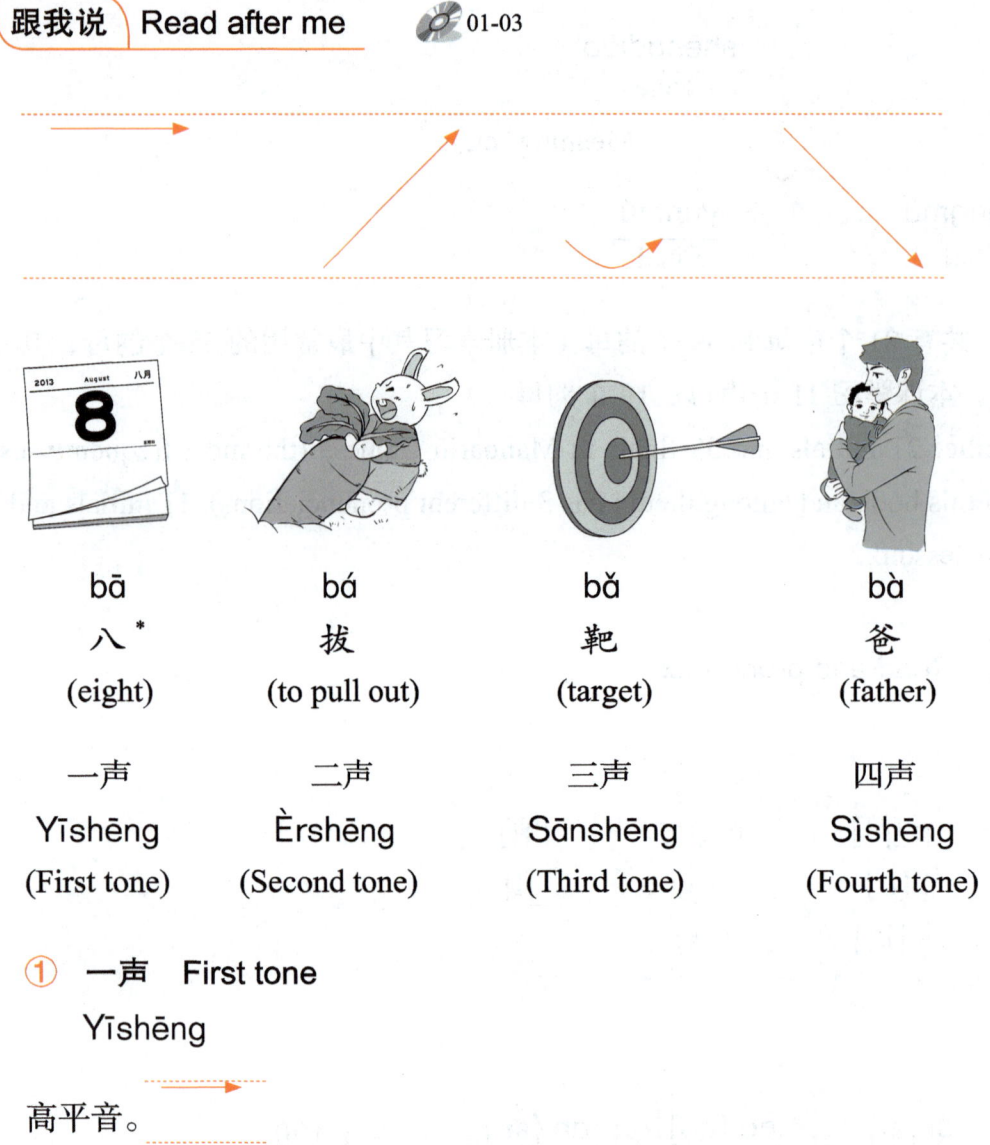

① 一声 First tone
Yīshēng

高平音。

发出一个相对高的音，并适当延长。好像音符 𝄞 5 。例如：bā。

It is a high and level tone. Pronounce in a relatively high voice, and appropriately extend the sound, like the musical note 𝄞 5. For example, bā.

＊本书所有音节对应的汉字为示例汉字。
All the Chinese characters corresponding to the syllables in this book are example characters.

② 三声　Third tone*
Sānshēng

低音。三声的发音有两种情况：

第一，单音节的发音。

在声带放松的情况下，找到自己声音的最低处，之后音高略有抬升。例如：bǎ (target)、bǎi (hundred)、kǔ (bitter)。

It is a low tone and has two cases of pronunciation:

Firstly, the pronunciation of a monosyllable.

Relax your vocal cord and pronounce the sound using your lowest voice and then raise your voice slightly. For example, bǎ (target), bǎi (hundred), and kǔ (bitter).

第二，除单音节以外的其他情况。

有其他音节（不包括三声）紧跟在三声音节后时，三声的音长变得很短，抬升的部分消失，使三声变成一个发到声音最低点为止的低短音。比如：mǎi huā (to buy flowers)、Gǔbā (Cuba)、liǎng tiān (two days)。

Secondly, other cases excluding monosyllables.

If a third-tone syllable is followed by another syllable (excluding the third tone), it becomes very short. Stop at the point of your lowest voice without raising it. For example, mǎi huā (to buy flowers), Gǔbā (Cuba), liǎng tiān (two days).

③ 二声　Second tone
Èrshēng

上挑音。

---

* 在这里，四种声调的解释及练习我们按照"一声、三声、二声、四声"的顺序，这跟以往"一声、二声、三声、四声"的顺序有所不同。这是由于"一声"是相对高音，"三声"是低音，二者之间对比明显，容易参照着掌握；其次，发好"三声"有助于找到发"二声"的起点，可以说发好"三声"是发好"二声"的基础，因此本教材把"三声"放在"二声"之前练习。

In contrast to traditionally following the order of the first, second, third and fourth tones, the teaching and exercises of the four tones are arranged in the order of the first, third, second and fourth tones. This is because the first tone is a relative high pitch in contrast to the third one, so it is easy to learn both by referring to each other. Secondly, learning to pronounce the third tone helps you find the starting point of the second tone. In other words, learning to pronounce the third tone lays the foundation for pronouncing the second tone. As a result, this set of teaching materials practices the third tone before the second tone.

找到自己声音的低点，然后音高迅速上升，达到大致发一声时的音高，好像没听清楚或者不明白时发出的反问的上挑调，类似说英语"What?"时的语调。例如：bá (to pull out)、lái (to come)、nán (difficult)。

It is a rising tone.

Find the point of your lowest voice and raise it quickly to the pitch approximate of the first tone as if you are not clear about or don't understand something. It is similar to the tone of "What?" in English. For example, bá (to pull out), lái (to come), nán (difficult).

④ 四声　Fourth tone
　　Sìshēng

下滑音。

找到发一声时的相对音高，然后以此为起点，迅速向下滑落至自己声音的最低点，几乎低到声音消失，好像英语感叹时发出"Oh!"的语调，或者发出"Let's go!"中"go"的语调。例如：bà (father)、dà (big)、kàn (to see)。

It is a falling tone.

Rapidly fall from a relatively high pitch of the first tone to the point of your lowest voice, like the tone of the English exclamatory expression "Oh!" or the tone of "go" in "Let's go!". For example, bà (father), dà (big) and kàn (to see).

读一读　Read　　01-04

一声　First tone
Yīshēng

bā	lā	dāo	māo		
eight	to pull	knife	cat		

ā	mā	gāo	bāo	tī	dōu
ah	mother	high	bag	to kick; to play	all

三声　Third tone
Sānshēng

bǎ	pǎo	bǐ	gǒu
target	to run	pen, pencil, etc.	dog

nǐ	lǎo	hǎo	nǎ	tǔ
you	old	good	which	soil

三声 + 一声

Gǔbā	nǎ tiān	huǎnghū	dǎkāi
Cuba	which day	in a trance	to open

一声 + 三声

fāngfǎ	dīgǔ	tiāntǐ	gāokǎo
method	low ebb	celestial body	college entrance examination

二声　Second tone
Èrshēng

ná	dú	pá	lóu
to take	to read	to climb	building

ái	bái	lán	tú	lái	guó
cancer	white	blue	picture	to come	country

三声 + 二声

tǎlóu	nǎ guó	diǎnmíng	mǎi fáng
tower building	which country	to call the roll	to buy a house

二声 + 三声

tiáolǐ	guótǔ	mínǐ	túbiǎo
to nurse one's health	national territory	mini-	chart

四声　Fourth tone
Sìshēng

bào	bìng	lù	fàn
newspaper	ill	road	food

dà	dài	tài	mài	dào	bà
big	to wear	too	to sell	to reach	father

三声 + 四声

bǎohù	lǐmào	dǎdòng	guǎnggào
to protect	courtesy	to move; to arouse one's feelings	advertisement

四声 + 三声

dàolǐ	dìlǐ	bànfǎ	bùmǎn
hows and whys	geography	method	discontented

② 三声变调　Third tone sandhi

两个三声连在一起读时，第一个三声要读成二声。

Where there are two consecutive third tones, the first one is pronounced a second tone.

跟我说　Read after me　 01-05

e.g.：nǐ hǎo (hello)
　　　yǔsǎn (umbrella)
　　　tǐng hǎo (very well)

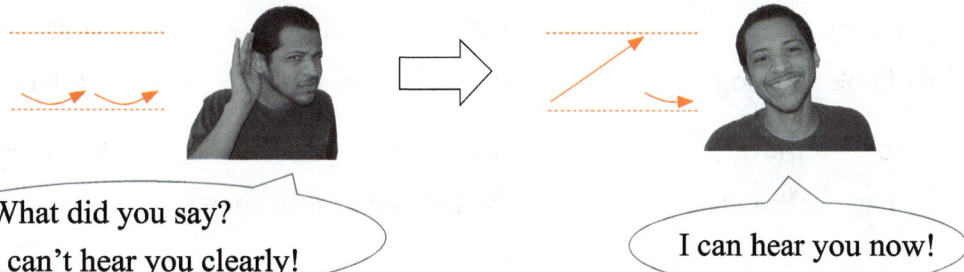

What did you say?
I can't hear you clearly!

I can hear you now!

读一读　Read　 01-06

| lǎobǎn | lǎohǔ | bǐtǒng | gǎnlǎn |
| boss | tiger | pen container | olive |

| dà lǎobǎn | dà lǎohǔ | dà bǐtǒng | dà gǎnlǎn |
| big boss | big tiger | big pen container | big olive |

| mǐngǎn | yǔsǎn | fǔdǎo | lǐngdǎo |
| sensitive | umbrella | to tutor | leader |

| tài mǐngǎn | dài yǔsǎn | nǐ fǔdǎo | hǎo lǐngdǎo |
| too sensitive | to take an umbrella (with sb.) | You work as a tutor. | good leader |

更多练习　More exercises

❶ 听写　Dictation　 01-07

（1）辨声调，用调号 ˉ ˊ ˇ ˋ 标出你听到的声调，调号标在变色的字母上方。

Distinguish the tones and mark the tones you hear using the tonal mark " ˉ ", " ´ ", " ˇ " or " ` ". Place the tonal marks on the coloured letters.

tí — tí	tīng — tíng	mā — mǎ
踢 to kick; to play 提 to lift	听 to listen 停 to park	妈 mother 马 horse

gōu — gǒu	fān — fàn	bāo — bào
钩 hook 狗 dog	帆 sail 饭 food	包 bag 报 newspaper

mào — māo	guà — guā	hǎo — hào
帽 hat 猫 cat	挂 to hang 刮 to shave	好 good 号 trumpet

tù — tǔ	bí — bǐ	dá — dǎ
兔 rabbit 土 soil	鼻 nose 笔 pen, pencil, etc.	答 to answer 打 to beat

（2）**辨声母，写出你听到的声母。**

Distinguish the initials and write down what you hear.

___ā — ___ā	___ú — ___ú	___án — ___án
八 eight 趴 to bend over	图 picture 读 to read	难 difficult 蓝 blue

___ǎo — ___ǎo	___àn — ___àn	___ā — ___ā
跑 to run 饱 to be full	干 to do 看 to see	他 he 搭 to put up

___òu — ___òu	___ǐ — ___ǐ	___ǐ — ___ǐ
够 enough 扣 to button up	匹 a measure word for horses	笔 pen, pencil, etc.

（3）**辨韵母，写出你听到的韵母。**

Distinguish the finals and write down what you hear.

l___ — l___	m___ — m___	l___ — l___
落 to fall 漏 to leak	民 people 名 name	脸 face 两 two

g___ — g___	b___ — b___		
瓜 any kind of melon or gourd 乖 well-behaved	掰 to break off with both hands 班 class		

t___ — t___	l___ — l___	d___ — d___
逃 to escape 条 article	搂 to embrace 裸 naked	淡 tasteless 档 grade

第1课 你好

（4）写出你听到的单音节。
Write down the monosyllables you hear.

披 to wrap around	鼻 nose	母 mother	怒 angry
干 to do	敢 to dare	乱 in a mess	还 to return
火 fire	扣 to button up	行 line; row	花 flower
两 two	店 shop	冰 ice	民 people

（5）写出你听到的双音节。
Write down the disyllables you hear.

| 发呆 to stare blankly | 抛锚 to drop anchor | 方法 method | 包括 to include |
| 白天 daytime | 徘徊 to linger about | 国土 national territory | 图画 picture |

2 声调组合 Combination of tones 01-08

- -	- ́	- ̌	- ̀
mā mā	mā má	mā mǎ	mā mà
bāogōng to contract for a job	bāohán to contain	bāoguǒ parcel	bāokuò to include
́ -	́ ́	́ ̌	́ ̀
má mā	má má	má mǎ	má mà
míngtiān tomorrow	míngnián next year	míngliǎo clear	míngliàng bright
̌ -	̌ ́	̌ ̌	̌ ̀
mǎ mā	mǎ má	mǎ mǎ	mǎ mà
dǎkāi to open	dǎ pái to play cards	lǐngtǔ territory	nǔlì to make great efforts

13

ˋ ˉ	ˋ ˊ	ˋ ˇ	ˋ ˋ
mà mā	mà má	mà mǎ	mà mà
bàofā to break out	bàomíng to sign up	bùmǎn dissatisfied; discontented	bàodào to report

3 朗读　Read aloud　🔊 01-09

Tā míngtiān lái Zhōngguó, bā diǎn dào Běijīng.
(he/she) (tomorrow) (to come) (China) (eight o'clock) (to arrive) (Beijing)

汉字　Characters

练一练　Exercises

1 看一看，圈出最右列汉字的正确发音
Read and circle the correct pronunciation of the characters on the right

nī	ní	nǐ	nì	你
hāo	háo	hǎo	hào	好
māng	máng	mǎng		忙

2 认一认，连一连　Read and match

你　　　bù
好　　　máng
忙　　　ma
吗　　　hǎo
不　　　nǐ

3 给汉字标上拼音　Mark *pinyin* for the following characters

吗_____　忙_____　好_____　你_____　不_____

4 认读汉字　Read the characters

你
好　你好！
忙　你忙吗？
不　不忙。

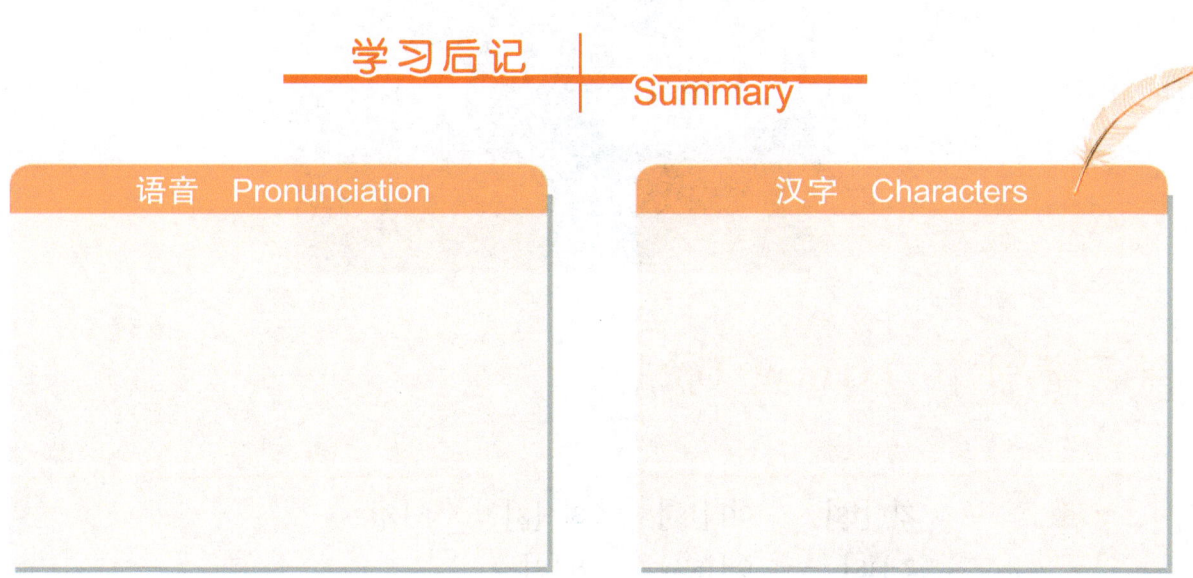

学习后记　Summary

语音　Pronunciation

汉字　Characters

2 早上好
Good Morning

学习提示 Learning Tips

声母 Initials	zh [tʂ]　　ch [tʂʻ]　　sh [ʂ]　　r [ʐ] z [ts]　　c [tsʻ]　　s [s]
韵母 Finals	e [ɤ]　　en [ən]　　eng [əŋ]
轻声 Neutral tone	māma　　hútu　　nǎinai　　dìdi 妈妈　　糊涂　　奶奶　　弟弟 (mother)　(confused)　(paternal grandma)　(younger brother)

- 你会读以下几组音吗？它们有什么不一样？
  Can you read the following groups of syllables? What's the difference between the two syllables in each pair?

第2课 早上好

（1）sān — shān
three   mountain

（2）zǎo — zhǎo
early   to look for

（3）cā — chā
to wipe   to insert

（4）zhàng — chàng — ràng
account   to sing   to let

（5）huāshēng   shēntǐ   chéngrén
peanut   body   adult

zhèngzài   shàngkè   zěnme
to be (doing)   to have class   how

zhēn de   zǎoshang   kèrén
really   morning   guest

课文 Text

02-01

生词 New words

（1）A：早上 好！
Zǎoshang hǎo!

B：早上 好！
Zǎoshang hǎo!

（2）A：中国 大不大？
Zhōngguó dà bu dà?

B：中国 很大，人 很 多。
Zhōngguó hěn dà, rén hěn duō.

（3）A：中国 的茶 好不好？
Zhōngguó de chá hǎo bu hǎo?

B：很 不错。
Hěn búcuò.

词语 Word	拼音 Pinyin	词性 Word Class	英文释义 Meaning in English
早上	zǎoshang	N	morning
大	dà	A	large; big
很	hěn	Adv	very; quite
人	rén	N	person; people
多	duō	A	many
的	de	Pt	(used after an attribute) of
茶	chá	N	tea
不错	búcuò	A	not bad

专有名词 Proper noun

| 中国 | Zhōngguó | China |

17

练一练　Exercises

1. 听一听，说一说　Listen and read.

2. 跟老师读　Read after the teacher.

3. 两人一组，分角色读　Work in pairs to play the roles and read the text.

4. 两人一组，分角色表演　Work in pairs and play the roles.

语音　Pronunciation

边学边练　Study and practice

声母和韵母　Initials and finals

本课学习 7 个声母、3 个韵母。

7 initials and 3 finals will be taught in this lesson.

看一看，读一读　Read and pronounce　 02-02

声母　Initials

| zh [tʂ] | ch [tʂʻ] | sh [ʂ] | r [ʐ] |
| z [ts] | c [tsʻ] | s [s] | |

韵母　Finals

e [ɤ]　　en [ən]　　eng [əŋ]

练一练　Exercises　 02-03

（1）注意声母的发音　Pay attention to the pronunciation of the initials.

| zhòu | chòu | shòu | ròu |
| wrinkle | smelly | thin | meat |

18

zǎo	cǎo	sǎo
early	grass	to sweep

(2) 辨音　Distinguish the syllables.

zh — ch — sh

zhá — chá — shá	zhǎo — chǎo — shǎo
brake　tea　what	to look for　to quarrel　few; little

zhuō — chuō — shuō	zhuài — chuài — shuài
table　to poke　to say	to drag　to kick (with the sole of one's foot)　handsome

r — l

ruò — luò	rǎn — lǎn
weak　to fall	to dye　lazy

réng — léng	ròu — lòu
still; yet　ridge	meat　to leak

z — c

zāi — cāi	zǎo — cǎo
to plant　to guess	Chinese date　grass

zèng — cèng	zuò — cuò
to give...as a present　to scrape	to do　wrong

z — zh

zú — zhú
ethnic group   bamboo

zǒu — zhǒu
to walk   elbow

zài — zhài
at; in; on   debt

zēng — zhēng
to increase   to steam

c — ch

cǎo — chǎo
grass   noisy

còu — chòu
to gather together   smelly

céng — chéng
floor   city; town

cáng — cháng
to hide   long

s — sh

sān — shān
three   mountain

sù — shù
plain   tree

sè — shè
colour   to shoot; to fire

sēng — shēng
Buddhist monk   to give birth to

（3）注意韵母的发音　Pay attention to the pronunciation of the finals.

gē	è	kě	hé
song	hungry	thirsty	river

hěn	bèn	pén	mén
very	stupid	basin	door; gate

chē	zhè	rè	shé
vehicle	this	hot	snake

chén	gēn	shēn	zhēn
a surname	with	deep	needle

② **轻声　Neutral tone**
Qīngshēng

汉语除了四个基本声调之外，还有"轻声"，发音特点是轻、短、松弛。轻声不是一个独立的声调，它总是附着在另一个音节之后，大致有高低两种：跟在三声后的轻声相对较高，跟在其他声调后的轻声相对较低。

Besides the four basic tones, there is a neutral tone in Chinese, which is light, short and relaxed. The neutral tone is always attached to another syllable rather than being used by itself. It is pronounced with a relatively high pitch if followed by a third tone, or a relatively low pitch if followed by other tones.

看一看，读一读　Read and pronounce　02-04

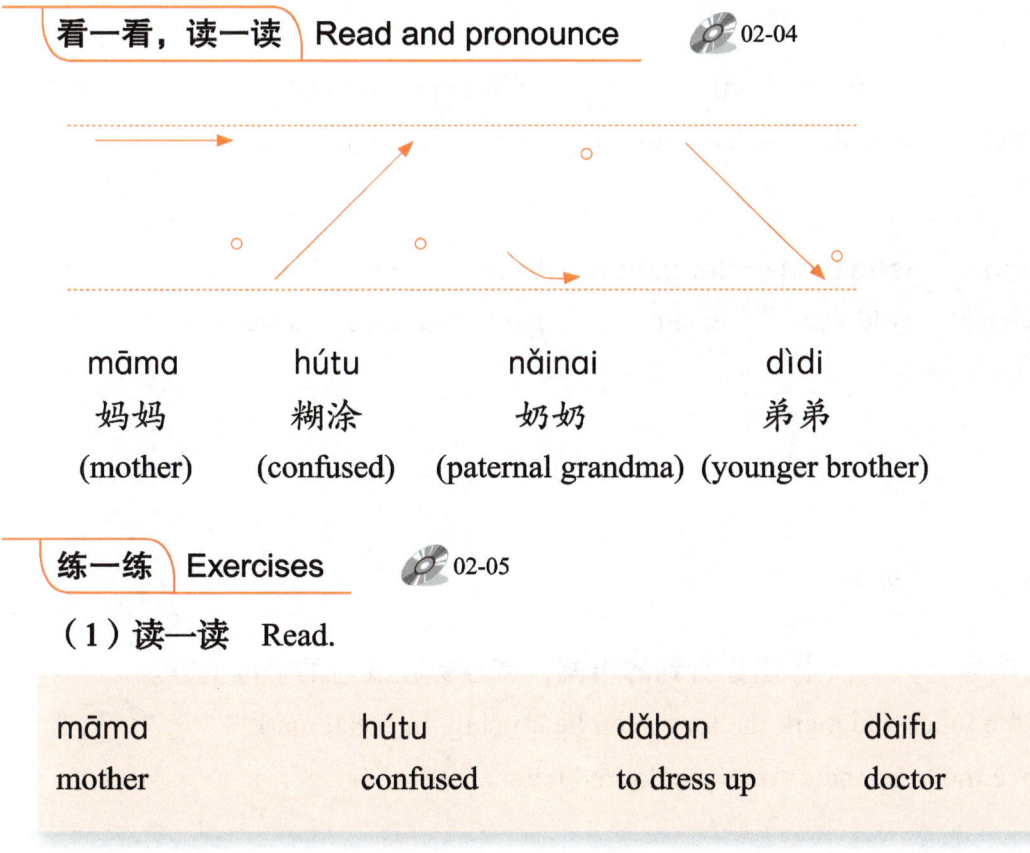

māma	hútu	nǎinai	dìdi
妈妈	糊涂	奶奶	弟弟
(mother)	(confused)	(paternal grandma)	(younger brother)

练一练　Exercises　02-05

（1）读一读　Read.

māma	hútu	dǎban	dàifu
mother	confused	to dress up	doctor

dāla	zhuōzi	bāofu
to slouch	table	cloth-wrapper

míngbai	máfan	liángkuai
to understand	troublesome	cool

nǎinai	lǐtou	lǎba
paternal grandma	inside	loudspeaker

lìhai	dìdao	gàosu
severe	authentic	to tell

（2）辨音　Distinguish the syllables.

kuàilè — kuài le	dìfāng — dìfang	dìdào — dìdao
happy　soon	locality　place	tunnel　authentic

shūfù — shūfu	fùyù — fùyu	kāitōng — kāitong
uncle　comfortable	wealthy　to have surplus	to open up　open-minded

bāohán — bāohan	lěngzhàn — lěngzhan	lìhài — lìhai
to contain　to excuse	cold war　to shiver	gains and losses　severe

更多练习　More exercises

1　听写　Dictation　02-06

（1）辨声调，用调号 ‾ ˊ ˇ ˋ 标出你听到的声调，调号标在变色的字母上方。
Distinguish the tones and mark the tones you hear using the tonal mark "‾", "ˊ", "ˇ" or "ˋ". Place the tonal marks on the coloured letters.

zhen — zhen　　chan — chan　　sheng — sheng
针 needle　枕 pillow　铲 shovel　馋 greedy　绳 rope　生 to give birth to

san — san　　cang — cang　　ren — ren
三 three　伞 umbrella　舱 cabin　藏 to hide　人 human being　忍 to endure

（2）辨声母，写出你听到的声母。
Distinguish the initials and write down what you hear.

___ǎo — ___ǎo　　___āi — ___āi　　___ù — ___ù
找 to look for　吵 to quarrel　栽 to plant　猜 to guess　素 element　树 tree

___áng — ___áng　　___ǔ — ___ǔ　　___uān — ___uān
长 long　藏 to hide　组 group　煮 to cook　钻 to drill　酸 sour

___ǎn — ___ǎn　　___ài — ___ài
染 to dye　懒 lazy　赛 to match　菜 food

（3）辨韵母，写出你听到的韵母。
Distinguish the finals and write down what you hear.

zh___ — zh___　　d___ — d___　　sh___ — sh___
真 real　争 to strive　得 to get　夺 to take... by force　剩 to be left over　上 up

c___ — c___　　l___ — l___　　ch___ — ch___
惨 miserable　踩 to step on　落 to fall　漏 to leak　船 boat　床 bed

（4）写出你听到的单音节。
Write down the monosyllables you hear.

_____　　_____　　_____　　_____
冷 cold　　特 very　　跟 with　　能 can

_____　　_____　　_____　　_____
这 this　　整 whole　　沉 to sink　　撑 to prop up

_____　　_____　　_____　　_____
僧 Buddhist monk　神 god　　省 to save　　触 to touch

| 长 long | 车 vehicle | 忍 to endure | 热 hot |

（5）写出你听到的双音节。
Write down the disyllables you hear.

| 苍天 Heavens | 真诚 sincere | 真理 truth | 真正 true |
| 认真 conscientious | 任何 any | 赦免 to remit (a punishment) | 让步 to make a concession |

❷ 声调组合　Combination of tones  02-07

- -	- ˊ	- ˇ	- ˋ	- ・
fēnzhōng minute	shēngrén stranger	shēntǐ body	shēngbìng to get ill	gēge elder brother
gāo shān high mountain	sēnlín forest	huācǎo flowers and plants	zhōubào weekly newspaper	duōshao how many

ˊ -	ˊ ˊ	ˊ ˇ	ˊ ˋ	ˊ ・
pá shān to climb a mountain	páichú to get rid of	chéngpǐn end product	nénglì ability	mántou steamed bun
rénshēng life	réngrán still; yet	rénkǒu population	zérèn responsibility; duty	liángkuai cool

ˇ -	ˇ ˊ	ˇ ˇ	ˇ ˋ	ˇ ・
hǎitān seashore	běnlái originally	fǔdǎo to tutor	zǎofàn breakfast	nuǎnhuo warm
huǒchē train	děng rén to wait for sb.	zhěnglǐ to put...in order	fěnsè pink	zěnme how

第 2 课　早上好

ˋ ˉ	ˋ ˊ	ˋ ˇ	ˋ ˋ	ˋ 。
zhèngshū certificate; credential	kètáng classroom	hècǎi to acclaim; to cheer	zhùhè to congratulate	dìfang place
rènzhēn take...seriously	dàmén gate	kèkǔ assiduous	shàngkè to have a class	kèren guest; visitor

3 趣味朗读　　Interesting reading materials　　🔘 02-08

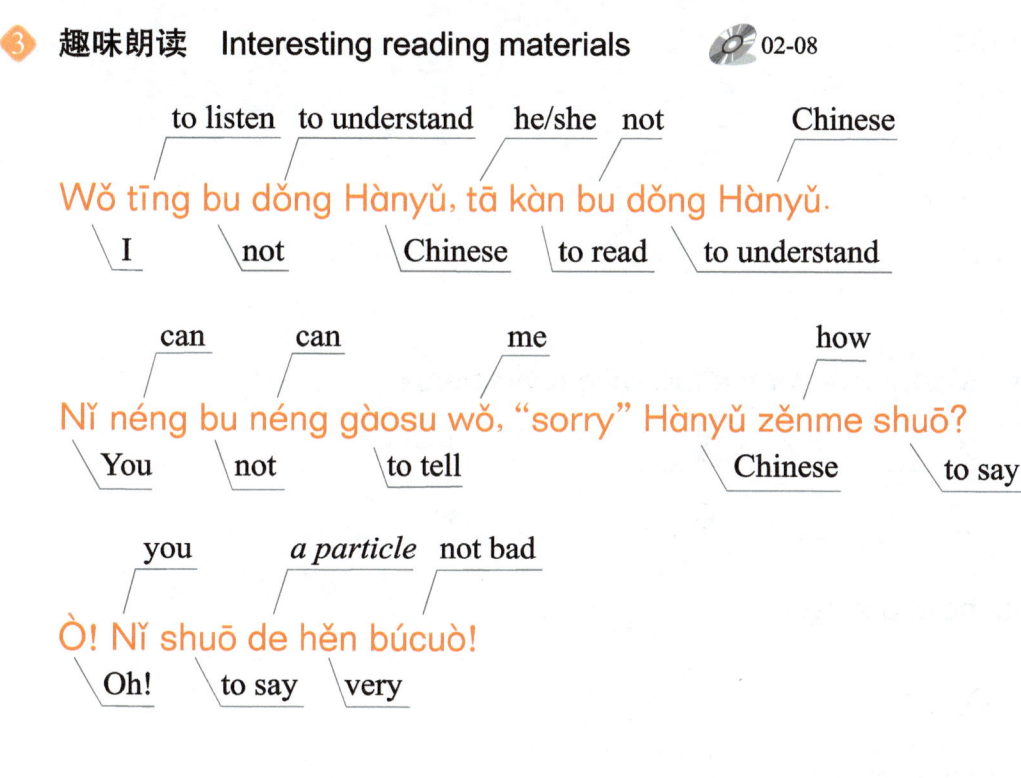

　　　　　　　to listen　to understand　he/she　not　　　　Chinese
　　　Wǒ tīng bu dǒng Hànyǔ, tā kàn bu dǒng Hànyǔ.
　　　　 I　　 not　　 Chinese　to read　to understand

　　　　　can　　can　　　　me　　　　　　　how
　　　Nǐ néng bu néng gàosu wǒ, "sorry" Hànyǔ zěnme shuō?
　　　　You　　not　　to tell　　　　　　　Chinese　　to say

　　　　　you　　a particle　not bad
　　　Ò! Nǐ shuō de hěn búcuò!
　　　　Oh!　　to say　　very

---汉字 | Characters---

👤 练一练　　Exercises

1 看一看，圈出最右列汉字的正确发音
Read and circle the correct pronunciation of the characters on the right

zāo	záo	zǎo	zào	早
zhōng		zhǒng	zhòng	中
guō	guó	guǒ	guò	国
dā	dá	dǎ	dà	大
	hén	hěn	hèn	很

• 25

	rén	rěn	rèn	人
duō	duó	duǒ	duò	多
chā	chá	chǎ	chà	茶
cuō	cuó	cuǒ	cuò	错

❷ 认一认，连一连　Read and match

早　　　　　hěn
大　　　　　chá
错　　　　　zǎo
茶　　　　　cuò
中　　　　　duō
人　　　　　zhōng
很　　　　　rén
多　　　　　dà

❸ 给汉字标上拼音　Mark *pinyin* for the following characters

早_____　人_____　多_____　大_____

茶_____　很_____　中_____　错_____

❹ 认读汉字　Read the characters

早上　　　早上好！
中国　　　中国大不大？
人　　　　人很多。
中国的茶　中国的茶好不好？
不错　　　很不错。

第 2 课 早上好

学习后记 Summary

语音 Pronunciation

汉字 Characters

3 打电话
Making a Phone Call

学习提示 Learning Tips

韵母 Finals	o [o] ie [iɛ] ei [eɪ] uei [ueɪ]	ong [uŋ] iou [iəu] uen [uən]	iong [iuŋ] ueng [uəŋ]

- 拼音拼写规则（1）：与 i、u 相关的拼写规则

    Spelling rules of *pinyin* (1): spelling rules of i and u

- 你会发下面的音吗？

    Can you read the following syllables?

wǒ	yī	wǔ	yóu	yào	wèn
I; me	one	five	oil	medicine	to ask

课文 Text

A：你有中国朋友吗？
　　Nǐ yǒu Zhōngguó péngyou ma?

B：有，我有一个中国朋友。我常问他问题。
　　Yǒu, wǒ yǒu yí ge Zhōngguó péngyou. Wǒ cháng wèn tā wèntí.

A：你们常打电话吗？
　　Nǐmen cháng dǎ diànhuà ma?

B：我们常打电话。
　　Wǒmen cháng dǎ diànhuà.

生词 New words

词语 Word / Phrase	拼音 Pinyin	词性 Word Class	英文释义 Meaning in English
有	yǒu	V	to have
朋友	péngyou	N	friend
我	wǒ	Pr	I; me
一	yī	Num	one
个	gè	M	a measure word of general use
常	cháng	Adv	often; usually
问	wèn	V	to ask
他	tā	Pr	he; him
问题	wèntí	N	question; problem
你们	nǐmen	Pr	you (*pl.*)
打电话	dǎ diànhuà		to make a phone call
我们	wǒmen	Pr	we; us

练一练 Exercises

1. 听一听，说一说　Listen and read.
2. 跟老师读　Read after the teacher.
3. 两人一组，分角色读　Work in pairs to play the roles and read the text.
4. 两人一组，分角色表演　Work in pairs and play the roles.

语音 | Pronunciation

边学边练 Study and practice

❶ 韵母 Finals

本课学习 9 个韵母。
9 finals will be taught in this lesson.

看一看，读一读 Read and pronounce  03-02

韵母 Finals

o [o]	ong [uŋ]	
ie [iɛ]	iou [iəu]	iong [iuŋ]
ei [eɪ]		
uei [ueɪ]	uen [uən]	ueng [uəŋ]

练一练 Exercises  03-03

注意韵母的发音　Pay attention to the pronunciation of the finals.

fēicháng	bù dǒng	dǎléi	mèimei
very	not to understand	to thunder	younger sister

bóbo	gǎndòng	pòhuài	fómén
uncle	to be moved	to destroy	Buddhism

❷ 拼音拼写规则（1） Spelling rules of *pinyin* (1)

（1）i 以及其他以 i 开头的韵母前边没有声母时，写法如下：
If there is not an initial before i or a final starting with i, the spelling rules are as follows:

① i、in、ing 自成音节时，要在前边加上 y，写成 yi、yin、ying。声调符号标在 i 上，同时去掉 i 上的 "·"。例如：

If i, in and ing form syllables of their own, they are preceded by y and written as yi, yin and ying. The tonal marks are placed above i with the dot of i omitted. For example,

ī → yī īn → yīn īng → yīng
one   because   eagle

② 其他以 i 开头的韵母自成音节时，i 要写成 y，如 ia、ie、iao、iou、ian、iang、iong，要写成 ya、ye、yao、you、yan、yang、yong。

For other finals starting with i, if they form syllables of their own, i is written as y. For example, ia, ie, iao, iou, ian, iang or iong is written as ya, ye, yao, you, yan, yang or yong respectively.

iá → yá ié → yé iào → yào iòu → yòu
tooth   paternal grandfather   medicine   again

iǎn → yǎn iáng → yáng iòng → yòng
eye   sheep   to use

读一读　Read　 03-04

| yáyī | yíngyǎng | piányi | chōu yān |
| dentist | nutrition | cheap | to smoke |

| yòuyīn | zhòngyào | dāying | zuòyè |
| incentive | important | to respond | homework |

（2）u 以及其他以 u 开头的韵母前边没有声母时，写法如下：

If there is not an initial before u or a final starting with u, the spelling rules are as follows:

① u 自成音节时，要在前边加上 w，写成 wu。例如：

If u forms a syllable of its own, it is preceded by w and written as wu. For example,

ǔ → wǔ
five

② 其他以 u 开头的韵母自成音节时，u 要写成 w，如 ua、uo、uai、uei、uan、uen、uang、ueng，要写成 wa、wo、wai、wei、wan、wen、wang、weng。例如：

For other finals starting with u, if they form syllables of their own, u is written as w. For instance, ua, uo, uai, uei, uan, uen, uang or ueng is written as wa, wo, wai, wei, wan, wen, wang or weng respectively. For example,

uǎ → wǎ watt	uǒ → wǒ I; me	uài → wài out	uèi → wèi stomach
uán → wán to complete	uēng → wēng old man	uàng → wàng to forget	uèn → wèn to ask

读一读 Read 03-05

fángwū house	wǒmen we; us	wàiguó foreign country

yīnwèi because	wèntí question; problem	wángguó kingdom

lǎowēng old man	wánchéng to accomplish; to finish	shàngwǎng to surf the Internet

更多练习 More exercises

1 读一读 Read  03-06

（1）辨音　Distinguish the syllables.

dōu — duō　　　　　　yòng — yòu
all; both　many; much　to use　again

yè — yìn　　　　　　　wài — wèi
night　seal　　　　　　out　stomach

róng — réng　　　　　　miè — miàn
to melt　still　　　　　to extinguish　noodle

（2）辨调　Distinguish the tones.

yǐwài — yìwài　　　　　　　　yìyàng — yíyàng
beyond　unexpected　　　　　unusual　the same

zhòngyào — zhōngyào　　　　　yāyì — yáyī
important　traditional Chinese medicine　to constrain　dentist

（3）双音节连读 Practice the liaison of the disyllabic words.

mófǎng to imitate	guǎngbō to broadcast	kèren guest
tèbié special	méiyòng useless	hépíng peace
làngfèi to waste	róngyì easy	zhōngcān Chinese food
yǒude some	yīnwèi because	wèntí question; problem

② 听写 Dictation 　03-07

（1）辨声调，用调号 ‾ ˊ ˇ ˋ 标出你听到的声调，调号标在变色的字母上方。

Distinguish the tones and mark the tones you hear using the tonal mark " ‾ ", " ˊ ", " ˇ " or " ˋ ". Place the tonal marks on the coloured letters.

bo — bo
播 to broadcast　伯 uncle; father's elder brother

dong — dong
懂 to understand　洞 hole

you — you
优 excellent　右 right

ye — ye
也 also; too　爷 paternal grandfather

mei — mei
煤 coal　每 every

wen — wen
吻 to kiss　问 to ask

wei — wei
围 to surround　味 taste

tong — tong
痛 ache　铜 copper

wo — wo
我 I; me　窝 nest

（2）辨声母，写出你听到的声母。

Distinguish the initials and write down what you hear.

___ōng — ___ōng
钟 clock　冲 to rush

___iē — ___iē
跌 to fall　贴 to stick

___òng — ___òng
送 to send　纵 vertical

___óng — ___óng
从 from　虫 insect; worm

___éi — ___éi
陪 to accompany　肥 fat

___ǎng — ___ǎng
躺 to lie　挡 to block

___ǒu — ___ǒu
口 mouth　狗 dog

___ào — ___ào
绕 to go round　闹 noisy

（3）辨韵母，写出你听到的韵母。
Distinguish the finals and write down what you hear.

zh____ — zh____　　　　　　　y___ — y____
种 kind; sort　整 whole　　　　又 again　用 to use

l___ — l___　　　　　　　　　t___ — t___
累 tired　裂 to split　　　　　头 head　驮 to bear on the back

zh____ — zh____　　　　　　　ch____ — ch____
张 a surname　睁 to open (one's eyes)　馋 greed　长 long

ch____ — ch____　　　　　　　l____ — l____
穿 to wear　窗 window　　　　　脸 face　两 two

（4）写出你听到的单音节。
Write down the monosyllables you hear.

_____　　_____　　_____　　_____
破 broken　有 to have　攻 to attack　叠 to fold

_____　　_____　　_____　　_____
夜 night　吻 to kiss　拥 to crowd　围 to surround

_____　　_____　　_____　　_____
东 east　碗 bowl　油 oil　用 to use

_____　　_____　　_____　　_____
黑 black　稳 steady　浓 thick　累 tired

（5）写出你听到的双音节。
Write down the disyllables you hear.

_____　　_____　　_____
高中 high school　中国 China　冬泳 winter swimming

_____　　_____　　_____
医药 medicine　鸟窝 bird's nest　吻别 to kiss goodbye

_____　　_____　　_____
往返 to come and go　晚饭 supper; dinner　文化 culture

❸ 趣味朗读　Interesting reading materials　🔘 03-08

　　　　　Chinese　　　friend　　　　many　　　happy
　　　　　　＼　　　　　＼　　　　　＼　　　＼
　　Shuō Hànyǔ, zhǎo péngyou. Péngyou duō, hěn kuàilè.
　　　　＼　　　　＼　　　　　　＼　　　＼
　　　　speak　　look for　　　　friend　　very

　　　onomatopoeia　　tone　　　　to say　　pronunciation
　　　　　＼　　　＼　　　　　＼　　　＼
　　Yī yī yā yā liàn shēngdiào, rénrén shuō wǒ fāyīn hǎo.
　　　　　　＼　　　　　＼　　＼　　　＼
　　　　　to practice　　everybody　I (my)　good

汉字　| Characters

👤 练一练　Exercises

❶ 看一看，圈出最右列汉字的正确发音
Read and circle the correct pronunciation of the characters on the right

yōu	yóu	yǒu	yòu	有
wō		wǒ	wò	我
pēng	péng	pěng	pèng	朋
chāng	cháng	chǎng	chàng	常
wēn	wén	wěn	wèn	问
tī	tí	tǐ	tì	题
tā		tǎ	tà	他
dā	dá	dǎ	dà	打
diān		diǎn	diàn	电
huā	huá		huà	话

❷ 认一认，连一连　Read and match

我	cháng		朋	dǎ
他	wǒ		打	péng
电	diàn		问	tí
话	huà		题	wèn
常	tā		有	yǒu

❸ **给汉字标上拼音** Mark *pinyin* for the following characters

常_____ 电_____ 话_____ 打_____

我_____ 有_____ 问_____ 题_____

❹ **认读汉字** Read the characters

朋友　　　中国朋友
　　　　　一个中国朋友
　　　　　我有一个中国朋友。

问题　　　问问题
　　　　　常问问题
　　　　　我常问他问题。

打电话　　常打电话
　　　　　我们常打电话。

学习后记 | Summary

语音　Pronunciation

汉字　Characters

4 对不起
I'm Sorry

学习提示 Learning Tips

声母 Initials	j [tɕ]	q [tɕʰ]	x [ɕ]
韵母 Finals	ü [y] üan [yɛn]	üe [yɛ] ün [yn]	

- 拼音拼写规则（2）：与 ü 相关的拼写规则

  Spelling rules of *pinyin* (2): spelling rules of ü

- 你会读下面各组拼音吗？每组有什么不同的地方？

  Can you read the following groups of syllables? What is the difference between the two syllables in each pair?

  jiāo — qiāo   xiǎo — shǎo
  to teach to knock   small   few; little

  zǎo — jiǎo   cā — qiā
  early   foot   to wipe to pinch

  jù — quán — xué — yūn
  sentence whole   to study dizzy; faint

课文　Text　　　　生词　New words　　04-01

（1）A：对不起！
　　　　Duìbuqǐ!

　　B：没　关系。
　　　　Méi guānxi.

（2）A：谢谢！
　　　　Xièxie!

　　B：不 客气。
　　　　Bú kèqi.

（3）A：再见！
　　　　Zàijiàn!

　　B：再见！明天 见！
　　　　Zàijiàn! Míngtiān jiàn!

（4）A：你 去 上课 吗？
　　　　Nǐ qù shàngkè ma?

　　B：去。
　　　　Qù.

　　A：我 也 去。
　　　　Wǒ yě qù.

词语 Word / Phrase	拼音 *Pinyin*	词性 Word Class	英文释义 Meaning in English
对不起	duìbuqǐ	V	I'm sorry.
没关系	méi guānxi		Never mind; It doesn't matter.
谢谢	xièxie	V	to thank
不客气	bú kèqi		You're welcome.
再见	zàijiàn	V	to see you later
明天	míngtiān	N	tomorrow
见	jiàn	V	to see
去	qù	V	to go
上课	shàngkè	VO	to go to class (both for students and teachers)
也	yě	Adv	too; also

练一练　Exercises

1. 听一听，说一说　Listen and read.

2. 跟老师读　Read after the teacher.

3. 两人一组，分角色读　Work in pairs to play the roles and read the text.

4. 两人一组，分角色表演　Work in pairs and play the roles.

语音 Pronunciation

边学边练 Study and practice

1 声母和韵母 Initials and finals

本课学习 3 个声母、4 个韵母。
3 initials and 4 finals will be taught in this lesson.

看一看，读一读 Read and pronounce  04-02

声母 Initials

    j [tɕ]　　　q [tɕʰ]　　　x [ɕ]

韵母 Finals

    ü [y]　　　üe [yɛ]
    üan [yɛn]　　　ün [yn]

读一读 Read  04-03

j — q — x

（1）单音节 Monosyllables

| jí — qí — xí | jiǎo — qiǎo — xiǎo |
| urgent　to ride　to study | foot　coincidental　small |

| jīn — qīn — xīn | jiā — qiā — xiā |
| golden　to kiss　new | family　to pinch　shrimp |

| jiàn — qiàn — xiàn | jiǎng — qiǎng — xiǎng |
| sword　to owe　county | to talk　to rob　to think |

（2）双音节　Disyllables

jīqì machine	jiānqiáng strong; firm	jíxiàn the limit	yíqiè everything
jiéshù to finish; to end	jiāotōng traffic	tiānqiáo overpass	xiāoqiǎn pastime
qīnqiè cordial; kind	qiǎngjié to rob	jīngcháng often; frequently	jiàqī vacation
yīngxióng hero	xiàtiān summer	jiānglái future	jìnbù progress
xiāngxìn to believe	jiējìn to be close to	qíjì miracle	xiǎoxīn to be careful

❷ 拼音拼写规则（2）　Spelling rules of *pinyin* (2)

（1）ü 以及其他以 ü 开头的韵母前边没有声母时，要在 ü 前边加上 y，同时去掉 ü 上边的两点"‥"，写法如下：

If there is not an initial before ü or a final starting with ü, add y before ü and remove the two dots above ü. It is written as follows:

ú → yú fish	üè → yuè month	üǎn → yuǎn far	ún → yún cloud

读一读 Read　04-04

dǎyú to go fishing	yuèdú to read	yáoyuǎn remote	bái yún white cloud

（2）ü以及其他以ü开头的韵母在j、q、x后边时，要去掉ü上边的两点"‥"，写法如下：

If ü or a final starting with ü is preceded by j, q or x, the two dots above ü are removed. It is written as follows:

j+ǔ → jǔ   q+ù → qù   x+ū → xū
   to lift   to go   must

j+üè → juè   q+üē → quē   x+üé → xué
   stubborn   to lack   to study

j+üān → juān   q+üán → quán   x+üǎn → xuǎn
   to donate   whole   to choose

j+ün → jūn   q+ún → qún   x+ùn → xùn
   army   skirt   to scold

（3）u以及其他以 u 开头的韵母在 l、n 后边时，写法不变。如：

If ü or a final starting with ü is preceded by l or n, the two dots above ü are not removed. For example,

l+ú → lú   n+ǔ → nǔ
   donkey   female

l+üè → lüè   n+üè → nüè
   to omit   to maltreat

读一读 Read  04-05

jūnyún	juānxiàn	yóuyù
well-distributed	to donate	to hesitate

quēshǎo	yuánquán	xuànyào
to lack	source	to show off

xuéwen	juédìng	yǒuqù
knowledge	to decide	interesting

nǔrén	shěnglüè	nüèdài
women	to omit	to maltreat

更多练习 More exercises

1 读一读 Read 🔊 04-06

(1) 注意韵母的发音 Pay attention to the pronunciation of the finals.

xǔ — xǐ	xún — xióng	lù — lǜ	xié — xué
to allow to wash	to look for bear	road green	shoes to learn

nǚ — nǔ	lüè — liè	qiē — quē	xú — xún
female to exert (efforts)	to omit line; row	to cut to lack	a surname to look for

(2) 双音节连读 Practice the liaison of the disyllabic words.

yùndòng	nǚshēng	lǜsè
sports	girl student	green

nüèdài	yùxí	jiéshěng
to maltreat	to preview	to save

(3) 辨调 Distinguish the tones.

Yīngyǔ — yíngyú	dàyú — dàyǔ
English language surplus	big fish heavy rain

jièyuè — jiěyuē	yóuyù — yóuyú
to borrow books to read to cancel a contract	to hesitate squid

yuànyì — yuányì	yǔxuě — yǔxuē
to be willing original intention	rain and snow rain boots

2 听写 Dictation 🔊 04-07

(1) 辨声调，用调号 ‾ ´ ˇ ˋ 标出你听到的声调，调号标在变色的字母上方。
Distinguish the tones and mark the tones you hear using the tonal mark " ‾ ", " ´ ", " ˇ " or " ˋ ". Place the tonal marks on the coloured letters.

guan — guan	mei — mei
关 to close 管 to administer	没 not to have 妹 younger sister

第 4 课　对不起

qi　—　qi
起 to get up　气 to make sb. angry

xie　—　xie
谢 to thank　鞋 shoe

ke　—　ke
课 class　渴 thirsty

ye　—　ye
也 also; too　爷 paternal grandfather

qu　—　qu
去 to go　取 to fetch

juan　—　juan
捐 to donate　卷 volume

（2）辨声母，写出你听到的声母。

Distinguish the initials and write down what you hear.

___iāo　—　___iāo
教 to teach　敲 to knock

___ián　—　___ián
钱 money　咸 salty

___ué　—　___ué
学 to study　瘸 to be lame

___ù　—　___ù
去 to go　聚 to get together

___uǎn　—　___uǎn
选 to choose　犬 dog

___uán　—　___uán
船 boat　全 whole

___àn　—　___àn
暂 of short duration　灿 bright; illuminating

___āng　—　___āng
张 a surname　伤 wound

（3）辨韵母，写出你听到的韵母。

Distinguish the finals and write down what you hear.

j__　—　j__
聚 to get together　俊 handsome

x__　—　x__
雪 snow　写 to write

x____　—　x____
悬 to hang　咸 salty

q___　—　q___
缺 to lack　圈 circle

l__　—　l__
略 to omit　裂 to split (open)

n___　—　n___
脑 brain　鸟 bird

x_____　—　x___
熊 bear　寻 to look for

q____　—　q___
千 thousand　切 to cut

（4）写出你听到的单音节。
Write down the monosyllables you hear.

去 to go	徐 a surname	靴 boots	写 to write
撅 to stick up	卷 to roll up	权 right; power	雀 sparrow
虐 to maltreat	训 to lecture	想 to think	先 first

（5）写出你听到的双音节。
Write down the disyllables you hear.

具体 concrete	履历 resume	省略 to omit
捐献 to donate	缺陷 defect	一切 everything
同学 schoolmate; classmate	全面 overall; comprehensive	兴趣 interest

3 朗读 Read aloud 🔘 04-08

to come / to study / because / to like

Wǒ lái Zhōngguó xué Hànyǔ, yīnwèi wǒ xǐhuan.
I \ China \ Chinese \ I

to go / to study / later on / interpreter

Tā qù Hánguó xué Hányǔ, yǐhòu dāng fānyì.
he/she \ Korea \ Korean \ to serve as

汉字 Characters

练一练 Exercises

1 看一看，圈出最右列汉字的正确发音
Read and circle the correct pronunciation of the characters on the right

guān		guǎn	guàn	关
	méi	měi	mèi	没
qī	qí	qǐ	qì	起
xiē	xié	xiě	xiè	谢
kē	ké	kě	kè	客
yē	yé	yě	yè	也
qū	qú	qǔ	qù	去
kē	ké	kě	kè	课

2 认一认，连一连 Read and match

明　　zài　　　　　没　　kè
天　　jiàn　　　　关　　xiè
见　　míng　　　　谢　　guān
再　　tiān　　　　课　　méi

3 给汉字标上拼音 Mark *pinyin* for the following characters

没_____　关_____　起_____

明_____　课_____　见_____

4 认读汉字 Read the characters

对不起！　　谢谢！　　再见！
没关系。　　不客气。　　明天见！

nǐ qù.
你去。
nǐ qù shàng kè ma?
你去上课吗？
wǒ qù.
我去。
wǒ yě qù.
我也去。

学习后记 | Summary

语音 Pronunciation	汉字 Characters

汉语不难
Chinese Is Not Difficult

学习提示　Learning Tips

- 拼音拼写规则（3）：iou、uei、uen 的拼写规则

  Spelling rules of *pinyin* (3): spelling rules of iou, uei and uen

- 你会读下面各组拼音吗？每组有什么共同的地方？

  Can you read the following groups of syllables? What is the difference between the two syllables in each pair?

yóu — niú	wèi — duì	wěn — zhǔn
oil　cattle	stomach　right	to kiss　accurate

课文 Text

05-01

A：你 学 什么？
Nǐ xué shénme?

B：我 学 汉语。
Wǒ xué Hànyǔ.

A：汉语 难 吗？
Hànyǔ nán ma?

B：汉语 不 难。
Hànyǔ bù nán.

A：你 为 什么 学 汉语？
Nǐ wèi shénme xué Hànyǔ?

B：因为 汉语 很 有用。
Yīnwèi Hànyǔ hěn yǒuyòng.

生词 New words

词语 Word / Phrase	拼音 Pinyin	词性 Word Class	英文释义 Meaning in English
学	xué	V	to study; to learn
什么	shénme	Pr	what
汉语	Hànyǔ	N	Chinese language
难	nán	A	difficult
为什么	wèi shénme		why
因为	yīnwèi	Conj	because
有用	yǒuyòng	A	useful

练一练 Exercises

1. 听一听，说一说 Listen and read.

2. 跟老师读 Read after the teacher.

3. 两人一组，分角色读 Work in pairs to play the roles and read the text.

4. 两人一组，分角色表演 Work in pairs and play the roles.

语音 Pronunciation

边学边练 Study and practice

I 拼音拼写规则（3） Spelling rules of *pinyin* (3)

（1）iou 自成音节时写成 you。例如：
If iou forms a syllable of its own, it is written as you. For example,

48

ióu → yóu
   oil

iou 前边有声母时写成 iu。例如：
If iou is preceded by an initial, it is written as iu. For example,

d+iōu → diū   q+iōu → qiū   n+ióu → niú
to lose   autumn   cattle

读一读 Read 05-02

| liúxué | nòngdiū | píjiǔ |
| to study abroad | to lose | beer |

| yāoqiú | xiūxi | zúqiú |
| to demand | to rest | soccer; football |

（2）uei 自成音节时写成 wei。例如：
If uei forms a syllable of its own, it is written as wei. For example,

uèi → wèi
   stomach

uei 前边有声母时写成 ui。例如：
If uei is preceded by an initial, it is written as ui. For example,

d+uèi → duì   g+uèi → guì   sh+uěi → shuǐ
right   expensive   water

读一读 Read 05-03

| zuìhǎo | suīrán | hē shuǐ |
| had better | although | to drink water |

| chuīniú | guīzé | huí guó |
| to boast | rule | to go back to one's country |

（3）uen 自成音节时写成 wen。例如：

If uen forms a syllable of its own, it is written as wen. For example,

    uèn → wèn
       to ask

uen 前边有声母时写成 un。例如：

If preceded by an initial, uen is written as un. For example,

  l+uén → lún   c+uēn → cūn   k+uèn → kùn
   wheel   village   sleepy

读一读　Read　05-04

chūntiān	lùnwén	lúntāi
spring	thesis	tyre

zūnshǒu	sǔnhuài	hǎitún
to abide by	to damage	dolphin

❷ 声调符号的标注　Place the tonal marks

（1）声调要标在韵母的主要元音上。主要元音指发音时开口度大、声音响亮的元音。当一个韵母中包含两个或三个元音时，按以下优先顺序确定标声调的元音字母。

A tonal mark is placed on the main vowel of a final. The main vowel refers to the vowel you pronounce loudly with your mouth widely open. When there are two or three vowels, the tonal mark is placed on the vowel earlier in the sequence:

  a > o > e > i / u / ü

例如：For example,

dà	dāo	kuài	dōu	lèi
big	knife	quick	all	tired
kùn	wǔ	jiě		xuě
sleepy	five	elder sister		snow

（2）如果声调在 i 上，要先去掉 i 上的"·"，然后再标调。例如：yī。需要注意的是，韵母是 iu 和 ui 时，声调都要标在后边的字母上。

If the tonal mark is placed on i, the dot above i needs to be removed first. For example, yī.
Note: If the final is iu or ui, the tonal mark is placed on the last vowel.

duì	tuǐ	diū	qiú
right	leg	to lose	ball

读一读 Read  05-05

jiàoshòu	huàn qián	kāihuì
professor	to exchange money	to have a meeting

liúxué	guójiā	qíguài
to study abroad	country	strange

yǒuxiē	wèile	zuòwén
some	in order to	composition

更多练习 More exercises

❶ 读一读 Read  05-06

lánqiú	niú ròu	nóngcūn	shūguì	yóujú
basketball	beef	countryside	bookcase	post office
wénhuà	pínkùn	chēlún	bú duì	rè shuǐ
culture	poverty	vehicle wheel	incorrect	hot water
wèikǒu	yōuxiù	yāoqiú	kùnnan	duì cuò
appetite	excellent	requirement	difficulty	right or wrong

❷ 听写 Dictation  05-07

（1）辨声调，标出你听到的声调。

Distinguish the tones and mark the tones you hear.

you — you　　　　　niu — niu
有 to have　油 oil　　牛 cattle　扭 to turn round

qiu — qiu
球 ball　秋 autumn

shui — shui
水 water　睡 to sleep

dui — dui
对 right　堆 to pile up

jiu — jiu
揪 to hold tight and pull　旧 old

kun — kun
捆 to tie　困 sleepy

tun — tun
吞 to swallow　臀 buttocks

（2）辨声母，写出你听到的声母。

Distinguish the initials and write down what you hear.

____ūn — ____ūn
吨 ton　吞 to swallow

____òu — ____òu
臭 smelly　皱 to wrinkle up

____éi — ____éi
陪 to accompany　肥 fat

____án — ____án
男 male　蓝 blue

____áng — ____áng
常 often　藏 to hide

____iū — ____iū
秋 autumn　修 to repair

____uī — ____uī
追 to chase after　吹 to blow

____uì — ____uì
会 meeting　愧 ashamed

（3）辨韵母，写出你听到的韵母。

Distinguish the finals and write down what you hear.

d____ — d____
炖 to stew　队 team

y____ — y____
右 right　用 to use

j____ — j____
尖 pointed　街 street

l____ — l____
留 to reserve; to keep　楼 building

r____ — r____
人 human being　仍 still; yet

x____ — x____
歇 to rest　靴 boots

w____ — w____
吻 to kiss　尾 tail

y____ — y____
眼 eye　远 far

第5课 汉语不难

（4）写出你听到的单音节。
Write down the monosyllables you hear.

春 spring	穷 poor	球 ball	雨 rain
学 to study	训 to lecture	南 south	喊 to shout
揪 to hold tight and pull	姐 elder sister	瘸 to be lame	汗 sweat

（5）写出你听到的双音节。
Write down the disyllables you hear.

| 有用 useful | 因为 because | 什么 what | 学习 to study |
| 留学 to study abroad | 足球 soccer | 酒吧 bar | 吹牛 to talk big |

3 趣味朗读　Interesting reading materials  05-08

　　　　　　　Chinese
Xué Hànyǔ, jiāo péngyou.
　to learn　　　to make friends

　　　　　many　　to worry
Péngyou duō, bù fāchóu.
　　friend　　not

　　to say　　　too
Nǐ shuō shēngdiào tài nán le?
　you　　tones　　　difficult

　　　　　　much; more; a lot　no problem
Méi shénme. Duō liànxí, méi wèntí.
　　nothing　　　　to practice

53

汉字 Characters

边学边练　Study and practice

◆ **汉字的种类**　The categories of Chinese characters

最早的汉字是从图画演变而来的。人们用简单的线条画出事物的样子，叫象形字。后来又加了一些符号，产生了指事字。还有的用物体的图形组合起来，变成一个意思，叫会意字。最多的一类是形声字，字的一部分是与它相同或相似的读音，另一部分表示它的意义。汉字有 3000 多年的历史。瞧，汉字多神奇！

The earliest characters, originated from pictures, depict the shapes of things using simple lines. Characters constructed in this way are known as pictographic characters. Later, some symbols were added and self-explanatory characters made their appearance. Some characters combining the images of objects and denoting a new meaning are known as the associative compounds. Pictophonetic characters account for the largest number, with the phonetic element denoting its identical or similar pronunciation and the semantic component indicating its meaning. Chinese characters have a history of over 3,000 years. How amazing they are!

（1）象形字　Pictographic characters
　　　Xiàngxíng zì

　　日　rì　sun

（2）指事字　Self-explanatory characters
　　　Zhǐshì zì

　　上　shàng　up

（3）会意字　Associative compounds
　　　Huìyì zì

　　好　hǎo　good
　　　女 (woman) + 子 (child)
　　　nǚ　　　　　zǐ

　　明　míng　bright
　　　日 (sun) + 月 (moon)
　　　rì　　　　yuè

（4）形声字　Pictophonetic characters
　　　Xíngshēng zì

妈　mā　　mother

女 (woman) + 马 (the phonetic element of "妈")
nǚ　　　　 mǎ

更多练习　More exercises

1 看一看，圈出最右列汉字的正确发音
Read and circle the correct pronunciation of the characters on the right

wēi	wéi	wěi	wèi	为
xuē	xué	xuě	xuè	学
hān	hán	hǎn	hàn	汉
yū	yú	yǔ	yù	语
yōng	yóng	yǒng	yòng	用

(Circled: xué, yǔ)

2 认一认，连一连　Read and match

语　　　nán
难　　　xué
学　　　yòng
汉　　　yǔ
用　　　hàn

3 给汉字标上拼音　Mark *pinyin* for the following characters

学_____　　汉_____　　语_____

难_____　　用_____　　为_____

4 认读汉字　Read the characters

xué
学

shénme　　　Nǐ xué shénme?
什么　　　　你学什么？

Hànyǔ　　　Wǒ xué Hànyǔ.
汉语　　　　我学汉语。

nán 难	Hànyǔ nán ma? 汉语难吗?
	Hànyǔ bù nán. 汉语不难。
wèi shén me 为什么	Nǐ wèi shén me xué Hànyǔ? 你为什么学汉语?
yǒu yòng 有用	Hànyǔ hěn yǒu yòng. 汉语很有用。

学习后记 | Summary

语音 Pronunciation	汉字 Characters

6 快点儿
Hurry up

学习提示 Learning Tips

特殊韵母 er The special final er	ér son	ěr ear	èr two
	nǎr where	nàr there	zhèr here
	huār flower	rénr kernel	tiáor strip

- 你会读下面这些音吗？
Can you read the following syllables?

xiàngliànr　　　shǒujuànr　　　rùménr
necklace　　　　handkerchief　　to learn the ABC of

méizhǔnr　　　 gàn huór　　　 dǎgér
maybe; not sure　to work　　　　to hiccup

57

课文 Text

（1） A：你去哪儿？
　　　　Nǐ qù nǎr?

　　　B：去商店。
　　　　Qù shāngdiàn.

　　　A：我也去。你等我一会儿。
　　　　Wǒ yě qù. Nǐ děng wǒ yíhuìr.

　　　B：你快点儿。
　　　　Nǐ kuài diǎnr.

（2） A：请问，这儿有卫生间吗？
　　　　Qǐngwèn, zhèr yǒu wèishēngjiān ma?

　　　B：有。在二层。
　　　　Yǒu. Zài èr céng.

生词 New words

06-01

词语 Word	拼音 Pinyin	词性 Word Class	英文释义 Meaning in English
哪儿	nǎr	Pr	where
商店	shāngdiàn	N	store; shop
等	děng	V	to wait
一会儿	yíhuìr		a little while
快	kuài	A	fast; quick
（一）点儿	(yì)diǎnr		a little; a few
请问	qǐngwèn	V	May I ask…; Excuse me…
这儿	zhèr	Pr	here
卫生间	wèishēngjiān	N	toilet
在	zài	V	to be (at; in; on); to be (here; there)
二	èr	Num	two
层	céng	M	floor

练一练 Exercises

1. 听一听，说一说　Listen and read.

2. 跟老师读　Read after the teacher.

3. 两人一组，分角色读　Work in pairs to play the roles and read the text.

4. 两人一组，分角色表演　Work in pairs and play the roles.

语音 Pronunciation

边学边练 Study and practice

1. 特殊韵母 er The special final "er"

（1）er 不能与声母拼合，只能单用，只有以下三种发音：
er is not spelled with any initials. Rather, it is independently used with the following three pronunciations:

ér	ěr	èr
son	ear	two

读一读 Read 06-02

érsūn	érqiě	nǚ'ér
children and grandchildren	(not only)...but also...	daughter

ěrduo	èrděng	èrbǎi
ear	second-class	two hundred

（2）儿化韵 Retroflex ending

er 可以作为"儿化韵"的标记，附在一个拼音的最后，要写成"r"。
er, written as r, is attached to the end of a syllable as a retroflex ending.

跟我说 Read after me 06-03

zhè+er → zhèr	nà+er → nàr	diǎn+er → diǎnr	huā+er → huār
here	there	dot	flower

wèi+er → wèir	yàng+er → yàngr	wán+er → wánr	yú+er → yúr
taste	appearance	to play	fish

读一读　Read　06-04

guǎiwānr	tǔdòur	xiǎochǒur	xiǎohái r
to make a turn	potato	clown	child

bǎobèir	hǎowánr	yìdiǎnr	fāhuǒr
baby	interesting	a little	to get angry

gànhuór	liǎndànr	xīnyǎnr	xiāngwèir
to work	cheek; face	heart	fragrance

❷ 隔音符号　Syllable-dividing mark

多音节中，当后一个拼音以 a、o、e 开头时，与前一个拼音之间要用 ' 隔开。例如：

For a polysyllable, if the latter syllable starts with a, o or e, a syllable-dividing mark is used to separate it from the former syllable. For example,

Tiān'ānmén	jī'è	hǎi'ōu	Xī'ān	dá'àn
Tian'anmen	hungry	seagull	name of a Chinese city	answer

更多练习　More exercises

❶ 读一读　Read　06-05

（1）单音节　Monosyllables

gài — gàir	huà — huàr	kòu — kòur
to cover　cover	to draw　drawing	to button up　button

gè — gèr	yǎn — yǎnr	xìn — xìnr
a measure word of general use　height	eye　small hole	letter　message

tóu — tóur	wān — wānr	juǎn — juǎnr
head　chief	curved; bent　turn; curve	to roll up　roll

（2）双音节　Disyllables

méiménr no way	bájiānr tiptop; the very best	bīnggùnr ice-lolly
pòlànr junk	méijìnr to feel weak	lǎotóur old man
jīnrge today	míngrge tomorrow	yíkuàir together
zhāduīr to flock together	kōuménr stingy; miserly	chàdiǎnr almost; on the verge of

❷ 听写　Dictation  06-06

（1）辨声调，标出你听到的声调。

Distinguish the tones and mark the tones you hear.

deng — deng 灯 light　等 to wait		wanr — wanr 弯儿 curve　玩儿 to play	
qing — qing 请 to invite　晴 fine; clear		huor — huor 活儿 work　火儿 to get angry	
sheng — sheng 生 unripe　胜 to win		nar — nar 那儿 there　哪儿 where	
hui — hui 会 meeting　回 to return		er — er 儿 son　耳 ear	

（2）辨声母，写出你听到的声母。

Distinguish the initials and write down what you hear.

___uài — ___uài 快 fast　怪 strange	___ān — ___ān 单 single　贪 greedy
___uǎn — ___uǎn 款 sum of money　管 to administer	___í — ___í 提 to lift　笛 flute
___uán — ___uán 悬 to hang　全 whole	___ài — ___ài 败 to lose　派 to send

___éi — ___éi   　　　　　　___ǎng — ___ǎng
肥 fat   赔 to compensate   　　掌 palm   厂 factory

（3）辨韵母，写出你听到的韵母。
Distinguish the finals and write down what you hear.

g___ — g___   　　　　　　d____ — d___
锅 pot   沟 ditch   　　　　　懂 to understand   躲 to avoid

l___ — l____   　　　　　　b____ — b___
淋 to drench   零 zero   　　　变 to change   半 half

f___ — f____   　　　　　　h___ — h___
饭 meal   放 to set...free   　灰 dust; ash   昏 faint

d___ — d___   　　　　　　h____ — h_____
带 to bring   但 but   　　　　环 ring   黄 yellow

（4）写出你听到的单音节。
Write down the monosyllables you hear.

_____　　　_____　　　_____　　　_____
商 trade   尖 sharp   店 shop   在 at; in; on

_____　　　_____　　　_____　　　_____
等 to wait   您 you   请 to invite   还 still; yet

（5）写出你听到的双音节。
Write down the disyllables you hear.

_____　　　　_____　　　　_____
普通 ordinary   比如 such as   久别 long separation

_____　　　　_____　　　　_____
左右 about   汽车 automobile   特别 special

_____　　　　_____　　　　_____
正在 to be (doing)   那么 then   最好 best

3 趣味朗读　Interesting reading materials　06-07

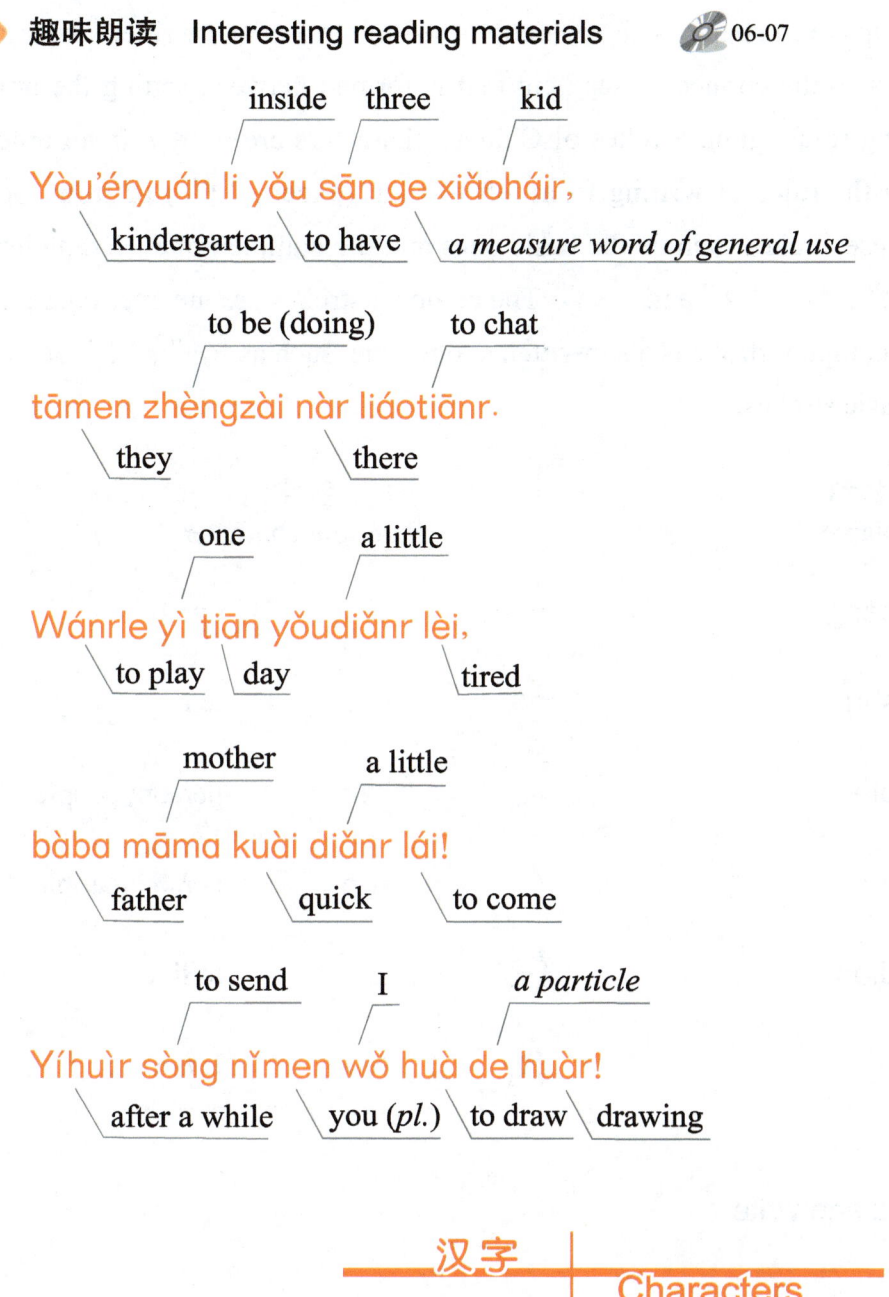

汉字 | Characters

边学边练　Study and practice

1 汉字的基本笔画　Basic strokes of Chinese characters

汉字是方块字，每个汉字都是由笔画组成的，每个笔画都是一笔，写的时候笔不离纸，一次性写出。汉字的笔画是有走势的，起笔一般都是从左到右（撇"丿"除外）或者从上到下（提"㇀"除外）。汉字的笔画包括基本笔画和复杂笔画。基本笔画如"一丨丿丶"等；复杂笔画是由两个或两个以上的基本笔画连接成的，也是一笔写出，如"㇆ ㇄ ㇋"等。下面我们学习几种基本笔画。

Chinese characters are square in shape, with each composed of strokes and written one stroke at a time. One "stroke" refers to the connected segment that is formed between setting the brush/pen down on paper and lifting it up again. Strokes of Chinese characters are written in an orderly manner, generally following the rules of writing from left to right (except "丿") or from top to bottom (except "㇀"). Chinese strokes include the basic ones and the complex ones. Examples of the basic strokes include "一", "丨", "丿" and "㇏". The complex strokes are the ones combining two or more basic strokes. A complex stroke is also written at one time, such as "⁊", "凵" or "∠". Let's look at the following basic strokes.

笔画 Stroke	名称 Name	例字 Example character		
一	héng	一	yī	one
丨	shù	十	shí	ten
丿	piě	人	rén	person; people
㇏	nà	人	rén	person; people
丶	diǎn	住	zhù	to live
㇀	tí	我	wǒ	I; me

看一看，写一写 Read and write

一

十

人 丿人

住 丿亻亻亻亻住住

我 一二于手我我我

2 笔画之间的位置关系　The positions of strokes

笔画之间的位置关系大致有三种，分别为"分离"、"相连"和"交叉"，位置关系的不同会影响到汉字的意义。

Strokes are usually positioned in three ways, i.e., they are separated from, connected with or crossed to each other. Different positions of strokes result in different meanings of Chinese characters.

（1）分离。例如：八、儿、二、小。
　　　Strokes separated from each other, e.g. "八", "儿", "二" and "小".
（2）相连。例如：人、几、天、上。
　　　Strokes connected with each other, e.g. "人", "几", "天" and "上".
（3）交叉。例如：大、九、夫、土。
　　　Strokes crossed to each other, e.g. "大", "九", "夫" and "土".

写一写　Write

天 一二于天 （tiān, sky）

夫 一 二 丰 夫　（fū, husband）

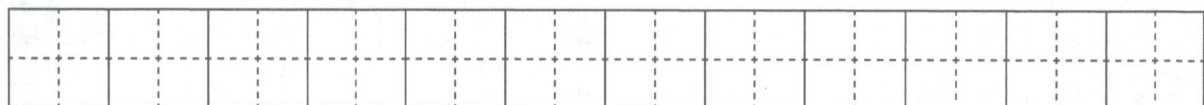

午 丿 𠂉 𠂉 午　（wǔ, noon）

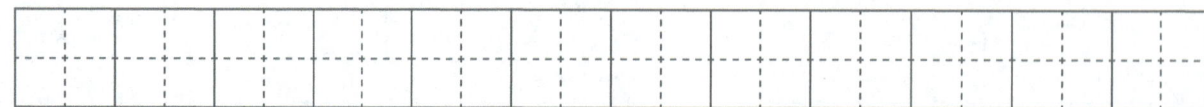

牛 丿 𠂉 𠂉 牛　（niú, cattle）

③ **认写基本汉字**　Read and write the basic Chinese characters

（1）一　yī　one

　　一　1 stroke

（2）二　èr　two

　　一 二　2 strokes

（3）三　sān　three

　　一 二 三　3 strokes

（4）十　shí　ten

　　一 十　2 strokes

（5）土　tǔ　soil

　　一 十 土　3 strokes

（6）八　bā　eight

　　丿 八　2 strokes

（7）人　rén　person; people

　　丿 人　2 strokes

（8）个　gè　*a measure word of general use*

丿 人 个　3 strokes

（9）木　mù　wood

一 十 才 木　4 strokes

（10）六　liù　six

丶 亠 六 六　4 strokes

更多练习　More exercises

1 看一看，圈出最右列汉字的正确发音
Read and circle the correct pronunciation of the characters on the right

shāng	sháng	shǎng	shàng	商
diān		diǎn	diàn	店
dēng		děng	dèng	等
qīng	qíng	qǐng	qìng	请
wēi	wéi	wěi	wèi	卫
shēng	shéng	shěng	shèng	生
jiān		jiǎn	jiàn	间
zāi		zǎi	zài	在

2 认一认，连一连　Read and match

卫　　　céng　　　　　哪儿　　　qǐng
生　　　wèi　　　　　 商　　　　nǎr
间　　　zhèr　　　　　店　　　　shāng
在　　　zài　　　　　 请　　　　diàn
二　　　shēng　　　　快　　　　děng
层　　　èr　　　　　　等　　　　kuài
这儿　　jiān

3 给汉字标上拼音　Mark *pinyin* for the following characters

卫_____　　层_____　　等_____

请_____　　快_____　　商_____

4 认读汉字 Read the characters

哪儿	你去哪儿？
商店	我去商店。
一会儿	等我一会儿。
点儿	快点儿！
卫生间	有卫生间。
	这儿有卫生间吗？
	请问，这儿有卫生间吗？
二层	在二层。

学习后记 | Summary

语音 Pronunciation

汉字 Characters

7 你叫什么名字
What Is Your Name

学习提示 Learning Tips

- 韵母 i 的不同读音

  Different pronunciations of the final i

bi	pi	mi		
di	ti	ni	li	→ i [i]
ji	qi	xi		
zi	ci	si		→ i [ɿ]
zhi	chi	shi	ri	→ i [ʅ]

- 你会读下面这些音吗?

  Can you read the following syllables?

zì	cí	sì	
character	word	four	

zhǐ	chī	shí	rì
paper	to eat	ten	sun

课文　Text　　　生词　New words　　　07-01

A：你 叫 什么 名字？
　　Nǐ jiào shénme míngzi?

B：我 叫 爱子。
　　Wǒ jiào Àizǐ.

A：你 是 哪 国 人？
　　Nǐ shì nǎ guó rén?

B：我 是 日本 人。
　　Wǒ shì Rìběn rén.

A：你 住 哪儿？
　　Nǐ zhù nǎr?

B：我 住 十四 号 楼。
　　Wǒ zhù shísì hào lóu.

词语 Word	拼音 Pinyin	词性 Word Class	英文释义 Meaning in English
叫	jiào	V	to be called
名字	míngzi	N	name
是	shì	V	to be
哪	nǎ	Pr	which
国	guó	N	country; nation
住	zhù	V	to live
十四	shísì	Num	fourteen
号	hào	M	used after a number to mark the order
楼	lóu	N	building

专有名词　Proper nouns

爱子（山口爱子）	Àizǐ (Shānkǒu Àizǐ)	Yamaguchi Aiko, name of a girl student from Japan. Please refer to the "Introduction to the Main Characters" for more details.
日本	Rìběn	Japan

练一练　Exercises

1. 听一听，说一说　Listen and read.

2. 跟老师读　Read after the teacher.

3. 两人一组，分角色读　Work in pairs to play the roles and read the text.

4. 两人一组，分角色表演　Work in pairs and play the roles.

第7课 你叫什么名字

语音 Pronunciation

边学边练 Study and practice

韵母 i 的不同读音 Different pronunciations of the final "i"

韵母 i 在拼音里有三个读音：[i]、[ɿ]、[ʅ]。i 与 b、p、m、d、t、n、l、j、q、x 拼合时读 [i]；i 与声母 z、c、s 拼合时，读 [ɿ]；i 与声母 zh、ch、sh、r 拼合时，读 [ʅ]。

The final i has three pronunciations, namely [i], [ɿ] and [ʅ]. When preceded by b, p, m, d, t, n, l, j, q or x, it is pronounced [i]; when preceded by z, c or s, it is pronounced [ɿ]; when preceded by zh, ch, sh or r, it is pronounced [ʅ].

跟我说 Read after me 07-02

| bǐ | nì | qī | i → [i] |
| pen, pencil, etc. | greasy | seven | |

| zì | cí | sǐ | i → [ɿ] |
| character | word | to die | |

| zhǐ | chī | shí | rì | i → [ʅ] |
| only | to eat | ten | day | |

读一读 Read 07-03

(1) 辨音 Distinguish the syllables.

| cí — chí | zhī — chī | sī — zī | zǐ — zhǐ |
| word pool | to knit to eat | to tear fund | purple paper |

| zhí — shí | rì — shì | zì — cì | sǐ — shǐ |
| straight ten | day to be | character (a measure word) time | to die history |

（2）双音节连读　Practice the liaison of the disyllabic words.

yǐzi	dìtiě	diàntī	zázhì
chair	subway	elevator	magazine

zìsī	shēngcí	shēngrì	zhīshi
selfish	new word	birthday	knowledge

xiǎochī	cízhí	zìzhì	mílù
snack	to resign	self-control	to lose one's way

❷ 注意三声的发音　Pay attention to the pronunciations of the third tone

如前所述，一个三声的音节在实际使用时，声调会有三种可能的情况：一种是短而低的"低调"，如 hǎo ma、yǒuyòng；一种是发三声单字调时先低之后再略有抬升的情况，如 nǐ、hǎo；一种是两个三声音节连读，前一个变为二声，如 nǐ hǎo、lǎobǎn (boss)。但是，有时为了强调处于停顿前的三声音节，也会出现一个自然的抬升和拉长，如"Wǒ mài (to sell) bǐ (pen), tā mài sǎn (umbrella)"。要注意的是，从低点抬升到一个仍然相对较低的位置后，声音在水平方向上自然拉长，而不是继续上挑。这点跟三声单字调的情况是相同的。如图所示：

As mentioned earlier, a third-tone syllable can be pronounced in three ways: one being a short "low tone", like hǎo ma and yǒuyòng, one low first and then rising, as the way a third-tone monosyllable is pronounced, like in nǐ and hǎo, and another a second tone, as in nǐ hǎo and lǎobǎn (boss). However, to stress a third-tone syllable before a pause, there is a natural rise and stretch of the tone, as in "Wǒ mài (to sell) bǐ (pen), tā mài sǎn (umbrella)". Note that the natural drawl of the tone is horizontal rather than continuing to rise. This is the same case as the third-tone monosyllables, which is shown in the following diagram:

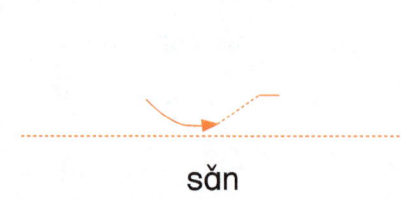

sǎn

读一读 Read  07-04

shuǐ → Wǒ hē shuǐ.	yǔ → Jīntiān yǒu yǔ.
water I drink water.	rain It will rain today.

dǒng → Wǒ bù dǒng.	shǎ → Tā hěn shǎ.
to understand I don't understand.	stupid He/She is very stupid.

nǎr → Nǐ qù nǎr?
where   Where are you going?

三声的声调符号标记为ˇ，它反映了三声发音的三种可能，并不是三声发音的实际走势。这点请特别注意。

Note that the third tone is marked " ˇ ", which shows its possible pronunciation rather than its actual pronunciation.

更多练习 More exercises

❶ 读一读 Read  07-05

（1）辨音 Distinguish the syllables.

shísì — sìshí	shíliù — liùshí
fourteen forty	sixteen sixty

tuīcí — cítuì	sì cì — cìsǐ
to decline to dismiss	four times to stab and kill

shīcí — císhí	zìsī — sīzì
verse; poetry magnet	selfish without sb.'s permission

zīshì — shízì	zhǐshì — shízhì
posture to learn to read	only; just essence

rìshí — shírì	cìwei — wèicǐ
solar eclipse time and date	hedgehog for this reason

（2）双音节连读　Practice the liaison of the disyllabic words.

shízài honest	zhǐshǐ to instigate	érnǚ children	shízhǐ index finger
xià cì next time	rìzi days	sīshì privacy	lǎoshī teacher
xuǎnjǔ to elect	chǐzi ruler	yǐngxiǎng influence	shǒuyǔ sign language
chǐcùn size	qǐshǐ origin	érsūn children and grandchildren	rìjì diary

（3）声调组合　Combination of tones.

‐ ‐	‐ ˊ	‐ ˇ	‐ ˋ	‐ ˳
jiāoshū to teach	Zhōngguó China	hē jiǔ to drink wine	yīyuàn hospital	yīfu clothes
chūfā to start off	jīnnián this year	zhījǐ bosom friend	zūnjìng to respect	guānxi relation

ˊ ‐	ˊ ˊ	ˊ ˇ	ˊ ˋ	ˊ ˳
xióngmāo panda	xuéxí to study	cháguǎnr teahouse	niú ròu beef	piányi cheap
shíjiān time	huí guó to return to one's country	nánnǚ men and women	yíyàng same	qúnzi skirt

ˇ ‐	ˇ ˊ	ˇ ˇ	ˇ ˋ	ˇ ˳
lǎoshī teacher	lǚxíng to travel	nǐ hǎo hello	gǔpiào stock	yǐzi chair
Běijīng Beijing, capital of China	zhěngróng plastic surgery	Kǒngzǐ Confucius	kǎoshì examination	nuǎnhuo warm

ˋ ˉ	ˋ ˊ	ˋ ˇ	ˋ ˋ	ˋ ˚
chènshān shirt	wèntí question; problem	lùkǒu crossing	zàijiàn goodbye	yàoshi key
qìchē automobile	sìshí forty	Hànyǔ Chinese language	Hànzì Chinese character	shìqing matter

2 听写 Dictation  07-06

（1）辨声调，标出你听到的声调。

Distinguish the tones and mark the tones you hear.

ming — ming jiao — jiao shi — shi
名 name 命 fate 叫 to call 交 to hand over 事 matter; affair 十 ten

na — na guo — guo ren — ren
哪 which 那 that 国 country 锅 pot 人 human being 忍 to endure

lou — lou zhu — zhu si — si
楼 building 漏 to leak 住 to live 猪 pig 四 four 死 to die

（2）辨声母，写出你听到的声母。

Distinguish the initials and write down what you hear.

___ì — ___ì ___ǐ — ___ǐ
字 character 刺 to stab 纸 paper 尺 ruler

___ī — ___ī ___ué — ___ué
湿 wet 汁 juice 学 to learn 绝 matchless

___ēn — ___ēn ___í — ___í
真 really 深 deep 梨 pear 泥 mud

___uē — ___uē ___ǐng — ___ǐng
缺 to lack 靴 boots 请 to invite 挺 quite

（3）辨韵母，写出你听到的韵母。

Distinguish the finals and write down what you hear.

sh___ — sh___ 　　　　　g___ — g_____
市 city　树 tree　　　　　根 root　羹 thick soup

l___ — l_____ 　　　　　h___ — h___
楼 building　龙 dragon　　喊 to shout　很 very

y_____ — y___ 　　　　　k_____ — k_____
怨 to complain　月 month　空 empty　坑 pit

l_____ — l___ 　　　　　j___ — j_____
聊 to chat　牢 jail　　　　酒 wine　窘 awkward

（4）写出你听到的单音节。

Write down the monosyllables you hear.

_____　　_____　　_____　　_____
市 city　　死 to die　　吃 to eat　　紫 purple

_____　　_____　　_____　　_____
只 only　　词 word　　人 human being　　最 most

（5）写出你听到的双音节。

Write down the disyllables you hear.

_____　　　　_____　　　　_____
昨天 yesterday　食堂 canteen　　词典 dictionary

_____　　　　_____　　　　　　　　_____
一共 in all　　后天 the day after tomorrow　绿茶 green tea

_____　　　　_____　　　　_____
电影 movie　　最近 recently　　客气 modest

3 趣味朗读　Interesting reading materials　🔊 07-07

　　　　　　nephew　Japan
Wǒ zhízi zài Rìběn liúxué,
　　I (my)　to be in　to study abroad

tā yǐhòu xiǎng dāng lǜshī.
(he / later on / to want / to serve as / lawyer)

Wǒ zhínǚr zài Ruìshì shēnghuó.
(I (my) / niece / to be in / Switzerland / to live)

tā zhǐ huì yìdiǎnr Hànyǔ.
(she / only / to be acquainted with / a little / Chinese)

汉字 | Characters

练一练　Exercises

1 看一看，圈出最右列汉字的正确发音
Read and circle the correct pronunciation of the characters on the right

lōu	lóu	lǒu	lòu	楼
jiāo	jiáo	jiǎo	jiào	叫
zhū	zhú	zhǔ	zhù	住
bēn		běn	bèn	本
shī	shí	shǐ	shì	是
nā	ná	nǎ	nà	哪
guō	guó	guǒ	guò	国
	rén	rěn	rèn	人

2 认一认，连一连　Read and match

名	nǎ		国	lóu
叫	shì		人	guó
是	míng		住	zhù
哪	jiào		楼	rén

77

3 给汉字标上拼音   Mark *pinyin* for the following characters

叫_____   名_____   字_____   是_____   哪_____

国_____   人_____   住_____   号_____   楼_____

4 认读汉字   Read the characters

什么

名字   你叫什么名字？

哪国人   你是哪国人？

日本人   我是日本人。

哪儿   你住哪儿？

十四号楼   我住十四号楼。

学习后记 | Summary

语音　Pronunciation

汉字　Characters

8 你的电话是多少
What Is Your Telephone Number

学习提示　Learning Tips

- 注意区别以下几组声母的发音

  Distinguish the pronunciations of several pairs of initials

b — p	d — t	g — k	f — p
j — zh	q — ch	x — sh	

- 注意以下各组中韵母相同部分的发音

  Pay attention to the pronunciations of the identical part of the finals in several groups

ai an → a [a]	a ia → a [ɑ]
ao ang → a [ɑ]	ian üan → a [ɛ]
bo po mo fo wo → o [uo]	
e → e [ɤ]	en eng → e [ə]
ie üe → e [ɛ]	ei → e [e]
fu → u [ʊ]	

- 你会读下面这些音吗？

  Can you read the following syllables?

  wǒ — mō
  I; me　to touch

  dàn — yán — yuǎn
  egg　salt　far

  è — jiè — xué
  hungry　to borrow　to study

课文 Text　　生词 New words　08-01

A：你的 电话 是 多少？
　　Nǐ de diànhuà shì duōshao?

B：13402079568
　　Yāo sān sì líng èr líng qī jiǔ wǔ liù bā.

A：你 在 哪儿 上课？
　　Nǐ zài nǎr shàngkè?

B：我 在 407 教室 上课。
　　Wǒ zài sì líng qī jiàoshì shàngkè.

A：你 去 吃饭 吗？
　　Nǐ qù chīfàn ma?

B：去，一起 去 吧。
　　Qù, yìqǐ qù ba.

词语 Word	拼音 Pinyin	词性 Word Class	英文释义 Meaning in English
电话	diànhuà	N	telephone
多少	duōshao	Pr	how many; how much
教室	jiàoshì	N	classroom
吃饭	chīfàn	VO	to eat (a meal)
一起	yìqǐ	Adv	together
吧	ba	Pt	*a modal particle*

练一练　Exercises

1. 听一听，说一说　Listen and read.

2. 跟老师读　Read after the teacher.

3. 两人一组，分角色读　Work in pairs to play the roles and read the text.

4. 两人一组，分角色表演　Work in pairs and play the roles.

语音 Pronunciation

边学边练　Study and practice

① 注意区别以下几组声母的发音
Distinguish the pronunciations of several pairs of initials

读一读 Read  08-02

(1) b — p　d — t　g — k　f — p

gǎn — kǎn	tú — dú
to dare　to chop	picture　to read

bā — pā	fàng — pàng
eight　to bend over	to let...go　fat

túshū — dúshū	pízi — bízi
books　to go to school	leather　nose

gǔlì — kǔlì	fùbù — pùbù
to encourage　coolie	abdomen; belly　waterfall

(2) j — zh　q — ch　x — sh

jiǎo — zhǎo	zhàn — jiàn	jiāng — zhāng
foot　to look for	to stand　to see	ginger　*a surname*

qiā — chā	cháng — qiáng	chōu — qiū
to pinch　to insert	long　wall	to take out　autumn

xiǎo — shǎo	xiù — shòu	xiàng — shàng
small　few; little	rust　thin	to resemble　upper

❷ 注意以下各组中韵母相同部分的发音

Pay attention to the pronunciations of the identical part of the finals in several groups

（1）ai、an：a [a]　　a、ia：a [A]　　ao、ang：a [ɑ]　　ian、üan：a [ɛ]

这四组韵母中 a 的读音有所不同。受后一个音的影响，ai、an 中的 a 位置靠前，发 [a]；ao、ang 中的 a 位置靠后，发 [ɑ]。a、ia 中的 a 后面没有其他音，不受影响，位置适中，

发 [A]。ian、üan 中 a 的发音与前三组有较大的不同，分别受前、后的音影响，开口度明显变小，发 [ɛ]。

In the four instances, the pronunciations of a are not quite the same. Influenced by the following sound, a in ai and an is a front vowel and pronounced [a]; a in ao and ang is a back vowel and pronounced [ɑ]; a in a and ia is a central vowel since it is not followed by other sound. It is pronounced [A]. The pronunciation of a in ian and üan is much different from the other three groups. Influenced by the preceding and following sounds, it is pronounced [ɛ] with the opening of the speaker's mouth becoming much smaller.

读一读 Read  08-03

注意 a 的不同发音　Pay attention to the different pronunciations of a.

| yuán — chuán | juǎn — jiǎn |
| round　boat | to roll up　to cut |

| xuǎn — quǎn | xián — qián |
| to choose　dog | salty　money |

| fàngjià | wánxiào | fācái |
| to have a vacation | joke | to make a fortune |

| shànliáng | jiǎnduǎn | quánmiàn |
| kind-hearted | brief; short | all-round |

| xiànzài | ànnà | yuánquán |
| now | to restrain | source |

（2）bo、po、mo、fo、wo：o [uo]

bo、po、mo、fo、wo 中的 o 实际发音是 [uo]，不是 [o]。

o in bo, po, mo, fo and wo is actually pronounced [uo] instead of [o].

读一读 Read  08-04

注意 o 的发音　Pay attention to the pronunciation of o.

bōluó	ànmó	pōmò
pineapple	to massage	splash-ink

wǒmen	Fójiào	bǎwò
we	Buddhism	to grasp; to seize

bóruò	pòhuài	shuōcuò
weak	to destroy	to speak wrongly

（3）e：e [ɤ]　　en、eng：e [ə]　　ie、üe：e [ɛ]　　ei：e [e]

这四组韵母中 e 的读音各有不同。发单韵母 e 时舌位相对其他来说较高、较后，发 [ɤ]。en、eng 中的 e 发音状态较松弛，舌位适中，发 [ə]。ie、üe 中的 e 发音时舌位在四组韵母中最低，较为靠前，发 [ɛ]。ei 中的 e 发音时舌位比 [ɛ] 更前、更高一些，发 [e]。

Of the four groups of finals, the pronunciations of e are not quite the same. The single final e is pronounced [ɤ], with your tongue in a relatively high and backward position. e in en and eng is loosely articulated and is pronounced [ə], with your tongue in a central position; e in ie and üe is pronounced [ɛ], with your tongue at the lowest and a relatively front position among the four groups of finals. e in ei is pronounced [e], with your tongue at a more forward and higher position.

读一读 Read  08-05

注意 e 的不同发音　Pay attention to the different pronunciations of e.

yéye	hēisè	shěnglüè
paternal grandfather	black (colour)	to omit

zěnme	xuéwèi	zhèxiē
how	academic degree	these

mēnrè muggy	shénme what	děng rén to wait for sb.
quèqiè exact; precise	jiějué to solve	gēge elder brother
èliè very bad	tèsè characteristic	xuéwen knowledge

（4）fu：u [ʋ]

fu 中的 u 发音比较特别，它受声母 f 的影响，实际发浊辅音 [ʋ]，不发元音 [u]，发音时口型不是圆的，嘴也不向前噘起。

u in fu has a special pronunciation. Under the influence of the initial f, it is actually a voiced consonant [ʋ] rather than a vowel [u]. Neither do you round nor push forward your mouth when pronouncing this syllable.

读一读　Read　 08-06

注意 u 的发音　Pay attention to the pronunciation of u.

yīfu clothes	dàifu doctor; physician	fūfù husband and wife
fùxí to review	pífū skin	fǔdǎo to tutor
fúqi good fortune	fǔbài to corrupt	fùqin father
fúlǔ captive	fúwù to serve	fùzá complicated

3 声母的实际发音及其字母名称　The actual pronunciation of initials and their names

声母 Initial	实际发音 Actual pronunciation	字母名称 Name
b	[p]	[puo]
p	[pʻ]	[pʻuo]
m	[m]	[muo]
f	[f]	[fuo]
d	[t]	[tɤ]
t	[tʻ]	[tʻɤ]
n	[n]	[nɤ]
l	[l]	[lɤ]
g	[k]	[kɤ]
k	[kʻ]	[kʻɤ]
h	[x]	[xɤ]
j	[tɕ]	[tɕi]
q	[tɕʻ]	[tɕʻi]
x	[ɕ]	[ɕi]
zh	[tʂ]	[tʂɿ]
ch	[tʂʻ]	[tʂʻɿ]
sh	[ʂ]	[ʂɿ]
r	[ʐ]	[ʐɿ]
z	[ts]	[tsɿ]
c	[tsʻ]	[tsʻɿ]
s	[s]	[sɿ]

唱一唱　Sing

唱声母　Sing the song of initials.

```
‖ 1  2  3  1  | 1  2  3  1  |
  b  p  m  f  | d  t  n  l  |

  3  4  5  —  | 3  4  5  —  ‖
  g  k  h     | j  q  x
```

```
| 5  6   5  4   3  3   1     | 5  6   5  4   3  3   1     |
| zh ch  sh r   z  c   s     | èr shí  yī ge  shēng mǔ    |

| 3  3   5  5   1   —        | 3  3   5  5   1   —        |
| wǒ dōu xué huì le          | wǒ dōu xué huì le          |
```

I have all learned.

更多练习　More exercises

1 读一读　Read　　08-07

（1）双音节连读　Practice the liaison of the disyllabic words.

wòshǒu	xiě zì	tiān'é	luóbo
to shake hands	to write characters	swan	radish
ānquán	diǎncài	dǎban	xiàtiān
safe	to order food	to dress up	summer
zǎoshang	shūfu	quēshǎo	zhǔfù
morning	comfortable	to lack	housewife
fēngfù	měinǚ	gǎn'ēn	lěngmò
abundant	beauty	to feel grateful	indifferent

（2）课堂用语　Classroom expressions.

Dàjiā hǎo!	Hello, everyone!
Lǎoshī hǎo!	Hello, teacher!
Gēn wǒ shuō.	Read after me.
Yìqǐ shuō.	Read together.
Zài shuō yí biàn.	Say it again.
Bú kàn shū.	Don't look at your textbook.
Xiànzài tīngxiě.	Now let's do the dictation.
Qǐng náchū běnzi.	Take out your exercise books.
Yǒu wèntí ma?	Any questions?
Duì!	Right!
Bú duì.	Not right.

Xiànzài zuò liànxí.	Now let's do the exercises.
……shì shénme yìsi?	What's the meaning of…
Qǐng dú shēngcí.	Please read the new words.

(3) 朗读 Read aloud.

Hànyǔ nán ma? Hànyǔ bù nán.
Pīnyīn Hànzì, hěn yǒu yìsi.
Yì zhōu rùménr, dǎhǎo jīchǔ.
Biāozhǔn Hànyǔ, zhèli qǐbù.

yǒu yìsi	interesting
yì zhōu	one week
rùménr	to get started
dǎhǎo jīchǔ	to build a good foundation
biāozhǔn	standard
zhèli	here
qǐbù	to start

2 听写　Dictation  08-08

(1) 辨声调，标出你听到的声调。

Distinguish the tones and mark the tones you hear.

duo ― duo　　　　　　　　dian ― dian
多 many　夺 to take by forces　店 shop　点 to check; to count

hua ― hua　　　　　　　　men ― men
画 to draw；花 flower　　　闷 stuffy　门 door
　to paint

wan ― wan　　　　　　　　cha ― cha
碗 bowl　万 ten thousand　　茶 tea　叉 fork

jie ― jie　　　　　　　　　he ― he
接 to pick...up　借 to borrow　喝 to drink　和 and

(2) 辨声母，写出你听到的声母。

Distinguish the intials and write down what you hear.

____ǒu ― ____ǒu　　____ǎo ― ____ǎo　　____ái ― ____ái
手 hand　丑 ugly　　跑 to run　饱 to be full　白 white　牌 card

___ǐ — ___ǐ 　　___í — ___í 　　___è — ___è
挤 crowded　起 to get up　　池 pool　直 straight　　各 each　克 gram

___ān — ___ān 　　___ǎi — ___ǎi 　　___iè — ___iè
三 three　山 mountain　　买 to buy　奶 milk　　借 to borrow　谢 to thank

(3) 辨韵母，写出你听到的韵母。
Distinguish the finals and write down what you hear.

p___ — p___　　　　　z___ — z___
票 ticket　泡 to steep　　走 to walk　左 left

h___ — h___　　　　　x___ — x___
河 river　活 alive　　　心 heart　星 star

l___ — l___　　　　　zh___ — zh___
来 to come　栏 column　　肿 to be swollen　准 exact

g___ — g___　　　　　sh___ — sh___
高 high; tall　刚 just　　税 tax　顺 fluent and well-arranged

(4) 写出你听到的单音节。
Write down the monosyllables you hear.

_____　　_____　　_____　　_____
电 electricity　多 many　话 word; talk　教 to teach

_____　　_____　　_____　　_____
再 again　吃 to eat　饭 meal　捡 to pick up

(5) 写出你听到的双音节。
Write down the disyllables you hear.

_____　　_____　　_____　　_____
卫生 hygiene　复习 to review　自己 oneself　上课 to attend class

_____　　_____　　_____　　_____
简单 simple　可能 perhaps　所以 so; therefore　点菜 to order food

3 趣味朗读　Interesting reading materials　08-09

汉字　Characters

边学边练　Study and practice

1 汉字的复杂笔画（1）　Complex strokes of Chinese characters (1)

笔画 Stroke	名称 Name	例字 Example character		
㇅	héng zhé	口	kǒu	mouth
㇆	héng zhé gōu	月	yuè	moon; month
㇚	shù gōu	小	xiǎo	small
㇄	shù wān gōu	儿	ér	son

（续表）

笔画 Stroke	名称 Name	例字 Example character		
㇆	héng piě	又	yòu	again; once more
㇏	piě diǎn	女	nǚ	female; woman

看一看，写一写 Read and write

口 丨 冂 口

月 丿 冂 月 月

小 亅 小 小

儿 丿 儿

又 ㇆ 又

女 ㇏ 夂 女

2 认写基本汉字　Learn and write the basic Chinese characters

(1) 口　kǒu　mouth

丨 冂 口　3 strokes

(2) 日　rì　sun; day

丨 冂 日 日　4 strokes

(3) 五　wǔ　five

一 丆 五 五　4 strokes

(4) 门　mén　door

丶 门 门　3 strokes

(5) 月　yuè　moon; month

丿 冂 月 月　4 strokes

(6) 小　xiǎo　small

亅 小 小　3 strokes

(7) 丁　dīng　*a family name*

一 丁　2 strokes

(8) 儿　ér　son

丿 儿　2 strokes

(9) 七　qī　seven

一 七　2 strokes

(10) 又　yòu　again; once more

𠃌 又　2 strokes

(11) 女　nǚ　female; woman

㇛ 女 女　3 strokes

更多练习　More exercises

1. 看一看，圈出最右列汉字的正确发音
Read and circle the correct pronunciation of the characters on the right

duō	duó	duǒ	duò	多
diān		diǎn	diàn	电
huā	huá		huà	话
shī	shí	shǐ	shì	室
zāi		zǎi	zài	在
chī	chí	chǐ	chì	吃
fān	fán	fǎn	fàn	饭

2. 认一认，连一连　Read and match

电　　　zài　　　　　室　　　chī
话　　　diàn　　　　吃　　　fàn
在　　　huà　　　　饭　　　shì

3. 给汉字标上拼音　Mark *pinyin* for the following characters

话_____　　多_____　　在_____

室_____　　吃_____　　起_____

4. 认读汉字　Read the characters

你的
电话　　　你的电话
多少　　　你的电话是多少？
在
教室　　　在教室
上课　　　在教室上课
一起
吃饭　　　一起吃饭吧。

92

第 8 课　你的电话是多少

学习后记　Summary

语音　Pronunciation

汉字　Characters

你是留学生吗
Are You an International Student

学习提示 Learning Tips

重点词 Key Words	你　好　是　留学生　吗　不　也
重点句 Key Sentences	1. 你好! 　　Nǐ hǎo! 2. 我是留学生。 　　Wǒ shì liúxuésheng. 3. 你是老师吗? 　　Nǐ shì lǎoshī ma? 4. 我不是老师，我也是学生。 　　Wǒ bú shì lǎoshī, wǒ yě shì xuésheng.
功　能 Function	打招呼、问候、询问身份 Exchanging greetings and asking sb.'s identity

第9课　你是留学生吗

课文　Text

李明：你 好！
Lǐ Míng: Nǐ hǎo!

杰克：你 好！
Jiékè: Nǐ hǎo!

李明：你 是 留学生 吗？
Lǐ Míng: Nǐ shì liúxuéshēng ma?

杰克：我 是 留学生，你 呢？
Jiékè: Wǒ shì liúxuéshēng, nǐ ne?

李明：我 不 是 留学生。
Lǐ Míng: Wǒ bú shì liúxuéshēng.

杰克：你 是 老师 吗？
Jiékè: Nǐ shì lǎoshī ma?

李明：我 不 是 老师，我 也[1] 是 学生。
Lǐ Míng: Wǒ bú shì lǎoshī, wǒ yě shì xuésheng.

练一练　Exercises

1. 听课文，说说你听到了什么　Listen to the text and talk about what you hear.

2. 跟老师读课文　Read the text after the teacher.

3. 两人一组，分角色读　Work in pairs to play the roles and read the text.

4. 回答问题　Answer the following questions.

　（1）杰克是留学生吗？
　（2）李明是留学生吗？
　（3）李明是老师吗？

5. 两人一组，分角色表演　Work in pairs and play the roles.

生词 New words

序号 No.	词语 Word	拼音 Pinyin	词性 Word Class	英文释义 Meaning in English	例子 Example
1	你	nǐ	Pr	you	
2	好	hǎo	A	good; fine; OK	你好
3	是	shì	V	to be	
4	留学生	liúxuésheng	N	student studying abroad; international student	是留学生
5	吗	ma	Pt	an interrogative particle for questions expecting a yes-or-no answer	
6	我	wǒ	Pr	I; me	
7	呢	ne	Pt	a modal particle used for elliptical questions	
8	不	bù	Adv	no; not	不是
9	老师	lǎoshī	N	teacher	是老师
10	也	yě	Adv	too; also	也是老师
11	学生	xuésheng	N	student	是学生

专有名词 Proper nouns

李明	Lǐ Míng	Li Ming, name of a Chinese boy student. Please refer to "Introduction to the Main Characters" for more details.
杰克	Jiékè	Jack, name of a boy student from the USA. Please refer to "Introduction to the Main Characters" for more details.

注释 Note

[1] 副词"也" The adverb "也"

副词"也"放在动词或形容词前，表示"同样"。

The adverb "也" is followed by a verb or an adjective, meaning "too" or "also".

（1）① 我是学生。
② 我也是学生。

（2）① 我是老师。

③ 你不是老师，我也不是老师。

② 我不是老师，我是学生。

练一练 Exercises

给"也"选择适当的位置　Put "也" in the right positions.

（1）杰克是学生，__A__ 我 __B__ 是 __C__ 学生。
（2）李明 __A__ 不是老师，__B__ 我 __C__ 不是老师。

语法 Grammar

❶ "是"字句（表示判断）　A sentence with "是"（to indicate making a judgement）

"是"字句，表示判断，否定形式是"不是"。例如：
A sentence with "是" is used to indicate making a judgement. Its negative form is "不是". For example,

主语（S）	谓语（P）			标点（Punctuation）
	副词（Adv）	是（V）	宾语（O）	
我		是	学生	。
我	不	是	老师	。

练一练 Exercises

给"是"选择适当的位置　Put "是" in the right positions.

（1）___A___ 我 ___B___ 学生 ___C___ 。

（2）___A___ 我 ___B___ 不 ___C___ 留学生。

② **用"吗"的是非疑问句　A yes-or-no question using "吗"**

陈述句句末加上"吗",变成是非疑问句,用来对不确定的事物提问。

A yes-or-no question is formed by using "吗" at the end of a declarative sentence. It is used to ask questions about something uncertain.

主语（S）	谓语（P）	吗	标点（Punctuation）
你	是学生	吗	？
你	是老师	吗	？

练一练 Exercises

根据回答完成会话　Complete the following dialogues according to the answers.

（1）A：_____？（吗）
　　　B：我不是老师。

（2）A：_____？（吗）
　　　B：我是留学生。

③ **汉语的语序及主要句子成分：主语、谓语、宾语**

Word order and the main sentence elements in Chinese: subject, predicate and object

汉语没有严格意义的形态变化,主要通过语序和虚词表示语法意义。汉语句子的基本语序为：主语+谓语。谓语里多包含宾语,因此汉语句子的主要结构也常用"主语+谓语+宾语"表示。

Chinese doesn't have strict morphological change. It mainly uses word order and function words to indicate grammatical meanings. Its basic word order is as follows: subject+ predicate. A predicate usually includes an object; as a result, the major structure of a Chinese sentence is often shown as: subject + predicate + object.

主语（S）	谓语（P）	宾语（O）	标点（Punctuation）
我	是	学生	。
我	不是	老师	。

三个人一组，其中两人当学生，一人当老师，表演老师和两个学生第一次见面，互相问话。准备时间：3～5分钟。

Work in groups of three, with two being students and one a teacher. The teacher and the two students are meeting for the first time and greeting each other. Preparation time: 3-5 minutes.

提示　Tips

老师　学生　留学生　是　也

◆ **添句成段**　Write more sentences to compose a paragraph

在所给句子前后加上两三句话，把它补充成一段完整的文字。

Write two or three sentences before or after the given sentence to make a complete passage.

杰克也不是老师

语音 Pronunciation

📔 **边学边练** Study and practice

◆ "不"的变调 Tone sandhi of "不"

"不（bù）"在四声音节前读为二声。

"不（bù）" is pronounced with a second tone if followed by a fourth-tone syllable.

bù + ˋ → bú ˋ

e.g.: bú shì   bú duì   bú qù   bú jiàn

练一练 Exercises  09-03

（1）读一读 Read.

不 hē	不 xué	不 hǎo	不 shì
不 duō	不 shú	不 shǎo	不 bì
不 shuō	不 máng	不 lǐ	不 xiè

（2）标出"不"的实际声调 Mark the actual tones of "不".

bu gàn   bu kàn   bu lái   bu xǔ
bu xíng   bu là   bu gāi   bu dǒng

📔 **更多练习** More exercises

❶ 辨声调 Distinguish the tones  09-04

bái — bǎi   dān — dàn   pēn — pén
white hundred   single but   to spray basin

tán — tān   féi — fèi   mǎn — màn
to talk greedy   fat to waste   full slow

pāibǎn — páibǎn   bàiběi — bǎi bèi
to make the final   to set type   to suffer defeat   a hundred times
decision

hěn màn	—	hěn mǎn	bēifèn	—	bèifèn
very slow		very full	sad and angry		backup

② 辨声母 Distinguish the initials 🔊 09-05

b — p — f

pén — fén
bái — pái
pǔ — fǔ
bēi — fēi

d — t

dài — tài
dàn — tàn
dī — tī
dú — tú

③ 辨韵母 Distinguish the finals 🔊 09-06

ai — ei

bāi — bēi
gǎi — gěi
pái — péi
bǎi — běi

an — en

fān — fēn
hǎn — hěn
bàn — bèn
pán — pén

④ 声调组合 Combination of tones 🔊 09-07

- -	- ́	- ̌	- ̀	- ˚
fēibēn to run at full speed	fēihuí to fly back	fēizǒu to fly away	fēiqù to fly to (some place)	fēi le to fly away
́ -	́ ́	́ ̌	́ ̀	́ ˚
báitiān daytime	báitáng sugar	bái zhǐ white paper	báisè white color	bái de white
̌ -	̌ ́	̌ ̌	̌ ̀	̌ ˚
běnzhōu this week	běnrén oneself	běnlǐng skill	běnyì original meaning	běnzi notebook
̀ -	̀ ́	̀ ̌	̀ ̀	̀ ˚
hànbīng roller-skating	Hànzú the Han ethnic group	Hànyǔ Chinese language	Hànzì Chinese character	hànzi true man

5 双音节连读 Practice the liaison of the disyllabic words 09-08

| fāyīn | pīnyīn | tóngxué | xuéxí |
| pronunciation | *pinyin* | classmate | to study |

| yǔfǎ | kǒuyǔ | Hànzì | huìhuà |
| grammar | spoken language | Chinese character | conversation |

6 多音节连读 Practice the liaison of the polysyllabic words 09-09

gōnggòng qìchē — bus
chūzūchē — taxi
tíngchēchǎng — parking lot

wèishēngjiān — restroom
jiànshēnfáng — fitness center

7 轻声练习 Practice the neutral tone 09-10

| māma | gēge | kū le | tā de |
| mother | brother | cried | his/her |

| bóbo | mántou | liángkuai | piányi |
| uncle; father's elder brother | steamed bun | cool | cheap |

| nǐmen | hǎo ba | ěrduo | nuǎnhuo |
| you (*pl.*) | OK | ear | warm |

| dìdi | bàba | kèqi | dìfang |
| younger brother | father | polite | place |

8 朗读 Read aloud 09-11

学生   老师
好学生   好老师
我是好学生。   你是好老师。

9 趣味朗读 Interesting reading materials 09-12

我 的 乐趣 (pleasure)
Wǒ de lèqù

他 是 学生, 他 在 (in; at) 国内 (domestic) 学习 法律 (law)。
Tā shì xuésheng, tā zài guónèi xuéxí fǎlǜ.

我 也 是 学生，我 在 中国 学习 汉语。
Wǒ yě shì xuésheng, wǒ zài Zhōngguó xuéxí Hànyǔ.

你 知道 (to know) 吗？
Nǐ zhīdao ma?

学习 汉语 是 我 最 (most) 大 (great) 的乐趣 (pleasure; joy)。
Xuéxí Hànyǔ shì wǒ zuì dà de lèqù.

汉字 | Characters

边学边练 Study and practice

1 汉字的复杂笔画（2） Complex strokes of Chinese characters (2)

笔画 Stroke	名称 Name	例字 Example character		
㇄	shù zhé	山	shān	mountain
㇂	shù tí	长	cháng	long
㇉	piě zhé	去	qù	to go
㇆	héng gōu	你	nǐ	you
㇃	xié gōu	我	wǒ	I; me
乙	héng zhé wān gōu	九	jiǔ	nine
㇌	héng zhé zhé piě	建	jiàn	to build
㇉	shù zhé zhé gōu	马	mǎ	horse

2 写汉字 Write characters

（1）山　　shān　　mountain

　　丨 凵 山　　3 strokes

(2) 长　cháng　long
　　ノ 一 长 长　4 strokes

(3) 去　qù　to go
　　一 十 土 去 去　5 strokes

(4) 你　nǐ　you
　　ノ 亻 亻 竹 你 你 你　7 strokes

(5) 我　wǒ　I; me
　　ノ 一 于 手 我 我 我　7 strokes

(6) 九　jiǔ　nine
　　ノ 九　2 strokes

(7) 这　zhè　this
　　丶 一 ナ 文 文 辽 这　7 strokes

(8) 马　mǎ　horse
　　コ 马 马　3 strokes

3 认写基本汉字　Learn and write the basic Chinese characters

(1) 尔　ěr　you
　　ノ ク 勹 尔 尔　5 strokes

(2) 刀　dāo　knife
　　コ 刀　2 strokes

(3) 田　tián　field
　　丨 冂 冃 田 田　5 strokes

(4) 生　shēng　to give birth to...
　　ノ 丨 一 牛 生　5 strokes

(5) 子　zǐ　child
　　フ 了 子　3 strokes

(6) 尼　ní　Buddhist nun
　　フ コ 尸 尸 尼　5 strokes

(7) 不　bù　no; not
　　一 ア 不 不　4 strokes

(8) 巾　jīn　a piece of cloth (*as used for a towel or scarf*)
　　丨 冂 巾　3 strokes

(9) 也　yě　also; too
　　フ 九 也　3 strokes

4 认写本课汉字　Learn and write the Chinese characters in this lesson

(1) 你　nǐ　you
　　你 → 亻 + 尔

(2) 是　shì　to be
　　是 → 日 + 疋

(3) 留学生　liúxuéshēng　international student
　　留 → 𠂉 + 刀 + 田　to study abroad
　　学 → 𭕄 + 子　to study

(4) 吗　ma　an interrogative particle for a question expecting a yes-or-no answer
　　吗 → 口 + 马

(5) 好　hǎo　good; fine; OK
　　好 → 女 + 子

(6) 呢　ne　a modal particle used for elliptical questions
　　呢 → 口 + 尼

（7）老师　lǎoshī　teacher

老　→　耂 + 匕　old

师　→　丿 + 一 + 巾　teacher

实践活动 Activity

◆ 走一走，问一问　Go for a survey

问几个不认识的人"你是老师吗？"或者"你是学生吗？""你是留学生吗？"，他们怎么回答的，在课上作报告。

Ask some strangers the following questions: "Are you a teacher?" or "Are you a student?", "Are you an international student?" Report your findings to the class.

文化点滴 Cultural Note

甲骨文　Oracle Inscriptions
Jiǎgǔwén

人 大 女 又 目 耳 口 齿

日 月 草 木 水 戈 户 门

牛 羊 犬 豕 马 鹿 弓 矢

连一连　Match

日　　　　月
丿　　　　门
門　　　　日

历经几千年的演变，这些古汉字你认识多少？

Chinese characters have gone through thousands of years' evolution. How many of these ancient characters can you recognize?

第 9 课 你是留学生吗

学习后记 | Summary

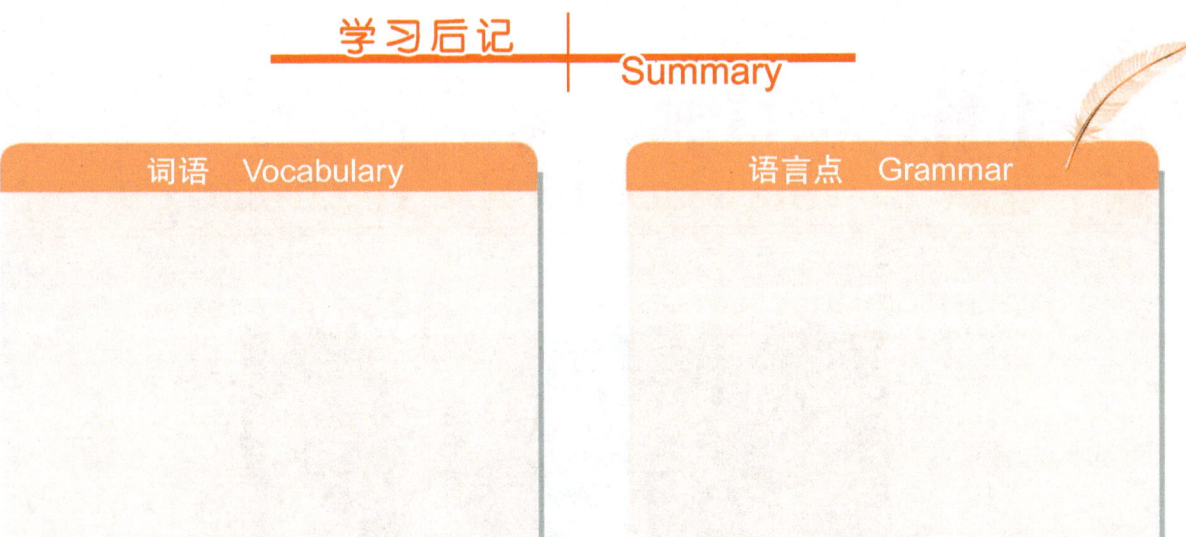

词语　Vocabulary

语言点　Grammar

10 你是哪国人
Which Country Are You from

学习提示 Learning Tips

重点词 Key Words	你们 哪 国 都 叫 什么 名字 姓 很
重点句 Key Sentences	1. 你是哪国人？ Nǐ shì nǎ guó rén? 2. 我们 都是 韩国 人。 Wǒmen dōu shì Hánguó rén. 3. 你叫 什么 名字？ Nǐ jiào shénme míngzi? 4. 我 姓 金，叫 金 大成。 Wǒ xìng Jīn, jiào Jīn Dàchéng. 5. 认识 你 很 高兴。 Rènshi nǐ hěn gāoxìng.
功能 Function	询问姓名、国籍 Asking one's name and nationality

课文 Text

金大成：你好。
Jīn Dàchéng: Nǐ hǎo.

金在元：你好。
Jīn Zàiyuán: Nǐ hǎo.

爱子：你们[1]好，你们是留学生吗？
Àizǐ: Nǐmen hǎo, nǐmen shì liúxuéshēng ma?

金大成：是。你呢？
Jīn Dàchéng: Shì. Nǐ ne?

爱子：我也是留学生。
Àizǐ: Wǒ yě shì liúxuéshēng.

金大成：你是哪国人？
Jīn Dàchéng: Nǐ shì nǎ guó rén?

爱子：我是日本人，你们呢？
Àizǐ: Wǒ shì Rìběn rén, nǐmen ne?

金大成：我们都[2]是韩国人。你叫[3]什么名字？
Jīn Dàchéng: Wǒmen dōu shì Hánguó rén. Nǐ jiào shénme míngzi?

爱子：我叫山口爱子。
Àizǐ: Wǒ jiào Shānkǒu Àizǐ.

金大成：我姓金，叫金大成。他也姓金，叫金在元。
Jīn Dàchéng: Wǒ xìng Jīn, jiào Jīn Dàchéng. Tā yě xìng Jīn, jiào Jīn Zàiyuán.

认识你很高兴。
Rènshi nǐ hěn gāoxìng.

金在元：你好，认识你很高兴。
Jīn Zàiyuán: Nǐ hǎo, rènshi nǐ hěn gāoxìng.

爱子：认识你们，我也很高兴。
Àizǐ: Rènshi nǐmen, wǒ yě hěn gāoxìng.

练一练 Exercises

1. 听课文，说说你听到了什么　Listen to the text and talk about what you hear.

2. 跟老师读课文　Read the text after the teacher.

3. 三人一组，分角色读　Work in groups of three to play the roles and read the text.

4. 回答问题　Answer the following questions.

（1）金大成、金在元是留学生吗？
（2）他们是哪国人？
（3）爱子是哪国人？

5. 三人一组，分角色表演　Work in groups of three and play the roles.

6. 根据课文内容填空，然后朗读　Fill in the blanks based on the text and then read it aloud.

金大成是_____人，金在元_____韩国人。山口爱子_____
____。他们_____留学生。

生词　New words  10-02

序号 No.	词语 Word	拼音 Pinyin	词性 Word Class	英文释义 Meaning in English	例子 Example
1	你们	nǐmen	Pr	you (pl.)	
2	哪	nǎ	Pr	which	
3	国	guó	N	country; nation	哪国　韩国　中国 (Zhōngguó)
4	人	rén	N	person; people	中国人　韩国人
5	我们	wǒmen	Pr	we; us	
6	都	dōu	Adv	all; both	都是学生
7	叫	jiào	V	to be called	
8	什么	shénme	Pr	what	叫什么　是什么
9	名字	míngzi	N	name	什么名字
10	姓	xìng	V/N	one's surname is… / surname	姓什么

11	他	tā	Pr	he; him		
	她	tā	Pr	she; her		
12	认识	rènshi	V	to meet; to know	认识他	认识中国人
13	很	hěn	Adv	very; quite	很好	
14	高兴	gāoxìng	A	glad; happy	很高兴	不高兴

专有名词　Proper nouns

金大成	Jīn Dàchéng	Jin Daesung, name of a boy student from Republic of Korea. Please refer to "Introduction to the Main Characters" for more details.
金在元	Jīn Zàiyuán	Jin Jae-won, name of a boy student from Republic of Korea. Please refer to "Introduction to the Main Characters" for more details.
山口爱子	Shānkǒu Àizǐ	Yamaguchi Aiko, name of a girl student from Japan. Please refer to the "Introduction to the Main Characters" for more details.
日本	Rìběn	Japan
韩国	Hánguó	Republic of Korea

注释　Notes

[1] **后缀"们"** The suffix "们"

"人称代词/名词＋们"表示复数，这里的名词一般是指人的。例如：

"Personal pronoun/noun ＋们" indicates the plural form, usually referring to people. For example,

你　　→　　你们
我　　→　　我们
他　　→　　他们
她　　→　　她们
学生　→　　学生们

练一练　Exercises

完成会话　Complete the following dialogues.

A：你好。

B：你好，我是金大成，_____是爱子，_____都是留学生。

A：认识_____很高兴。

B：认识你，我们也很高兴。

[2] **副词"都"**　The adverb "都"

"都"表示包括某一范围的全部成员。

"都" indicates including all the members within a certain scope.

（1）

她们都是日本人。

（2）

他们都是中国人，　　　　　他们也都是中国人。

（3）

他们不都是中国人。

（4）

他们都不是中国人，他们都是美国（Měiguó, America）人。

练一练　Exercises

看图片完成句子　Look at the pictures and complete the sentences.

（1）

他们_____是韩国人，_____是日本人。

（2）

他是韩国人，　　　　他们_____是韩国人。

（3）

他们_____是日本人。

[3] 动词"叫" The verb "叫"

一般第一次介绍某人的名字或某事物的名称时用"叫"。

"叫" is used to tell the name of somebody or something for the first time.

你好，我叫李明。

李明

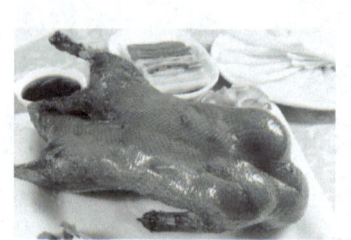

这个菜（cài, dish）叫北京烤鸭（Běijīng kǎoyā, Beijing roast duck）。

语法 | Grammar

1 动词谓语句 A sentence with a verbal predicate

动词谓语句的谓语部分是动词。这是大部分语言都有的一种句子结构。动词谓语句的基本结构是：

A verb is used as a predicate in a sentence with a verbal predicate, which is a structure used in most languages. Its basic structure is as follows:

主语（S）	谓语（P）				标点（Punctuation）
	副词（Adv）	动词（V）	宾语（O）	助词（Pt）	
我		叫	爱子		。
我	不	姓	金		。
你		认识	他	吗	？
我们		认识			。

> 练一练　Exercises

看图完成会话　Look at the pictures and complete the dialogues.

（1）

A：他叫李生吗？
B：他_____，
　　他叫成龙（Chéng Lóng）。

（2）

A：_____？
B：他不姓李，他姓 Jackson。

② **形容词谓语句**　A sentence with an adjectival predicate

形容词谓语句的谓语部分是形容词，形容词前常常有"很"等程度副词修饰。否定形式是"不＋形容词"，疑问形式是"形容词＋吗"。形容词谓语句的基本结构是：

An adjective, often preceded and modified by "很" or other adverb of degree, is used as a predicate in a sentence with an adjectival predicate. Its negative form is "不 ＋ adjective", and its interrogative form "adjective ＋ 吗". The basic structure of a sentence with an adjectival predicate is as follows:

主语（S）	谓语（P）			标点（Punctuation）
	副词（Adv）	形容词（A）	助词（Pt）	
他	很	高兴		。
我	不	高兴		。
你		好	吗	？

注意：形容词谓语句中没有"是"，因此下边的句子是不对的。

Note: "是" is not used in a sentence with an adjectival predicate, so the following sentences are wrong.

（1）他是高兴。（×）
（2）我是不高兴。（×）

> 练一练 Exercises

看图完成句子或会话　Look at the pictures and complete the sentences or dialogues.

（1）

她_____。

（2）

他_____。

（3）

A：_____？
B：他很忙（máng, busy）。

3 疑问代词"哪"　The interrogative pronoun "哪"

疑问代词"哪"，用来询问人或事物，从多个对象中确认一个时使用。在本课中，"哪+国"用来询问一个人的国籍。例如：

The interrogative pronoun "哪" is used to ask for a choice of somebody or something from several alternatives. "哪 + 国" in this lesson is used to ask somebody's nationality. For example,

主语（S）+是+哪国人？

A：他　是　哪国人？
B：他　是　中国人。

孔子（Kǒngzǐ, Confucius）

练一练　Exercises

看图选词填空　Look at the pictures and choose words to fill in the blanks.

哪国人　美国人（Měiguó rén, American）　英国人（Yīngguó rén, British）

（1）A：她们是_____？
　　B：她们是日本人。

（2）A：他是哪国人？
　　B：他是_____。

（3）A：他们是哪国人？
　　B：他们是_____。

练一练　Exercises

问问你同学的国籍　Ask your classmates about their nationality.

A：你是哪国人？
B：我是……。你呢？
A：我是……。

4 疑问代词"什么"　The interrogative pronoun "什么"

疑问代词"什么"用于询问事物。例如：

The interrogative pronoun "什么" is used to ask for information about something. For example,

练一练　Exercises

完成会话　Complete the dialogues.

（1）A：_____？
　　　B：我叫金大成。

（2）A：_____？
　　　B：他姓金。

情景交际 | Communication

两三个同学一组，互相介绍并询问对方的国籍。准备时间：3～5分钟。

Work in groups of two or three. Introduce each other and ask your partner's nationality. Preparation time: 3-5 minutes.

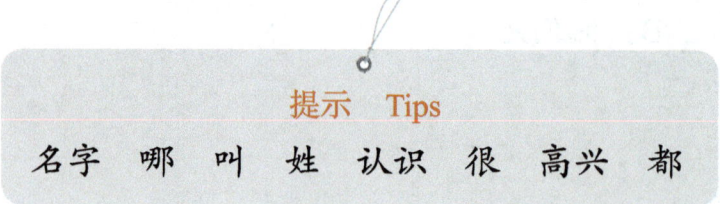

写作 | Writing

◆ **添句成段**　Write more sentences to compose a paragraph

在所给句子前后加上两三句话，把它补充成一段完整的文字。

Write two or three sentences before or after the given sentence to make a complete passage.

我是……人

_____

_____

_____

语音 Pronunciation

练一练 Exercises

1 辨声调 Distinguish the tones    10-03

guī — guì
tortoise   expensive

kuǎ — kuā
to collapse   to praise

huí guó — huǐguò
to go back to   to repent one's error
one's country

hěn guāi — hěn guài
well-behaved   very strange

huái — huài
bosom   bad

huó — huǒ
to live   fire

huǒhuā — huǒhuà
spark   to cremate

bùguǐ — bú guì
against the law   not expensive
or discipline

2 辨声母 Distinguish the initials    10-04

g — k — h

guó — huó
kuì — huì
kuài — huài
guā — huā

3. 辨韵母　Distinguish the finals　10-05

ua — uo	uai — ui
guǎ — guǒ	huài — huì
kuà — kuò	guǎi — guǐ
wā — wō	wài — wèi
huà — huò	guāi — guī

4. 声调组合　Combination of tones　10-06

− −	− ˊ	− ˇ	− ˋ	− ˚
huāshēng peanut	huāchá scented tea	huāduǒ flower	huāfèi to spend	huā de flowery

ˊ −	ˊ ˊ	ˊ ˇ	ˊ ˋ	ˊ ˚
huíshēng echo	huídá to answer	huíxiǎng to think back	huíhuà to reply	huíqu to go back

ˇ −	ˇ ˊ	ˇ ˇ	ˇ ˋ	ˇ ˚
wǒ chī I eat	wǒ lái I come	wǒ mǎi I buy	wǒ qù I go	wǒ de my/mine

ˋ −	ˋ ˊ	ˋ ˇ	ˋ ˋ	ˋ ˚
wàiyī coat	wàiguó foreign country	wàiyǔ foreign language	wàihuì foreign exchange	wàibian outside

5. 双音节连读　Practice the liaison of the disyllabic words　10-07

Yīngguó England	Zhōngguó China	Déguó Germany	Hánguó Republic of Korea
Měiguó America	Fǎguó France	Tàiguó Thailand	Yuènán Vietnam

6. 多音节连读　Practice the liaison of the polysyllabic words　10-08

Yīngguó rén British	Hánguó rén Korean	Měiguó rén American	Tàiguó rén Thai

Xīnjiāpō rén	Hélán rén	Yìdàlì rén	Àodàlìyà rén
Singaporean	Dutch	Italian	Australian

7 儿化练习 Practice the retroflex ending 🔊 10-09

xiānhuār	guǒzhīr	liáotiānr	guǎiwānr
flower	juice	to chat	to make a turn
hǎowánr	xiǎoháir	xiǎoyúr	gànhuór
interesting	child	little fish	to work
yìdiǎnr	fāhuǒr	xīnyǎnr	lǎotóur
a little bit	to get angry	mind	old man
zài zhèr	zài nàr	yǒu shìr	bǎobèir
to be here	to be there	to be occupied	baby

8 朗读 Read aloud 🔊 10-10

好

很好

你很好。

我也很好。

9 趣味朗读 Interesting reading materials 🔊 10-11

我 叫 钱 爱国
Wǒ jiào Qián Àiguó

我 介绍 (to introduce) 一下 自己 (oneself)：
Wǒ jièshào yíxià zìjǐ:

我 姓 钱，叫 钱 爱国。
Wǒ xìng Qián, jiào Qián Àiguó.

我 很 爱钱 (money)，也 很 爱国 (to love one's country)。
Wǒ hěn ài qián, yě hěn ài guó.

别 (don't) 笑 (to laugh)！别 笑！
Bié xiào! Bié xiào!

请 (please) 记住 (to bear in mind) 我。
Qǐng jìzhù wǒ.

汉字 Characters

边学边练 Study and practice

① 汉字的笔顺　Stroke order of Chinese characters

一个汉字是由一个或一个以上的笔画组成的。先写哪一笔、后写哪一笔也是有顺序的，这就是笔顺。学习笔顺是为了把汉字写得更快、更漂亮，也是为了查字典更方便。

A Chinese character is composed of one or more strokes. The order in which strokes are written is the stroke order. Having learned the stroke order, you can write characters faster and more beautiful and consult a dictionary more easily.

例字 Example character	笔顺 Stroke order	笔顺规则 Rules of stroke order
十	一 十	先横后竖 Horizontal strokes before vertical strokes
个	丿 人 个	从上到下 Upper strokes before lower strokes
儿	丿 儿	从左到右 Left strokes before right strokes
月	丿 几 月 月	先外后内 Enclosing strokes before enclosed strokes
日	丨 冂 日 日	先外后内再封口 First write enclosing strokes, then enclosed strokes and finally the strokes at the bottom
小	亅 小 小	先中间后两边 Vertical strokes in the middle before strokes on both sides

2 认写基本汉字　Learn and write the basic Chinese characters

(1) 者　zhě　person

一 十 土 耂 耂 者 者 者　8 strokes

(2) 玉　yù　jade

一 二 干 王 玉　5 strokes

(3) 夕　xī　sunset

丿 夕 夕　3 strokes

(4) 只　zhǐ　only

丶 口 口 尸 只　5 strokes

3 认写本课汉字　Learn and write the Chinese characters in this lesson

(1) 哪　nǎ　which

哪 → 口 + 月 + 阝

(2) 国　guó　country; nation

国 → 囗 + 玉

(3) 你们　nǐmen　you (pl.)

们 → 亻 + 门

(4) 都　dōu　all; both

都 → 者 + 阝

(5) 叫　jiào　to be called

叫 → 口 + 丩

(6) 什么　shénme　what

什 → 亻 + 十

么 → 丿 + 厶

123

（7）名字　　míngzi　　name

名 → 夕 + 口　　name

字 → 宀 + 子　　style name, taken at the age of twenty, by which a man is sometimes called; character

（8）姓　　xìng　　one's surname is...; surname

姓 → 女 + 生

（9）他　　tā　　he; him

他 → 亻 + 也

（10）她　　tā　　she; her

她 → 女 + 也

（11）认识　　rènshi　　to meet; to know

认 → 讠 + 人　　to recognize

识 → 讠 + 只　　to know

（12）很　　hěn　　very; quite

很 → 彳 + 艮

（13）高兴　　gāoxìng　　glad; happy

高 → 亠 + 口 + 冂 + 口　　high

兴 → 䒑 + 八　　mood; excitement

实践活动 | Activity

● **走一走，问一问**　Go for a survey

问一问你们班同学的姓名和国籍，要求问 3 位以上，把他们的姓名、国籍填在下面的表里（可以写拼音），下次课汇报。

Ask three or more of your classmates about their names and nationalities. Fill in the following table (*pinyin* can be used) and report your findings to the class next time.

第10课　你是哪国人

姓名　Name	国籍　Nationality

他/她叫_____，他/她是_____（国）人。

文化点滴　Cultural Note

百家姓　The Book of Family Names
Bǎijiāxìng

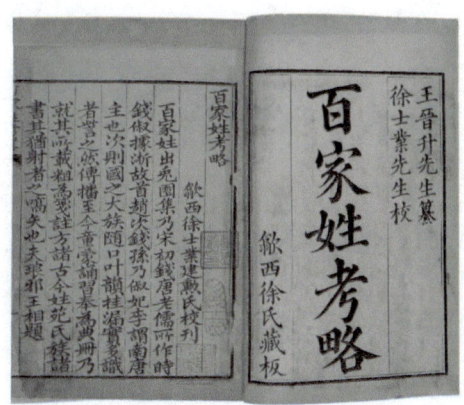

中国有13亿人口、100多个常用姓氏。

China has a population of 1.3 billion with over 100 family names frequently used.

目前中国姓氏前100位排名 *

王 李 张 刘 陈 杨 黄 吴 赵 周 徐 孙 马 朱 胡 林 郭
何 高 罗 郑 梁 谢 宋 唐 许 邓 冯 韩 曹 曾 彭 萧 蔡
潘 田 董 袁 于 余 叶 蒋 杜 苏 魏 程 吕 丁 沈 任 姚
卢 傅 钟 姜 崔 谭 廖 范 汪 陆 金 石 戴 贾 韦 夏 邱
方 侯 邹 熊 孟 秦 白 江 阎 薛 尹 段 雷 黎 史 龙 陶
贺 顾 毛 郝 龚 邵 万 钱 严 赖 覃 洪 武 莫 孔

答一答 Answer the following questions

1. 你知道哪些中国人的姓？请写一写。
   Write the Chinese family names you know.

2. 中国人口最多的姓是什么？
   Which is the most popular family name in China?

学习后记 | Summary

词语 Vocabulary	语言点 Grammar

---

* 来源：《新华每日电讯》, 2013 年 4 月 15 日载。

11 你住哪儿
Where Do You Live

学习提示 Learning Tips

重点词 Key Words	住 哪儿 宿舍 几 的 电话 号码 多少
重点句 Key Sentences	1. 你住哪儿？ Nǐ zhù nǎr? 2. 我 住 留学生 宿舍。 Wǒ zhù liúxuéshēng sùshè. 3. 你住几号楼？ Nǐ zhù jǐ hào lóu? 4. 8 号 楼 401 房间。 Bā hào lóu sì líng yāo fángjiān. 5. 你的 电话 号码是 多少？ Nǐ de diànhuà hàomǎ shì duōshao?
功能 Function	询问住址、电话 Asking one's address and telephone number

课文 Text

杰克：你 住 哪儿？
Jiékè: Nǐ zhù nǎr?

爱子：我 住 留学生 宿舍。
Àizǐ: Wǒ zhù liúxuéshēng sùshè.

杰克：几个 人 住？
Jiékè: Jǐ ge rén zhù?

爱子：我 一个 人 住。你 住 哪儿？
Àizǐ: Wǒ yí ge rén zhù. Nǐ zhù nǎr?

杰克：我 住 校外。你 住 几号 楼？
Jiékè: Wǒ zhù xiàowài. Nǐ zhù jǐ hào lóu?

爱子：8 号楼 401 房间。
Àizǐ: Bā hào lóu sì líng yāo fángjiān.

杰克：你 的 电话 号码 是 多少？[1]
Jiékè: Nǐ de diànhuà hàomǎ shì duōshao?

爱子：62318015。
Àizǐ: Liù èr sān yāo bā líng yāo wǔ.

杰克：我 的 电话 号码 是 13801057259。
Jiékè: Wǒ de diànhuà hàomǎ shì yāo sān bā líng yāo líng wǔ qī èr wǔ jiǔ.
住 校内 方便 吗？
Zhù xiàonèi fāngbiàn ma?

爱子：很 方便。
Àizǐ: Hěn fāngbiàn.

练一练 Exercises

1. 听课文，说说你听到了什么　Listen to the text and talk about what you hear.

2. 跟老师读课文　Read the text after the teacher.

3. 两人一组，分角色读　Work in pairs to play the roles and read the text.

4. 回答问题　Answer the following questions.

（1）爱子住哪儿？

（2）杰克住留学生宿舍吗？

（3）杰克的电话号码是多少？

5. 两人一组，分角色表演　Work in pairs and play the roles.

6. 根据课文内容填空，然后朗读　Fill in the blanks based on the text and read it aloud.

爱子住_____，_____号楼_____房间，她的电话号码是_____。住校内很_____。杰克住_____，他的电话号码是_____。

生词　New words

11-02

序号 No.	词语 Word	拼音 Pinyin	词性 Word Class	英文释义 Meaning in English	例子 Example
1	住	zhù	V	to live	
2	哪儿	nǎr	Pr	where	住哪儿
3	宿舍	sùshè	N	dormitory	宿舍很好
4	几	jǐ	Pr	how many	几个人
5	个	gè	M	*a measure word of general use*	一个人
6	校外	xiàowài	N	off campus	住校外
7	号	hào	M	*used after a number to mark the order*	1号　几号
8	楼	lóu	N	building	4号楼　几号楼
9	房间	fángjiān	N	room	306房间
10	的	de	Pt	*(used after an attribute)* of	我的房间　我的宿舍　我的老师
11	电话	diànhuà	N	telephone	我的电话
12	号码	hàomǎ	N	number	电话号码
13	多少	duōshao	Pr	how many; how much	号码是多少
14	校内	xiàonèi	N	on campus	住校内
15	方便	fāngbiàn	A	convenient	很方便　不方便

注释 Note

[1] "……号码是多少？" "What's the number of...?"

"……号码是多少？"用于询问电话、房间、门牌、身份证等的号码。

"……号码是多少？" is used to ask about a person's telephone number, room number, house number or ID number, etc.

（1）A：你的电话号码是多少？
B：13801057259。

（2）A：你的房间号码是多少？
B：501。

练一练 Exercises

完成会话　Complete the following dialogues.

（1）A：你的房间_____？
B：301。

（2）A：_____？
B：61842735。

语法 Grammar

1 数字的读法（1） How numbers are read (1)

0	1	2	3	4	5	6	7	8	9
〇	一	二	三	四	五	六	七	八	九
líng	yī	èr	sān	sì	wǔ	liù	qī	bā	jiǔ

号码中的数字要一个一个地读出来，例如电话号码、门牌号码、护照号码、汽车车牌号码、身份证号码等。在读号码时，1通常都读成yāo。例如：

Digits in numbers such as a telephone number, house number, passport number car number and ID number, etc. are read one by one. The digit 1 is usually pronounced yāo. For example,

8号楼　　　　　　　bā hào lóu
401房间　　　　　　sì líng yāo fángjiān
13801057259　　　yāo sān bā líng yāo líng wǔ qī èr wǔ jiǔ

练一练　Exercises

读一读，写一写　Read and write.

（1）

电话号码（telephone number）：
_____

（2）

门牌号码（house number）：
_____

② **疑问代词"哪儿"　The interrogative pronoun "哪儿"**

"哪儿"用来询问地点，在句中可以做主语（S）或宾语（O）。

"哪儿" is used as a subject (S) or an object (O) in a sentence to ask about place.

（1）你住哪儿？（O）
（2）你去哪儿？（O）
（3）哪儿方便？（S）

练一练　Exercises

完成对话　Complete the dialogues.

（1）A：_____？
　　　B：我住宿舍。

（2）A：_____？
　　　B：我住校外。

③ **疑问代词"几"　The interrogative pronoun "几"**

"几"一般用来询问十以下的数字。"几"和名词之间一般要加上量词，例如：

The interrogative pronoun "几" is used to ask about numbers fewer than 10. A measure word is usually used between "几" and the noun. For example,

（1）A：你认识几个老师？

　　B：四个。

（2）A：你们宿舍住几个学生？

　　B：三个。

"几 + 号"常常用来问号码，例如：

The structure "几 + 号" is usually used to ask about a number. For example,

（1）A：你住几号房间？

　　B：401号房间。

（2）A：你住几号楼？

　　B：8号楼。

练一练 Exercises

用"几"完成会话　Complete the dialogues using "几".

（1）A：_____？

　　B：我住502号房间。

（2）A：_____？

　　B：我住6号楼。

（3）A：_____？

　　B：我们宿舍住四个学生。

4 结构助词"的" The structural particle "的"

汉语可以用"的"表示领属。

"的" in Chinese can be used to indicate a possessive relationship.

代词（Pr）/名词（N）	的	名词（N）
我	的	名字
我们	的	老师
老师	的	房间

"的"后跟的名词指的是工作单位、家人时，"的"字可以省略，例如：他们学校（xuéxiào, school），我妈妈（māma, mother）。

"的" is omitted if it is followed by an organization in which somebody works or somebody's family member. For example, 他们学校 (xuéxiào, school), 我妈妈 (māma, mother).

练一练　Exercises

用"的"完成句子　Complete the following sentences using "的".

（1）_____房间很好。

（2）_____老师很高兴。

（3）_____电话号码不是13801057259。

情景交际　Communication

与你的同学互相提问并回答：住哪儿，电话号码是多少。准备时间：3～5分钟。

Ask each other questions with your classmates and answer them about their addresses and telephone numbers. Preparation time: 3-5 minutes.

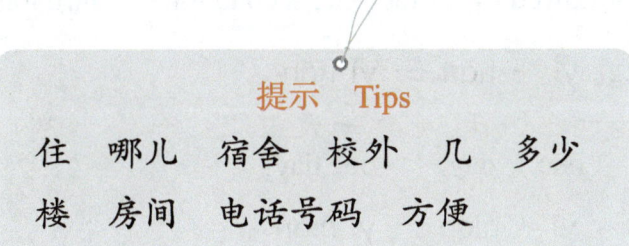

提示　Tips

住　哪儿　宿舍　校外　几　多少
楼　房间　电话号码　方便

写作　Writing

◆ **添句成段**　Write more sentences to compose a paragraph

在所给句子前后加上两三句话，把它补充成一段完整的文字。

Write two or three sentences before or after the given sentence to make a complete passage.

我的电话号码是……

_____

_____

_____

边学边练 Study and practice

◆ "一"的变调 Tone sandhi of "一"

（1）"一"后边是四声时，"一"读成二声 yí。

"一" is pronounced in second tone if it is followed by a fourth-tone syllable.

$$yī + ` → yí `$$

e.g.: yī + jù + huà → yí jù huà
　　　一　　句　　话　　一句话
　　　one　a measure word　word　one sentence

（2）"一"后边是一声、二声、三声时，"一"读成四声 yì。

"一" is pronounced in fourth tone if it is followed by a first tone, second tone or third tone.

$$yī + ˉ → yì ˉ$$
$$yī + ´ → yì ´$$
$$yī + ˇ → yì ˇ$$

e.g.: yī + tiān → yì tiān
　　　一　　天　　一天
　　　one　day　one day

yī + nián → yì nián
一　　年　　一年
one　year　one year

yī + qǐ → yìqǐ
一　起　一起
　　　together

（3）但需注意，"一"作为序数词使用时，读原调一声。例如：一楼（yī lóu, the first floor）、一号（yī hào, No. 1）。

But please note that "一" is pronounced in its original tone, the first tone, if it is used as a cardinal number. For example, 一楼 (yī lóu, the first floor), 一号 (yī hào, No. 1), etc.

◆ 练一练 Exercises  11-03

写出"一"的实际声调 Mark the tones of "一".

y__ biàn　　y__ zhí　　y__ tiān
y__ běn　　y__ huìr　　y__ gòng
y__ yàng　　y__ cì　　y__ qǐ

更多练习 More exercises

1. 辨声调 Distinguish the tones 🎧 11-04

ní — nǐ	lú — lù
mud you	donkey green

rě — rè	nuó — nuò
to offend hot	to move promise

róu — ròu	lóu — lòu
to rub meat	building to leak

nǐrén — nírén	èyú — Éyǔ
personification clay figure	crocodile Russian

yǔyī — yùyī	lóuyǔ — lòu yǔ
raincoat bathrobe	buildings leakage of rain

2. 辨声母 Distinguish the initials 🎧 11-05

l — n

lǚ — nǚ
luó — nuó
le — ne
lí — ní

l — r

lán — rán
lǎo — rǎo
lè — rè
lòu — ròu

3. 辨韵母 Distinguish the finals 🎧 11-06

i — ü

yì — yù
nǐ — nǚ
qī — qū
lí — lǘ

uo — e — ou

tuò — tè — tòu
wò — è — òu
zhuō — zhē — zhōu
guō — gē — gōu

④ 声调组合 Combination of tones  11-07

- -	- ˊ	- ˇ	- ˋ	- ∘
yīshēng doctor; physician	yī lóu the first floor	yīděng first-class	yījià coat hanger	yīfu clothing
ˊ -	ˊ ˊ	ˊ ˇ	ˊ ˋ	ˊ ∘
lóutī stairs	lóufáng a building of two or more floors	lóu bǎn floor	lóudào corridor	lóu li in the building
ˇ -	ˇ ˊ	ˇ ˇ	ˇ ˋ	ˇ ∘
nǐ shuō you speak	nǐ ná you take (sth.)	nǐ zǒu you go away	nǐ zuò you do (sth.)	nǐ de yours
ˋ -	ˋ ˊ	ˋ ˇ	ˋ ˋ	ˋ ∘
rèshēn warm-up	rèménr popular	règǒu hot dog	rè'ài to have deep love for	rè de hot

⑤ 双音节连读 Practice the liaison of the disyllabic words  11-08

yóujú
post office

chāoshì
supermarket

fànguǎnr
restaurant

xuéxiào
school

yīyuàn
hospital

yàodiàn
drugstore

gōngsī
company

mǎlù
road

⑥ 多音节连读 Practice the liaison of the polysyllabic words  11-09

tǐyùguǎn
gym

jiàoxuélóu
classroom building

sùshèlóu
dormitory building

bàngōngshì
office

wàishìchù
Foreign Affairs Department

7 根据拼写规则，写出下列韵母单独做音节时的汉语拼音

Based on the spelling rules, write down the *pinyin* in which finals are used as independent syllables

ī _____   ián _____   iòng _____   iǒu _____

ǔ _____   uǒ _____   uà _____   uài _____

uén _____   uēng _____   uǎng _____   ié _____

ú _____   üè _____   ūn _____   uèi _____

8 朗读 Read aloud   11-10

住哪儿

住宿舍

住哪儿的宿舍

住校内的宿舍

住校内的宿舍很方便

9 趣味朗读 Interesting reading materials   11-11

几 个 人 住 好
Jǐ ge rén zhù hǎo

一 个 人 住 安静 (quiet),
Yí ge rén zhù ānjìng,

两 个 人 住 热闹 (lively and bustling)。
liǎng ge rén zhù rènao.

各 (each) 有 (to have) 各 的 好 (advantage)。
Gè   yǒu   gè de hǎo.

就 看 (to depend on) 你 的 需要 (need)。
Jiù kàn   nǐ de xūyào.

汉字 | Characters

边学边练 Study and practice

1 认写基本汉字 Learn and write the basic Chinese characters

(1) 主　zhǔ　to host
丶 亠 宀 主 主　5 strokes

(2) 百　bǎi　hundred
一 丆 丆 百 百 百　6 strokes

(3) 几　jǐ　how many
丿 几　2 strokes

(4) 交　jiāo　to hand over
丶 亠 宀 六 交 交　6 strokes

(5) 米　mǐ　rice
丶 丷 䒑 半 米 米　6 strokes

(6) 户　hù　household
丶 丶 𠃋 户　4 strokes

(7) 方　fāng　square
丶 亠 宀 方　4 strokes

(8) 白　bái　white
丿 丨 白 白 白　5 strokes

(9) 勺　sháo　spoon
丿 勹 勺　3 strokes

(10) 电　diàn　electricity
丨 冂 日 曰 电　5 strokes

138

（11）舌　shé　tongue

一 二 千 千 舌 舌　6 strokes

（12）石　shí　stone

一 丆 丆 石 石　5 strokes

（13）少　shǎo　few; little

丨 丷 小 少　4 strokes

（14）更　gèng　more

一 厂 丂 亓 百 更 更　7 strokes

2 认写本课汉字　Learn and write the Chinese characters in this lesson

(1) 住　zhù　to live

住 → 亻 + 主

(2) 宿舍　sùshè　dormitory

宿 → 宀 + 亻 + 百　to stay overnight

舍 → 人 + 舌　house

(3) 个　gè　*a measure word of general use*

个 → 人 + 丨

(4) 校外　xiàowài　off campus

校 → 木 + 交　school

外 → 夕 + 卜　outside

(5) 号　hào　*used after a number to mark the order*

号 → 口 + 丂

(6) 楼　lóu　building

楼 → 木 + 米 + 女

(7) 房间　fángjiān　room
　　房 → 户 + 方　house
　　间 → 门 + 日　room

(8) 的　de　of
　　的 → 白 + 勺

(9) 电话　diànhuà　telephone
　　话 → 讠 + 舌　word; talk

(10) 号码　hàomǎ　number
　　码 → 石 + 马　code

(11) 多少　duōshao　how many; how much
　　多 → 夕 + 夕　many; much

(12) 校内　xiàonèi　on campus
　　内 → 冂 + 人　inside

(13) 方便　fāngbiàn　convenient
　　便 → 亻 + 更　convenient

实践活动 | Activity

◆ **走一走，问一问**　Go for a survey

问一问你们班老师和同学的住址和电话号码，填入下表中。要求问3个人以上，下次课汇报。

Ask three or more of your teachers and classmates about their addresses and telephone numbers. Fill in the following table and report your findings to the class next time.

姓名 Name	住址 Address	电话号码 Telephone number

文化点滴 Cultural Note

中国人常用的数字手势
Zhōngguó rén chángyòng de shùzì shǒushì
Chinese People's Frequently-Used Gestures for Numbers

> 用手势，说汉语。
> Speak Chinese while using gestures.

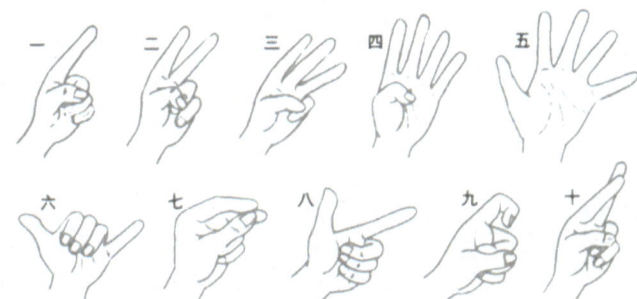

答一答　Answer the following questions

你们国家有这样的数字手势吗？如果有，怎么做？
Do you use gestures to express numbers in your country? If you do, what are they?

学习后记 Summary

词语 Vocabulary

语言点 Grammar

12 银行在哪儿
Where Is the Bank

学习提示 Learning Tips

重点词 Key Words	请问 银行 在 里 那儿 就 去 一起 吧
重点句 Key Sentences	1. 请问，银行在哪儿？ Qǐngwèn, yínháng zài nǎr? 2. 在办公楼里。 Zài bàngōnglóu li. 3. 在几层？ Zài jǐ céng? 4. 就在一层。 Jiù zài yī céng. 5. 一起去吧。 Yìqǐ qù ba.
功能 Function	询问处所 Asking the location

课文 Text

杰克：请问[1]，银行在哪儿？
Jiékè: Qǐngwèn, yínháng zài nǎr?

张小英：在办公楼里。
Zhāng Xiǎoyīng: Zài bàngōnglóu li.

杰克：办公楼在哪儿？
Jiékè: Bàngōnglóu zài nǎr?

张小英：在那儿，你看，那个红楼就[2]是。
Zhāng Xiǎoyīng: Zài nàr, nǐ kàn, nàge hóng lóu jiù shì.

杰克：在几层？
Jiékè: Zài jǐ céng?

张小英：就在一层。我也去银行，一起去吧。
Zhāng Xiǎoyīng: Jiù zài yī céng. Wǒ yě qù yínháng, yìqǐ qù ba.

杰克：行。
Jiékè: Xíng.

练一练 Exercises

1. 听课文，说说你听到了什么 Listen to the text and talk about what you hear.

2. 跟老师读课文 Read the text after the teacher.

3. 两人一组，分角色读 Work in pairs to play the roles and read the text.

4. 回答问题 Answer the following questions.

   （1）银行在哪儿？
   （2）办公楼是哪个楼？
   （3）银行在几层？
   （4）张小英去银行吗？

5. 两人一组，分角色表演 Work in pairs and play the roles.

6. 根据课文内容填空，然后朗读　Fill in the blanks based on the text and then read it aloud.

银行_____办公楼_____，在一_____。那个红楼_____是。杰克、张小英_____去银行。

生词　New words

 12-02

序号 No.	词语 Word	拼音 *Pinyin*	词性 Word Class	英文释义 Meaning in English	例子 Example
1	请问	qǐngwèn	V	May I ask…; Excuse me…	
	问	wèn	V	to ask	问老师
2	银行	yínháng	N	bank	中国银行　校内的银行
3	在	zài	V	to be (at; in; on); to be (here; there)	在哪儿　在宿舍　在校外　在8号楼
4	办公楼	bàngōnglóu	N	office building	在办公楼
5	里	li	N	inside	办公楼里
6	那儿	nàr	Pr	there	在那儿
	这儿	zhèr	Pr	here	在这儿
7	看	kàn	V	to look	你看
8	那个	nàge/nèige	Pr	that	那个楼
	这个	zhège/zhèige	Pr	this	这个学生
9	红	hóng	A	red	红楼
10	就	jiù	Adv	just	就是
11	层	céng	M	floor	一层　三层　几层楼
12	去	qù	V	to go	去银行　去办公楼
13	一起	yìqǐ	Adv	together	一起去　一起住
14	吧	ba	Pt	*a modal particle*	去吧
15	行	xíng	V	all right	

专有名词 Proper noun

| 张小英 Zhāng Xiǎoyīng | Zhang Xiaoying, name of a Chinese girl student. Please refer to "Introduction to the Main Characters" for more details. |

注释 Notes

[1] "请问，……?" "Excuse me, ...?"

提问题时先说"请问"是非常礼貌的表达。

"请问" is a very polite expression used before asking a question.

A：请问，你是留学生吗？
B：是，我是留学生。

练一练 Exercises

用"请问"完成会话　Complete the dialogues using "请问".

（1）A：_____，你叫什么名字？
　　　B：我叫金大成。

（2）A：_____，留学生宿舍在哪儿？
　　　B：在那儿。

[2] 副词"就" The adverb "就"

副词"就"可用于表示强调。
The adverb "就" can be used to indicate emphasis.

A：爱子在哪儿？
B：爱子就在那儿。

练一练 Exercises

用"就"完成会话　Complete the dialogues using "就".

（1）A：你住校内？
　　　B：是，我_____住留学生宿舍7号楼。

（2）A：老师在哪儿？
　　　B：看，老师_____在那儿。

146

语法 | Grammar

1 方位词"里"和"外" The nouns of locality "里" and "外"

名词+方位词"里/外",表示方位。例如:

The structure "noun + a noun of locality '里/外'" is used to indicate the position. For example,

名词(N)	里/外
办公楼	里
宿舍	外

练一练 Exercises

用"里""外"填空 Fill in the blanks with "里" or "外".

楼（　）

楼（　）

2 语气助词"吧" The modal particle "吧"

语气助词"吧"用在句末,可表达建议、商量、请求、命令等语气。例如:

The modal particle "吧" is used at the end of a sentence to make a suggestion, consultation, request, or command. For example,

（1）我们一起去银行吧。
（2）你去办公楼吧。
（3）你就在这儿吧。

练一练 Exercises

用"吧"完成会话　Complete the dialogues using "吧".

（1）A：我们去哪儿？

　　　B：_____。

（2）A：你看吗？

　　　B：我不看，_____。

情景交际 | Communication

两人或三人一组，介绍自己的国家（guójiā, country）在哪儿（我们国家……）。准备时间：3～5分钟。

Work in groups of two or three and introduce where your country is located with "我们国家...". Preparation time: 3-5 minutes.

提示　Tips
在　哪儿　这儿　你看　就

写作 Writing

◆ **添句成段** Write more sentences to compose a paragraph

在所给句子前后加上两三句话，把它补充成一段完整的文字。
Write two or three sentences before or after the given sentence to make a complete passage.

你看，……

_____

_____

_____

语音 Pronunciation

🏠 **练一练** Exercises

① 辨声调　Distinguish the tones　 12-03

| shān — shàn | chéng — chēng | ráng — ràng |
| mountain fan | city to weigh | flesh (of a melon) to let |

| zhǐ — zhī | rènshi — rénshì | chéngshì — chéngshí |
| paper juice | to know personnel | city honest |

| chíchěng — chìchéng | zhìshāng — zhǐ shang |
| to gallop sincere | IQ on paper |

② 辨声母　Distinguish the initials　 12-04

zh — ch

zhēng — chēng
zhí — chí
zhǐ — chǐ
zhàng — chàng

sh — r

shēng — rēng
shén — rén
shǎn — rǎn
shì — rì

149

3 辨韵母　Distinguish the finals　 12-05

an — ang

| bān — bāng |
| lán — láng |
| chǎn — chǎng |
| shàn — shàng |

en — eng

| zhēn — zhēng |
| mén — méng |
| zhěn — zhěng |
| mèn — mèng |

ang — eng

| fáng — féng |
| dǎng — děng |
| chàng — chèng |
| fāng — fēng |

4 声调组合　Combination of tones　 12-06

- -	- ´	- ˇ	- `	- ˙
zhīzhū spider	zhīchí to support	zhī chǐ to have a sense of shame	zhīzhù mainstay	zhīshi knowledge
´ -	´ ´	´ ˇ	´ `	´ ˙
chéngbāo to contract	chéngshí honest	chéngzhǎng to grow up	chéngshì city	chéng le to have accomplished
ˇ -	ˇ ´	ˇ ˇ	ˇ `	ˇ ˙
shǐzhōng from beginning to end	shǐshí historical facts	shǐzǔ earliest ancestor	shǐmìng misson	shǐshang in history
` -	` ´	` ˇ	` `	` ˙
rìchū sunrise	rìcháng daily	Rìběn Japan	rìlì calendar	rìzi life

5 双音节中的三声读音练习　Practice the third tone of the disyllables　 12-07

lǎoshī teacher	měi tiān every day	hǎo rén good person	mǎnzú to be satisfied	xiǎo shì trifle	kǎoshì exam
shīlǐ lack of manners	zhēn hǎo very good	lúnlǐ ethics	réntǐ human body	xià yǔ to rain	dàxuě heavy snow
měihǎo fine	liǎojiě to know	lǎobǎn boss	hǎojiǔ long time	hěn lěng very cold	suǒyǐ so

6 双音节连读　Practice the liaison of the disyllabic words　🔊 12-08

hùzhào	fēijī	qiānzhèng
passport	plane	visa

jīchǎng	jīpiào	tián biǎo
airport	air ticket	to fill in the form

qiánbāo	bàomíng	
wallet	to sign up	

7 多音节连读　Practice the liaison of the polysyllabic words　🔊 12-09

Rénmínbì	yínhángkǎ	xìnyòngkǎ
RMB	bank card	credit card

xuéshēngzhèng	shēnfènzhèng
student ID	ID

8 朗读　Read aloud　🔊 12-10

银行

办公楼

红楼

银行在办公楼里。

办公楼就是那个红楼。

9 趣味朗读　Interesting reading materials　🔊 12-11

我 就 在 你 的 心 里 (in your heart)
Wǒ jiù zài nǐ de xīn li

我 在 中国, 你 在 国内。
Wǒ zài Zhōngguó, nǐ zài guónèi.

我 在 这儿, 你 在 那儿。
Wǒ zài zhèr, nǐ zài nàr.

你 离 (to be away from) 我 很 远 (far)。
Nǐ lí　　　　　　　　wǒ hěn yuǎn.

我 的 心 (heart) 常 (often) 去 你 那儿 (your place),
Wǒ de xīn cháng qù nǐ nàr,

你 的 心 常 来 (to come) 我 这儿 (my place)。
nǐ de xīn cháng lái wǒ zhèr.

我 离 你 很 近 (close)。
Wǒ lí nǐ hěn jìn.

你 在 哪里 (where) ?
Nǐ zài nǎli?

我 就 在 这里 (here), 在 你 的 心 里 (in your heart)。
Wǒ jiù zài zhèli, zài nǐ de xīn li.

边学边练 Study and practice

❶ 汉字的部件（1） Components of Chinese characters (1)

构成汉字的结构单位有笔画和部件。笔画是最小的单位，是不代表意义的（"一"除外）。而部件则是由笔画组成的，是有意义的。有的部件本身就是一个汉字，例如："女""口"；有的部件不能独立构成汉字，例如："亻""讠"。从本课起，我们将陆续归纳已学过的常用部件。

The structural units of Chinese characters include the stroke and component, of which the stroke is the minimal unit and is meaningless (except "一"), while the component is made up by strokes and is meaningful. Some components are characters themselves, for example, "女" and "口"; while other components are not independent characters, for example, "亻" and "讠". The frequently-used components will be summarized starting from this lesson.

亻 dānrénpáng person	你 you	亻 + 尔
	们 plural suffix	亻 + 门
	什 assorted	亻 + 十
	他 he; him	亻 + 也
	便 convenient	亻 + 更
	住 to live	亻 + 主

讠 yánzìpáng speech	认 to recognize	讠 + 人
	识 to know	讠 + 只
	话 talk; word	讠 + 舌
	请 please	讠 + 青

口 kǒuzìpáng mouth	吗 an interrogative particle	口 + 马
	呢 a modal particle	口 + 尼
	哪 which	口 + 那
	叫 to be called	口 + 丩

② 汉字的结构（1） Structures of Chinese characters (1)

左右结构
Left-right structure

e.g.: 你 → 亻+尔
吗 → 口+马

③ 认写基本汉字 Learn and write the basic Chinese characters

（1）青　qīng　blue

一 = 丰 圭 丰 青 青 青　　8 strokes

（2）办　bàn　to do; to handle

フ 力 办 办　　4 strokes

（3）里　lǐ　inside

　7 strokes

（4）文　wén　script

丶 一 ナ 文　4 strokes

（5）目　mù　eye

丨 冂 冃 目 目　5 strokes

（6）工　gōng　work

一 丁 工　3 strokes

（7）京　jīng　the capital of a country

丶 一 六 亠 宁 亨 京 京　8 strokes

（8）尤　yóu　especially

一 ナ 尢 尤　4 strokes

（9）尸　shī　dead body

㇕ ㇐ 尸　3 strokes

（10）云　yún　cloud

一 二 云 云　4 strokes

（11）走　zǒu　to walk

一 十 土 キ キ 走 走　7 strokes

（12）己　jǐ　oneself

㇕ ㇐ 己　3 strokes

4 认写本课汉字　Learn and write the Chinese characters in this lesson

（1）银行　yínháng　bank

银 → 钅+艮　silver

行 → 彳+亍　business firm

（2）在　zài　to be (at; in; on); to be (here; there)

在 → 才+土

(3) 请问　qǐngwèn　excuse me
　　请 → 讠+青　please
　　问 → 门+口　to ask

(4) 办公楼　bàngōnglóu　office building
　　公 → 八+厶　public business

(5) 看　kàn　to look
　　看 → 手+目

(6) 那　nà/nèi　that
　　那 → 男+阝

(7) 这　zhè/zhèi　this
　　这 → 文+辶

(8) 红　hóng　red
　　红 → 纟+工

(9) 就　jiù　just
　　就 → 京+尤

(10) 层　céng　floor
　　层 → 尸+云

(11) 去　qù　to go
　　去 → 土+厶

(12) 一起　yìqǐ　together
　　起 → 走+己　to rise; to get up

(13) 吧　ba　*a modal particle*
　　吧 → 口+巴

实践活动 | Activity

◆ **走一走，问一问 Go for a survey**

调查你的住处附近有什么银行，写出这些银行的中英文名字和简称，下次课汇报。

Find out what banks there are around your residence. Write down their names and abbreviations in English and Chinese. Report your findings to the class next time.

银行的中文名字及拼音 The Chinese name of the bank (in characters and *pinyin*)	中文简称 Abbreviation in Chinese	英文名字 The English name of the bank	英文简称 Abbreviation in English

文化点滴 | Cultural Note

中国的银行 Banks in China
Zhōngguó de yínháng

银行——人们的保险箱。

The bank — a safe of people.

答一答　Answer the following questions

1. 你经常去的银行是哪家银行？是上边的银行吗？

   Which bank do you usually go to? Is it one of the banks above?

2. 你觉得中国的银行服务怎么样？请选择。

   What do you think of the service of Chinese banks? Please choose from the choices given.

   A. 很好　Very good　　　B. 一般　Average　　　C. 不好　Unsatisfactory

学习后记　Summary

词语　Vocabulary	语言点　Grammar

注释、语法：单元总结（一）(第9课～第12课)
Notes and Grammar: Unit Review 1 (Lesson 9 ~ Lesson 12)

课号 Lesson	注释/语法 Note / Grammar		页码 Page No.	例句 Example sentence	我的句子 My sentence
第9课	注释	副词"也"	96	我也是学生。	
	语法	"是"字句（表示判断）	97	我不是留学生。	
		用"吗"的是非疑问句		你是老师吗？	
		汉语的语序及主要句子成分：主语、谓语、宾语		我不是老师。	
第10课	注释	后缀"们"	111	你们是留学生吗？	
		副词"都"		我们都是韩国人。	
		动词"叫"		我叫金大成。	
	语法	动词谓语句	114	我叫爱子。	
		形容词谓语句		我很高兴。	
		疑问代词"哪"		你是哪国人？	
		疑问代词"什么"		你叫什么名字？	
第11课	注释	"……号码是多少？"	130	你的电话号码是多少？	
	语法	数字的读法（1）	130	我住8号楼401房间。	
		疑问代词"哪儿"		你住哪儿？	
		疑问代词"几"		几个人住？	
		结构助词"的"		我的电话号码是13801057259。	
第12课	注释	"请问，……？"	146	请问，银行在哪儿？	
		副词"就"（表示强调）		那个红楼就是。	
	语法	方位词"里"和"外"	147	银行在办公楼里。	
		语气助词"吧"		我也去银行，一起去吧。	

13 明天你有课吗
Will You Have Classes Tomorrow

学习提示 Learning Tips

重点词 Key Words	明天　有　节　点　半　上课　下课　没有
重点句 Key Sentences	1. 明天　你有课吗? Míngtiān nǐ yǒu kè ma? 2. 我　明天　上午　有四节课。 Wǒ míngtiān shàngwǔ yǒu sì jié kè. 3. 八　点　半　上课，十二　点　半　下课。 Bā diǎn bàn shàngkè, shí'èr diǎn bàn xiàkè. 4. 下午　呢? Xiàwǔ ne? 5. 明天　我去图书馆。 Míngtiān wǒ qù túshūguǎn. 6. 我们　三　点　去，好吗? Wǒmen sān diǎn qù, hǎo ma?
功能 Function	询问时间 Asking the time

课文 Text

安娜：明天你有课吗?
Ānnà: Míngtiān nǐ yǒu kè ma?

金大成：有，我明天上午有四节课。八点半上课，十二点半下课。
Jīn Dàchéng: Yǒu, wǒ míngtiān shàngwǔ yǒu sì jié kè. Bā diǎn bàn shàngkè, shí'èr diǎn bàn xiàkè.

安娜：下午呢?[1]
Ānnà: Xiàwǔ ne?

金大成：下午没有课。
Jīn Dàchéng: Xiàwǔ méiyǒu kè.

安娜：明天我去图书馆，那儿有很多外文书，你去吗?
Ānnà: Míngtiān wǒ qù túshūguǎn, nàr yǒu hěn duō wàiwén shū, nǐ qù ma?

金大成：图书馆远吗?
Jīn Dàchéng: Túshūguǎn yuǎn ma?

安娜：不远。
Ānnà: Bù yuǎn.

金大成：好，我也去。我们三点去，好吗?[2]
Jīn Dàchéng: Hǎo, wǒ yě qù. Wǒmen sān diǎn qù, hǎo ma?

安娜：行。
Ānnà: Xíng.

练一练 Exercises

1. 听课文，说说你听到了什么   Listen to the text and talk about what you hear.

2. 跟老师读课文   Read the text after the teacher.

3. 两人一组，分角色读   Work in pairs to play the roles and read the text.

4. 先回答问题，再根据课文内容互相提问
   Answer the questions and then ask each other questions based on the text.

   （1）金大成明天上午有课吗？下午呢？
   （2）安娜明天去哪儿？
   ……

5. 两人一组，分角色表演　Work in pairs and play the roles.

6. 根据课文内容填空，然后朗读　Fill in the blanks based on the text and then read it aloud.

   金大成明天上午有_____课，_____上课，_____下课。他下午_____课。安娜明天_____，图书馆有_____。金大成_____去图书馆，他们三_____去。

生词　New words  13-02

序号 No.	词语 Word	拼音 Pinyin	词性 Word Class	英文释义 Meaning in English	例子 Example
1	明天	míngtiān	N	tomorrow	明天去
2	有	yǒu	V	to have	有课　有电话
3	课	kè	N	lesson	有课
4	上午	shàngwǔ	N	morning	一个上午　明天上午
5	四	sì	Num	four	四个人　四个学生
6	节	jié	M	a measure word for class hours	三节课　几节课
7	八	bā	Num	eight	八个学生
8	点	diǎn	M	o'clock	上午九点
9	半	bàn	Num	half	八点半
10	上课	shàngkè	VO	to go to class (both for students and teachers)	八点上课　上四节课
11	十二	shí'èr	Num	twelve	十二点　十二点半
12	下课	xiàkè	VO	to dismiss the class	十二点半下课
13	下午	xiàwǔ	N	afternoon	一个下午　明天下午

14	没有	méiyǒu	V/Adv	not to have, there is not	没有课　没有人 没有去　没有买
15	图书馆	túshūguǎn	N	library	一个图书馆　去图书馆
16	多	duō	A	many	很多
17	外文	wàiwén	N	foreign language	很多外文书
18	书	shū	N	book	很多书
19	远	yuǎn	A	far	很远　不远
20	三	sān	Num	three	三个老师　三点

专有名词　Proper noun

| 安娜 | Ānnà | Anna, name of a girl student from Russia. Please refer to "Introduction to the Main Characters" for more details. |

注释　Notes

[1] 用"呢"的省略式问句　An elliptical interrogative sentence using "呢"

"……，……呢？"，是一种省略的疑问方式，省略的是上文提到过的内容。

"……，……呢？" is an elliptical interrogative sentence pattern, in which what is mentioned above is omitted.

（1）A：你好吗？
　　　B：我很好，你呢？
　　　A：我也很好。

（2）A：我们上午有四节课。
　　　B：下午呢？
　　　A：下午没有课。

练一练　Exercises

完成会话　Complete the following dialogues.

（1）A：我们下午三点有课，_____？
　　　B：我们下午没有课。

（2）A：我的电话号码是 13671351402，_____？

　　　B：我的电话号码是 13567892106。

[2] 用"……，好吗？"征求意见　Use "……，好吗？" to ask for sb.'s opinion

"……，好吗？"，以询问的方式提出建议，肯定回答时可用"行""好""好的""好吧"等。否定时可用"不行"，但语气较强，在实际交际中常用别的方式委婉拒绝。

"……，好吗？" is an interrogative sentence pattern used to make a suggestion. It has affirmative answers such as "行", "好", "好的" and "好吧". It can be negated by "不行", but the tone is quite strong, so people often politely refuse others in other ways in the real-life communication.

（1）A：你去，好吗？

　　　B：行 / 好 / 好的 / 好吧。

（2）A：明天八点我们去银行，好吗？

　　　B：明天八点我有课。

练一练　Exercises

完成会话　Complete the dialogues.

（1）A：我们三点半去银行，好吗？

　　　B：_____。

（2）A：_____，_____？

　　　B：好的。

语法 Grammar

❶ "有"字句（表示领有、具有）　A sentence with "有"（to indicate "have" or "possess"）

"有"字句，表示领有、具有。否定形式是"没有"。疑问形式是"有……吗？"或者"有没有……？"。

A sentence with "有" indicates "to have" or "to possess", with the negative form being "没有" and the interrogative form being "有……吗？" or "有没有……？".

163

主语（S）	谓语（P）			标点（Punctuation）
	副词（Adv）	V	宾语（O）	助词（Pt）	
我		有	课		。
我		没有	电话		。
你		有	电话	吗	？
你		有没有	电话		？

在回答问题时可以简要回答"有"或"没有"。

The question can be responded simply by "有" or "没有".

（1）A：你有课吗？

　　B：有。

（2）A：你有课吗？

　　B：没有。

练一练　Exercises

替换练习　Substitution drills.

A：你有<u>课</u>吗？　　　　　　　B：有，有<u>四节课</u>。

| 电话 |
| 外文书 |
| 中国朋友（péngyou, friend） |

| 一个电话 |
| 很多外文书 |
| 很多中国朋友 |

❷ 钟点表示法　Expressing the time

时间 Time	第一种读法 Expression 1	第二种读法 Expression 2	第三种读法 Expression 3
8：00	八 点 bā diǎn		
8：05	八 点 五 分 bā diǎn wǔ fēn	八 点 零 (zero) bā diǎn líng 五 分 wǔ fēn	

（续表）

时间 Time	第一种读法 Expression 1	第二种读法 Expression 2	第三种读法 Expression 3
8：15	八点 十五（分） bā diǎn shíwǔ (fēn)	八点 一刻 (quarter) bā diǎn yí kè	
8：30	八点 三十（分） bā diǎn sānshí (fēn)	八点 半 bā diǎn bàn	
8：45	八点 四十五（分） bā diǎn sìshíwǔ (fēn)	八点 三刻 bā diǎn sān kè	差 (to be lack of, short) chà 一刻九点 yí kè jiǔ diǎn 九点 差一刻 jiǔ diǎn chà yí kè
8：50	八点 五十（分） bā diǎn wǔshí (fēn)		差 十分九点 chà shí fēn jiǔ diǎn 九点 差 十分 jiǔ diǎn chà shí fēn

问　Question	答　Answer
现在（xiànzài, now）几点？	（9：30）现在九点半。 （6：50）现在差十分七点。 （11：07）现在十一点零七分。 ……
那儿现在几点？	（9：00）那儿现在九点。 ……

练一练　Exercises

读出下列时间　Please tell the following time.

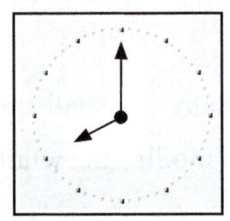 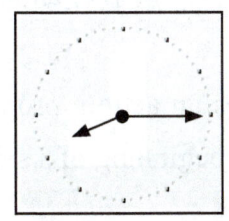 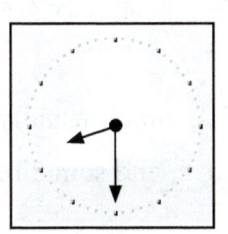

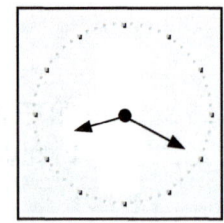 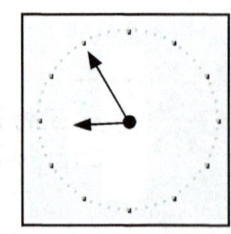 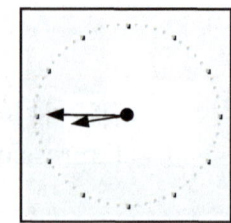

3 时间名词做状语　A noun of time used as an adverbial

时间名词一般放在动词前，做状语，修饰动词。有时也可放在主语前。例如：

A noun of time is generally used before a verb as an adverbial to modify a verb. It is sometimes used before a subject. For example,

我八点半上课。

我十二点半下课。

我下午三点去银行。

晚上（wǎnshang, evening）七点我去图书馆。

练一练　Exercises

一问一答　Ask questions and answer them.

例：A：你几点……？
　　B：我……点……。

qǐchuáng to get up 7：00	chī zǎofàn to have breakfast 7：30	qù xuéxiào to go to school 8：00	shàngkè to attend class 8：30
xiàkè class is over 16：00	duànliàn to do physical exercises 16：30	xǐzǎo to take a bath 21：30	shuìjiào to sleep 22：00

4 汉语的主要句子成分：状语　A main sentence element in Chinese: adverbial

状语是动作、性质、状态的修饰语，一般放在动词或形容词前，有时放在句首修饰整个句子。

An adverbial, which usually modifies an action, property or state, is usually placed before a verb or an adjective, and sometimes at the beginning of a sentence to modify the whole sentence.

（1）我<u>八点半</u>上课。
（2）我<u>很</u>高兴。
（3）<u>下午</u>金大成去图书馆。

练一练　Exercises

给括号中的词选择合适的位置　Put the words in the brackets in the right positions.

（1）你们__A__上__B__课__C__？（几点）
（2）__A__住校内__B__方便__C__。（很）
（3）__A__我__B__上午__C__上课__D__。（八点半）
（4）我们__A__不__B__去__C__银行__D__。（上午）

情景交际　Communication

和你的朋友互相问问每天的安排。准备时间：3～5分钟。
Talk with your friends about your daily schedules. Preparation time: 3-5 minutes.

提示　Tips
上午　下午　有　课　点
上课　下课　呢　……，好吗？

写作　Writing

◆ **添句成段**　Write more sentences to compose a paragraph

在所给句子前后加上两三句话，把它补充成一段完整的文字。
Write two or three sentences before or after the given sentence to make a complete passage.

下午没有课

_____
_____
_____

语音 Pronunciation

练一练 Exercises

① 辨声调 Distinguish the tones  13-03

sǐ — sì	zǐ — zì	cí — cì	suàn — suān
to die four	purple character	word to stab	garlic sour
zǐsì — zìsī	shīzi — shízì	zhízé — zhǐzé	shànzi — shànzì
son selfish	lion cross	duty to criticize	fan arbitrarily

② 辨声母 Distinguish the initials  13-04

z — c — s

zì — cì — sì
zuì — cuì — suì
zài — cài — sài
zǎo — cǎo — sǎo

③ 辨韵母 Distinguish the finals  13-05

uan — uang

chuán — chuáng
guān — guāng
huán — huáng
zhuān — zhuāng

uan — uen

wǎn — wěn
duān — dūn
chuān — chūn
shuàn — shùn

④ 双音节连读 Practice the liaison of the disyllabic words  13-06

qǐchuáng	duànliàn	gōngzuò	xǐzǎo
to get up	to do physical exercises	to work	to bath
zuò fàn	shuìjiào	kàn shū	zuòmèng
to cook	to sleep	to read	to dream

5 多音节连读　Practice the liaison of the polysyllabic words　🎵 13-07

tīng yīnyuè　　　　　　tīng lùyīn　　　　　　　zuò liànxí
to listen to the music　　to listen to the recording　to do an exercise

xiě Hànzì　　　　　　　yòng diànnǎo　　　　　fā yóujiàn
to write Chinese characters　to use a computer　　to send an email

bèi kèwén　　　　　　　kàn diànshì
to recite the text　　　　to watch TV

6 朗读　Read aloud　🎵 13-08

丶丶
下课

丶丶丶
去那儿

丶丶丶丶丶
下课就去那儿

丶丶丶丶丶丶丶
下课就去那儿上课

7 趣味朗读　Interesting reading materials　🎵 13-09

　　　我们　都　有　一　个　家 (family; home)
　　　Wǒmen dōu yǒu yí ge jiā

你 有 家，我 有 家，
Nǐ yǒu jiā, wǒ yǒu jiā,

我们　都　有　一　个　家。
wǒmen dōu yǒu yí ge jiā.

它 (it) 的　名字　叫　地球 (earth)。
Tā　　de míngzi jiào dìqiú.

我们　住 在 地球　上，
Wǒmen zhù zài dìqiú shang,

认识 你，认识 她，
rènshi nǐ, rènshi tā,

我们　的　朋友　遍 (all over) 天下 (the whole world)。
wǒmen de péngyou biàn　　　tiānxià.

汉字 Characters

📖 **边学边练** Study and practice

1 汉字的部件（2） Components of Chinese characters (2)

彳 shuāngrénpáng two persons	很 very	彳 + 艮
	行 to travel	彳 + 丁
木 mùzìpáng wood	校 school	木 + 交
	楼 building	木 + 娄

2 汉字的结构（2） Structures of Chinese characters (2)

上下结构
Up-down structure

e.g.: 字 → 宀 + 子

多 → 夕 + 夕

3 认写基本汉字 Learn and write the basic Chinese characters

(1) 果　guǒ　fruit

　　一 冂 曰 旦 甲 果 果　8 strokes

(2) 上　shàng　up

　　丨 卜 上　3 strokes

(3) 午　wǔ　noon

　　丿 𠂉 亠 午　4 strokes

(4) 四　sì　four

　　丨 冂 叨 四 四　5 strokes

(5) 占 zhàn to occupy
丨 卜 占 占 占 5 strokes

(6) 半 bàn half
丶 丷 丅 半 5 strokes

(7) 下 xià down
一 丁 下 3 strokes

(8) 冬 dōng winter
丿 夂 冬 冬 冬 5 strokes

(9) 书 shū book
乛 马 书 书 4 strokes

(10) 官 guān officer
丶 丷 宀 宀 宀 宫 官 官 8 strokes

(11) 元 yuán *a unit of Chinese currency*
一 二 亍 元 4 strokes

4 认写本课汉字 Learn and write the Chinese characters in this lesson

(1) 明天 míngtiān tomorrow
明 → 日 + 月 bright
天 → 一 + 大 day

(2) 有 yǒu to have
有 → 𠂇 + 月

(3) 节 jié *a measure word for class hours*
节 → 艹 + 卩

(4) 课 kè lesson
课 → 讠 + 果

171

（5）点　diǎn　o'clock
　　点 → 占 + 灬

（6）没有　méiyǒu　not to have
　　没 → 氵 + 殳　not

（7）图书馆　túshūguǎn　library
　　图 → 囗 + 冬　picture
　　馆 → 饣 + 官　a place for cultural activities; shop

（8）远　yuǎn　far
　　远 → 元 + 辶

实践活动 | **Activity**

◆ 走一走，问一问　Go for a survey

问问你的朋友：明天有没有课？有几节课？下课以后（yǐhòu, after）他们去哪儿，做什么？把你问到的情况填到表里，下次课汇报。

Ask your friends whether they will have classes tomorrow and how many classes they will have, where they will go and what they will do after class. Fill in the following table and report your findings to the class next time.

姓名	明天有没有课？	有几节课？	下课以后去哪儿，做什么？

文化点滴 Cultural Note

汉语热　Chinese Fever
Hànyǔ rè

孔子
（Kǒngzǐ, Confucius）

走进汉语，走进具有数千年历史的文明古国。

Getting to know Chinese language and China — the country with an ancient civilization and thousands years of history.

答一答　Answer the following questions

1. 你知道孔子是个什么样的人吗？
   Do you know what kind of a man Confucius was?

2. 你们国家有孔子学院吗？在哪个城市？
   Is there a Confucius Institute in your country? Which city is it located in?

3. 你现在在哪儿学汉语？　Where are you studying Chinese now?

4. 你为什么学汉语？　Why do you study Chinese?
   A. 喜欢中国，对汉语感兴趣　I like China and am interested in Chinese.
   B. 汉语很有用　Chinese is very useful.
   C. 父母让我学汉语　My parents want me to learn Chinese.
   D. 其他　Others _____

学习后记 Summary

词语 Vocabulary

语言点 Grammar

14 周末你做什么
What Do You Do on Weekends

学习提示 Learning Tips

重点词 Key Words	周末　做　打算　学习　休息　买　作业
重点句 Key Sentences	1. 周末　你做　什么？ Zhōumò nǐ zuò shénme? 2. 我　星期六　打算　去　故宫。 Wǒ xīngqīliù dǎsuan qù Gùgōng. 3. 后天　星期天。 Hòutiān xīngqītiān. 4. 我　上午　去　商店　买　东西。 Wǒ shàngwǔ qù shāngdiàn mǎi dōngxi.
功能 Function	表达日期（1）　Expressing the date (1) 描述活动　Describing an activity

175

课文 Text

爱子：周末 你 做 什么？
Àizǐ: Zhōumò nǐ zuò shénme?

金大成：我 星期六[1] 打算 去 故宫，你呢？
Jīn Dàchéng: Wǒ xīngqīliù dǎsuan qù Gùgōng, nǐ ne?

爱子：我 一天 学习，一天 休息。星期六 学习，星期天 休息。
Àizǐ: Wǒ yì tiān xuéxí, yì tiān xiūxi. Xīngqīliù xuéxí, xīngqītiān xiūxi.

金大成：后天 星期天，你 做 什么？
Jīn Dàchéng: Hòutiān xīngqītiān, nǐ zuò shénme?

爱子：我 上午 去 商店 买 东西，下午 游泳，你呢？
Àizǐ: Wǒ shàngwǔ qù shāngdiàn mǎi dōngxi, xiàwǔ yóuyǒng, nǐ ne?

金大成：我 星期天 上午 做 作业，下午 踢 足球。
Jīn Dàchéng: Wǒ xīngqītiān shàngwǔ zuò zuòyè, xiàwǔ tī zúqiú.

练一练 Exercises

1. 听课文，说说你听到了什么 Listen to the text and talk about what you hear.

2. 跟老师读课文 Read the text after the teacher.

3. 两人一组，分角色读 Work in pairs to play the roles and read the text.

4. 先回答问题，再根据课文内容互相提问
   Answer the questions and then ask each other questions based on the text.

   （1）金大成星期六打算去哪儿？
   （2）今天星期几？
   ……

5. 两人一组，分角色表演 Work in pairs and play the roles.

6. 根据课文内容填表 Fill in the blanks based on the text.

周末做什么\名字	星期六		星期天	
	上午	下午	上午	下午
金大成				
爱子				

生词 New words

 14-02

序号 No.	词语 Word	拼音 Pinyin	词性 Word Class	英文释义 Meaning in English	例子 Example
1	周末	zhōumò	N	weekend	一个周末　这个周末
2	做	zuò	V	to do	做什么
3	星期六	xīngqīliù	N	Saturday	
	星期	xīngqī	N	week	一个星期　上个星期 这个星期　下个星期
	星期天	xīngqītiān	N	Sunday	
	星期一	xīngqīyī	N	Monday	
	星期二	xīngqī'èr	N	Tuesday	
	星期三	xīngqīsān	N	Wednesday	
	星期四	xīngqīsì	N	Thursday	
	星期五	xīngqīwǔ	N	Friday	
4	打算	dǎsuan	V	to plan	打算做什么　打算去银行
5	天	tiān	M	day	一天
6	学习	xuéxí	V	to study; to learn	学习汉语
7	休息	xiūxi	V	to take a break; to rest	周末休息
8	后天	hòutiān	N	the day after tomorrow	后天星期天
9	商店	shāngdiàn	N	store; shop	一个商店
10	买	mǎi	V	to buy; to purchase	
11	东西	dōngxi	N	thing; stuff	买东西
12	游泳	yóuyǒng	V	to swim	学游泳　去游泳

177

13	作业	zuòyè	N	homework	做作业
14	踢	tī	V	to kick; to play	
15	足球	zúqiú	N	soccer	一个足球　踢足球

专有名词　Proper noun

| 故宫 | Gùgōng | the Forbidden City |

注释　Note

[1] 星期的表达方式　Expressing days of a week

星期一 xīngqīyī	星期二 xīngqī'èr	星期三 xīngqīsān	星期四 xīngqīsì	星期五 xīngqīwǔ	星期六 xīngqīliù	星期天 / 星期日 xīngqītiān/ xīngqīrì
周一 zhōuyī	周二 zhōu'èr	周三 zhōusān	周四 zhōusì	周五 zhōuwǔ	周六 zhōuliù	周日 zhōurì
Monday	Tuesday	Wednesday	Thursday	Friday	Saturday	Sunday

星期一　星期二……星期日　星期一　星期二……星期日　星期一　星期二……星期日

上（个）星期一
last Monday

今天

这（个）星期二
this Tuesday

下（个）星期二
next Tuesday

练一练　Exercises

一问一答　Ask questions and answer them.

（1）A：今天星期几？
　　　B：_____。

（2）A：明天星期几？
　　　B：_____。

1 名词谓语句　A sentence with a nominal predicate

在汉语中，名词、名词短语或数量短语可以直接做谓语，常常用来说星期（星期几）、日期（几号）、年龄（……岁）、价钱等，句子一般很短。

In Chinese, a noun, nominal phrase or quantitative phrase can be directly used as a predicate. This kind of sentences is usually short and often used to indicate days of a week, dates, ages, and prices, etc.

主语（S）	名词（N）/名词短语（NP）/数量短语（Num-M P）	标点（Punctuation）
明天	星期天	。
现在（xiànzài, now）	三点一刻	。
我	二十岁（suì, age）	。
这个足球	八十块钱（bāshí kuài qián, eighty *yuan*）	。

练一练　Exercises

一问一答　Ask questions and answer them.

（1）A：明天星期几？
　　B：_____。

（2）A：今天星期几？
　　B：_____。

（3）A：现在几点？
　　B：_____。

2 连动句（表示目的）　A sentence with serial verbal phrases (to indicate a purpose)

一个句子的谓语有两个动词或者动词短语，这样的句子我们叫连动句。本课介绍连动句中的一种：第二个动词/动词短语是第一个动词/动词短语的目的。

A sentence with two verbs or verbal phrases is known as a sentence with serial verbal phrases. In this lesson, a type of such sentences will be introduced, in which the second verb/verbal phrase indicates the purpose of the first one.

主语（S）	谓语（P）		标点（Punctuation）
	动词1（V1）/动词短语1（VP1）	动词2（V2）/动词短语2（VP2）	
我	去	买书	。
他	去商店	买东西	。
她	去图书馆	看书	。

练一练 Exercises

看图说话　Look at the pictures and talk about them.

星期六（……打篮球）　　周三（去图书馆……）　　晚上（去商店……）

情景交际 | Communication

和朋友互相问问周末的安排。准备时间：3～5分钟。
Talk about your plans for the weekend with your friends. Preparation time: 3-5 minutes.

提示　Tips
做　什么　打算　学习　休息

写作 Writing

◆ **添句成段** Write more sentences to compose a paragraph

在所给句子前后加上两三句话，把它补充成一段完整的文字。
Write two or three sentences before or after the given sentence to make a complete passage.

明天星期六

_____

_____

_____

语音 Pronunciation

🏠 **练一练** Exercises

❶ **辨声调** Distinguish the tones   💿 14-03

qiāng — qiáng	qián — qiān
gun wall	money thousand

xiān — xiàn   sān — sǎn
first   thread   three   umbrella

shíxí — shìxí   shíxiàn — shìxiān
to do an internship   to inherit   to realize   in advance

xiāngxìn — xiàngxīn   qiǎngxiān — qiǎngxiǎn
to believe   centripetal   to try to be the   emergency rescue
                                 first to do sth.

qìngxìng — qīngxǐng   xiànxiàng — xiǎnxiàng
to rejoice   clear-headed   phenomenon   dangerous sign or phenomenon

jìnxíng — jìnxìng
to carry on   to one's heart's content

shàngxiàng — shàngxiāng
photogenic   to burn incense and worship

xīnshǎng — xìn shang
to appreciate   in the letter

qīngchàng — qīngcháng
to sing opera arias   to pay off
(without make-up
and acting)

② 辨声母   Distinguish the initials   🎧 14-04

sh — x — s

shān	—	xiān	—	sān
shāng	—	xiāng	—	sāng
shēng	—	xīng	—	sēng
shēn	—	xīn	—	sēn

ch — q — c

chā	—	qiā	—	cā
chǎn	—	qiǎn	—	cǎn
cháng	—	qiáng	—	cáng
chéng	—	qíng	—	céng

③ 辨韵母   Distinguish the finals   🎧 14-05

in — ing

xīn	—	xīng
lín	—	líng
xìn	—	xìng
mín	—	míng

ian — iang

jiān	—	jiāng
liǎn	—	liǎng
yán	—	yáng
qiān	—	qiāng

④ 双音节连读   Practice the liaison of the disyllabic words   🎧 14-06

pǎobù
to run

sànbù
to take a walk

tiàowǔ
to dance

páshān
to climb the mountain

lǚyóu
to travel

ànmó
to massage

yùndòng
sports

zhōngyī
traditional Chinese medicine

⑤ 多音节连读   Practice the liaison of the polysyllabic words   🎧 14-07

dǎ lánqiú
to play basketball

dǎ wǎngqiú
to play tennis

dǎ páiqiú
to play volleyball

dǎ pīngpāngqiú to play table tennis	dǎ yǔmáoqiú to play badminton	dǎ tàijíquán to practice shadow boxing
liàn yújiā to practice yoga	xué wǔshù to learn martial arts	

6 朗读　Read aloud　🔘 14-08

周末我不去，
我去踢足球。
你们买东西，
我在宿舍休息。

7 趣味朗读　Interesting reading materials　🔘 14-09

周末　做　什么
Zhōumò zuò shénme

周末　不　上课，作业 也不 多。
Zhōumò bú shàngkè, zuòyè yě bù duō.

你　想　干 (to do) 什么？
Nǐ xiǎng gàn　　shénme?

我 去 看 大哥 (eldest brother)，他 在 这儿 工作。
Wǒ qù kàn dàgē,　　　　tā zài zhèr gōngzuò.

他 汉语 特别 好，也 非常 爱 中国。
Tā Hànyǔ tèbié hǎo, yě fēicháng ài Zhōngguó.

汉字　Characters

📓 **边学边练**　Study and practice

① 汉字的结构（3）　Structures of Chinese characters (3)

左中右结构
Left-middle-right structure

e.g.: 哪 → 口 + 月 + 阝

做 → 亻 + 古 + 攵

游 → 氵 + 方 + 子

上中下结构

Up-middle-down structure

e.g.: 算 → 竹 + 目 + 廾

② 认写基本汉字　Learn and write the basic Chinese characters

(1) 末　mò　end

一 二 丰 才 末　5 strokes

(2) 古　gǔ　ancient

一 十 古 古 古　5 strokes

(3) 其　qí　that; such

一 十 廿 甘 甘 其 其 其　8 strokes

(4) 习　xí　to practice

𠃌 习 习　3 strokes

(5) 自　zì　oneself

丿 亻 冂 白 自 自　6 strokes

(6) 心　xīn　heart

丶 心 心 心　4 strokes

(7) 头　tóu　head

丶 丷 二 头 头　5 strokes

(8) 东　dōng　east

一 七 东 东 东　5 strokes

(9) 西　xī　west

一ナ厂丙西西　6 strokes

(10) 永　yǒng　forever

丶亅刁永永　5 strokes

(11) 乍　zhà　for the first time

丿㇒午乍乍　5 strokes

(12) 业　yè　industry

丨丨丨业业　5 strokes

(13) 足　zú　foot

丨口口甲早足　7 strokes

(14) 勿　wù　not to do

丿勹勿勿　4 strokes

(15) 王　wáng　king

一二千王　4 strokes

(16) 求　qiú　to beg

一十十寸求求　7 strokes

3　认写本课汉字　Learn and write the Chinese characters in this lesson

(1) 周末　zhōumò　weekend

周 → 冂 + 土 + 口　week

(2) 做　zuò　to do

做 → 亻 + 古 + 攵

(3) 星期　xīngqī　week

星 → 日 + 生　star

期 → 其 + 月　phase

（4）打算　dǎsuan　to plan
　　打 → 扌+丁　to work out
　　算 → 竹+目+廾　to plan

（5）休息　xiūxi　to take a break; to rest
　　休 → 亻+木　to rest
　　息 → 自+心　to rest

（6）后天　hòutiān　the day after tomorrow
　　后 → 厂+一+口　after

（7）商店　shāngdiàn　store; shop
　　商 → 亠+丷+冂+八+口　trade
　　店 → 广+占　shop

（8）买　mǎi　to buy; to purchase
　　买 → 乛+头

（9）游泳　yóuyǒng　to swim
　　游 → 氵+方+𠂉+子　to swim
　　泳 → 氵+永　to swim

（10）作业　zuòyè　homework
　　作 → 亻+乍　task

（11）踢　tī　to kick; to play
　　踢 → 𧾷+日+勿

（12）足球　zúqiú　football; soccer
　　足 → 口+龰　foot
　　球 → 王+求　ball

第 14 课　周末你做什么

实践活动 | Activity

◆ 走一走，问一问　Go for a survey

问问你的朋友周末都做什么，至少问 3 个人，填入下表中，下次课汇报。

Talk with at least 3 of your friends about their plans for the weekend. Fill in the following table and report your findings to the class next time.

朋友	星期六做什么	星期天做什么

文化点滴 | Cultural Note

北京的名胜古迹
Běijīng de míngshèng gǔjì
Scenic Spots and Historic Sites in Beijing

　　一处名胜，一处历史。下面这些地方你一定要去。

　　Every place of interest has its history. These are the places you would love to visit.

长城
（Chángchéng, the Great Wall）

鸟巢
（Niǎocháo, Bird's Nest）

187

圆明园
（Yuánmíngyuán, the Old Summer Palace）

故宫
（Gùgōng, the Forbidden City）

天坛
（Tiāntán, the Temple of Heaven）

颐和园
（Yíhéyuán, the Summer Palace）

你知道这些名胜古迹原来的用途吗？请看一看，连一连。
Do you know what the following scenic spots and historic sites were originally used for? Please read the two columns and match each site with its usage.

长城 The Great Wall	封建帝王祈求丰收的地方 The place where emperors prayed for a good harvest
故宫 The Forbidden City	2008年北京奥运会主场馆 The stadium of the 2008 Beijing Olympics
鸟巢 Bird's Nest	封建帝王处理政务及与后妃的居住之所 The place where emperors attended to government affairs and lived with empresses
圆明园 The Old Summer Palace	清朝慈禧太后长期居住的大型皇家园林 The imperial garden where the Empress Dowager Cixi lived for a long time in the Qing Dynasty
颐和园 The Summer Palace	封建帝王夏季避暑的行宫 A summer palace for feudal emperors
天坛 The Temple of Heaven	军事防御工程，也具备通过点烽火传递重大军情等功能 A military defensive project with the function of sending military messages by setting beacon-fires, etc.

第 14 课　周末你做什么

学习后记 | Summary

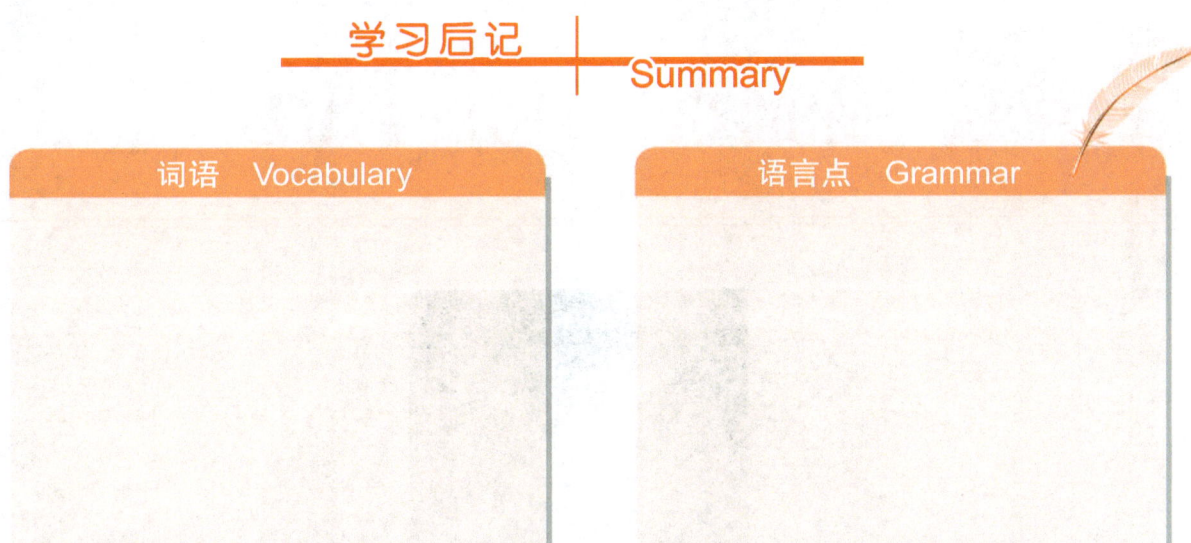

词语　Vocabulary

语言点　Grammar

15 你的生日是几月几号
When Is Your Birthday

学习提示 Learning Tips

重点词 Key Words	生日　祝　多大　属　出生　过
重点句 Key Sentences	1. 你今年多大? 　 Nǐ jīnnián duō dà? 2. 我十八岁，一九九四年出生。 　 Wǒ shíbā suì, yī jiǔ jiǔ sì nián chūshēng. 3. 你属狗。 　 Nǐ shǔ gǒu. 4. 你的生日是几月几号? 　 Nǐ de shēngrì shì jǐ yuè jǐ hào? 5. 我们打算今天晚上一起过生日。 　 Wǒmen dǎsuan jīntiān wǎnshang yìqǐ guò shēngrì.
功能 Function	表达日期（2） Expressing the date (2)

课文 Text

金大成：老师，今天是爱子的生日。
Jīn Dàchéng: Lǎoshī, jīntiān shì Àizǐ de shēngrì.

王老师：是吗？爱子，祝你生日快乐！你今年多大[1]？
Wáng lǎoshī: Shì ma? Àizǐ, zhù nǐ shēngrì kuàilè! Nǐ jīnnián duō dà?

爱子：我十九岁。
Àizǐ: Wǒ shíjiǔ suì.

王老师：你属鸡。
Wáng lǎoshī: Nǐ shǔ jī.

金大成：老师，我十八岁，一九九四年出生。我属什么？
Jīn Dàchéng: Lǎoshī, wǒ shíbā suì, yī jiǔ jiǔ sì nián chūshēng. Wǒ shǔ shénme?

王老师：你属狗。你的生日是几月几号？
Wáng lǎoshī: Nǐ shǔ gǒu. Nǐ de shēngrì shì jǐ yuè jǐ hào?

爱子：老师，他的生日也是九月。
Àizǐ: Lǎoshī, tā de shēngrì yě shì jiǔyuè.

金大成：我的生日是九月二十八号。
Jīn Dàchéng: Wǒ de shēngrì shì jiǔyuè èrshíbā hào.

爱子：我们打算今天晚上一起过生日。
Àizǐ: Wǒmen dǎsuan jīntiān wǎnshang yìqǐ guò shēngrì.

王老师：好主意。
Wáng lǎoshī: Hǎo zhǔyi.

练一练 Exercises

1. 听课文，说说你听到了什么　Listen to the text and talk about what you hear.

2. 跟老师读课文　Read the text after the teacher.

3. 三人一组，分角色读　Work in groups of three to play the roles and read the text.

4. 先回答问题，再根据课文内容互相提问

Answer the questions and then ask each other questions based on the text.

（1）今天是哪个学生的生日？

（2）金大成的生日也是九月吗？

……

5. 三人一组，分角色表演　Work in groups of three and play the roles.

6. 根据课文内容填表，然后叙述　Fill in the blanks based on the text and then narrate the text.

学生	多大	出生年月	属什么
金大成			
爱子			

生词　New words  15-02

序号 No.	词语 Word / Phrase	拼音 Pinyin	词性 Word Class	英文释义 Meaning in English	例子 Example
1	今天	jīntiān	N	today	今天星期一
	昨天	zuótiān	N	yesterday	昨天星期天
2	生日	shēngrì	N	birthday	他的生日
3	祝	zhù	V	to wish	
4	快乐	kuàilè	A	happy	很快乐　不快乐　生日快乐
5	今年	jīnnián	N	this year	
6	多大	duō dà		how old	你多大
	多	duō	Adv	how	多高（how tall） 多重（how heavy）
	大	dà	A	old	多大
7	十九	shíjiǔ	Num	nineteen	十九岁　十九个人
8	岁	suì	M	age	一岁　五岁　十九岁　六十岁
9	属	shǔ	V	to be born in the year of	属什么
10	鸡	jī	N	chicken	属鸡

192

11	十八	shíbā	Num	eighteen	十八个学生
12	年	nián	N/M	year	1988年　2010年 一年　三年
13	出生	chūshēng	V	to be born	1988年出生　哪年出生
14	狗	gǒu	N	dog	属狗
15	月	yuè	N	month	一月　二月　七月　十一月
16	号	hào	M	date	几月几号　十月一号
17	晚上	wǎnshang	N	evening	明天晚上　17号晚上
18	过	guò	V	to celebrate; to spend	过生日
19	主意	zhǔyi	N	idea	好主意　一个主意

专有名词　Proper noun

| 王 | Wáng | a family name |

注释　Note

[1] "多大"　"How old...?"

"多大"用来问年龄。在汉语里我们问年龄时，有不同的方法：

"多大" is used to ask somebody's age. We have different expressions to ask somebody's age in Chinese:

（1）

A：你今年多大？
B：我今年十八岁/二十岁。

二十岁　　　　　　　　　　　　　　　　　　十八岁

（2）

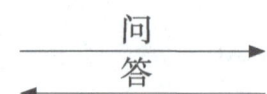

A：你今年多大？
B：我今年二十岁。

七十二岁　　　　　　　　　　　　　　　二十岁

（3）

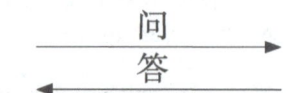

A：您（nín, meaning "you", the respectful form of "你"）今年多大岁数（suìshu, age）？
B：我今年七十二岁。

三十岁　　　　　　　　　　　　　　　七十二岁

（4）

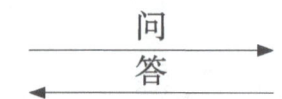

A：你今年几岁？
B：我今年四岁。

三十岁　　　　　　　　　　　　　　　四岁

练一练　Exercises

用"多大""几岁"或"多大岁数"完成会话

Complete the dialogues using "多大", "几岁" or "多大岁数".

（1）A：_____？
　　　B：我今年十五岁。

（2）A：_____？
　　　B：我今年八十岁。

（3）A：_____？
　　　B：我今年七岁。

语法 | Grammar

1 年、月、日的表示方法

Expressions of "年" (meaning "year") , "月" (meaning "month") and "日" (meaning "date")

（1）汉语里"年"的表示　Chinese expressions of "年" (meaning "year")

一九五九年（1959年）　　　二〇〇八年（2008年）
yī jiǔ wǔ jiǔ nián　　　　　èr líng líng bā nián

一九六三年（1963年）　　　二〇一一年（2011年）
yī jiǔ liù sān nián　　　　　èr líng yī yī nián

一九七八年（1978年）
yī jiǔ qī bā nián

（2）"月"的表示　Expressions of "月" (meaning "month")

一月 January yīyuè	七月 July qīyuè
二月 February èryuè	八月 August bāyuè
三月 March sānyuè	九月 September jiǔyuè
四月 April sìyuè	十月 October shíyuè
五月 May wǔyuè	十一月 November shíyīyuè
六月 June liùyuè	十二月 December shí'èryuè

（3）"日"的表示：在书写时一般写"一日、二日、三日……十五日……三十日、三十一日"；在口语里常常说"号"，而不说"日"。

Expressions of "日" (meaning "date"): It is usually written with the cardinal numbers 1～31 followed by "日". "号" instead of "日" is used in spoken Chinese.

日期的表示方法：

Expressions of dates:

年 + 月 + 日 + 星期

⇩

2008年8月17日，星期日

公元 2008 年 8 月						
日	一	二	三	四	五	六
					1	2
3	4	5	6	7	8	9
10	11	12	13	14	15	16
17	18	19	20	21	22	23
24	25	26	27	28	29	30
31						

8月17日是妈妈的生日。

练一练 Exercises

根据实际情况完成句子　Complete the sentences based on the actual situations.

（1）今天是_____月_____号星期_____。

（2）今年是_____年，明年是_____年。

（3）这个星期六是_____月_____号。

（4）我_____年_____月_____日出生，属_____。

2 数字的读法（2）　How numbers are read (2)

万	千	百	十	个	读法
			1	0	十 shí
		1	0	1	一百零一 yìbǎi língyī
		1	1	0	一百一十 yìbǎiyīshí

（续表）

万	千	百	十	个	读法
		1	1	5	一百一十五 yìbǎiyīshíwǔ
	1	0	1	0	一千零一十 yìqiānlíngyīshí
	1	1	0	0	一千一百 yìqiānyìbǎi
	1	1	1	0	一千一百一十 yìqiānyìbǎiyīshí
1	0	0	1	0	一万零一十 yíwànlíngyīshí
1	0	1	0	0	一万零一百 yíwànlíngyìbǎi
1	1	1	0	0	一万一千一百 yíwànyìqiānyìbǎi

练一练　Exercises

读出下面的数字　Read the following numbers.

| 11 | 20 | 59 | 101 | 314 | 550 | 999 |
| 4008 | 3115 | 9086 | 60345 | 10700 | 81290 | 70012 |

③ **汉语的主要句子成分：定语**　A main sentence element in Chinese: attribute

定语用来修饰名词和代词，常用来表示"谁的""什么样的""多少"等，定语和名词、代词之间有时用"的"，有时不用。例如：

An attribute, used to modify a noun and a pronoun, is often used to indicate the owner, property or quantity. "的" is sometimes used and sometimes omitted between an attribute and a noun/pronoun. For example,

（1）你的生日是几月几号？

（2）我住留学生宿舍。

（3）图书馆有**很多**外文书。
（4）**那个**红楼就是办公楼。

情景交际

问问你某个朋友或同学的生日，告诉他/她：你们打算给（gěi, for）他/她过生日。准备时间：3～5分钟。

Ask about the birthday of one of your friends or classmates and tell him/her you are going to celebrate his/her birthday. Preparation time: 3-5 minutes.

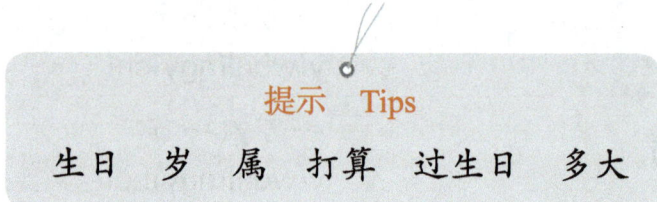

提示　Tips

生日　岁　属　打算　过生日　多大

写作

◆ **添句成段**　Write more sentences to compose a paragraph

在所给句子前后加上两三句话，把它补充成一段完整的文字。

Write two or three sentences before or after the given sentence to make a complete passage.

我属……

_____

_____

_____

语音 | Pronunciation

练一练 Exercises

1. 辨声调 Distinguish the tones  15-03

jiǎn — jiàn	xuè — xué	xīn — xìn	yuǎn — yuán
to cut to see	blood to study	heart letter	far round

jiéyuē — jièyuè
to economize to borrow a book to read

jiéjiǎn — jièjiàn
economical to use for reference

jiǎnyuè — jiǎnyuē
to inspect simple; concise

jiānjìn — jiànjìn
to imprison to advance gradually

2. 辨声母 Distinguish the initials  15-04

j — zh
- jiǎo — zhǎo
- jiā — zhā
- jī — zhī
- jiǔ — zhǒu

j — q
- jǐng — qǐng
- juē — quē
- jīn — qīn
- juǎn — quǎn

3. 辨韵母 Distinguish the finals  15-05

ian — üan
- qiān — quān
- jiān — juān
- xián — xuán
- qián — quán

in — ün
- jìn — jùn
- xìn — xùn
- xīn — xūn
- qín — qún

ie — üe
- jiè — juè
- xié — xué
- qiē — quē
- xiě — xuě

4. 双音节连读 Practice the liaison of the disyllabic words  15-06

shǔxiàng	niánlíng	nánrén	nǚrén
Chinese animal sign	age	man	woman

lǎorén	xiǎohái r	nánhái r	nǚhái r
the old	child	boy	girl

xià yǔ	xià xuě
to rain	to snow

5 多音节连读 Practice the liaison of the polysyllabic words 15-07

tiānqì yùbào	kàn xīnwén	fā duǎnxìn
weather forcast	to watch news	to send a text message
xiě rìjì	xiě zuòwén	niúzǎi kù
to keep a diary	to write a composition	jeans
T-xù shān	yùndòng xié	
T-shirt	gym shoes	

6 朗读 Read aloud 15-08

我今年二十一岁。

你明年二十二岁。

我们都属鸡，

今天晚上一起过生日。

7 学唱歌 Learn a song

生 日 歌

1=G 3/4

5 5 6 5 | 1 7 - | 5 5 6 5 | 2 1 - |
祝你 生 日 快 乐，   祝你 生 日 快 乐，

5 5 5 3 | 1 7 6 | 0 0 44 | 3 1 2 | 1 0 0 ‖
祝你 生 日 快 乐，   祝你 生 日 快 乐。

汉字 Characters

边学边练 Study and practice

1. 汉字的部件（3） Components of Chinese characters (3)

氵 sāndiǎnshuǐ water	没 not	氵+殳
	游 to swim	氵+斿
	泳 to swim	氵+永

日 rìzìpáng sun; time	明 bright	日+月
	是 to be	日+疋
	星 star	日+生
	晚 evening; night	日+免

2. 汉字的结构（4） Structures of Chinese characters (4)

全包围结构
Enclosed structure

e.g.: 国 → 囗+玉

半包围结构
Semi-enclosed structure

Left-top-right enclosed structure

e.g.: 周 → 冂+吉

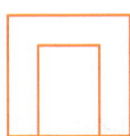

Top-left enclosed structure

e.g.: 房 → 户+方

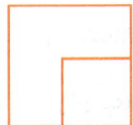

Left-bottom enclosed structure

e.g.: 过 → 寸+辶

3 认写基本汉字 Learn and write the basic Chinese characters

（1）今　jīn　today
丿 人 人 今　4 strokes

（2）乐　lè　happy; cheerful
一 二 乐 乐 乐　5 strokes

（3）年　nián　year
丿 一 二 午 仨 年　6 strokes

（4）虫　chóng　worm
丶 口 口 中 虫 虫　6 strokes

（5）鸟　niǎo　bird
丿 勹 勺 鸟 鸟　5 strokes

（6）出　chū　to go out
凵 凵 屮 出 出　5 strokes

（7）免　miǎn　to avoid
丿 勹 勺 负 色 争 免　7 strokes

（8）寸　cùn　*cun, a unit of length*
一 寸 寸　3 strokes

（9）立　lì　to stand
丶 二 六 立 立　5 strokes

4 认写本课汉字 Learn and write the Chinese characters in this lesson

（1）昨天　zuótiān　yesterday
昨 → 日 + 乍　yesterday

（2）祝　zhù　to wish
祝 → 礻 + 兄

（3）快乐　kuàilè　happy

快 → 忄 + 夬　quick; fast

（4）岁　suì　age

岁 → 山 + 夕

（5）属　shǔ　to be born in the year of

属 → 尸 + 一 + 虫 + 冂

（6）鸡　jī　chicken

鸡 → 又 + 鸟

（7）狗　gǒu　dog

狗 → 犭 + 勹 + 口

（8）晚上　wǎnshang　evening

晚 → 日 + 免　evening

（9）过　guò　to celebrate

过 → 寸 + 辶

（10）主意　zhǔyi　idea

意 → 立 + 日 + 心　idea; meaning

实践活动　Activity

◆ **走一走，问一问**　Go for a survey

问一问你周围同学、朋友、家人的生日和属相，填入下表中，下次课汇报。

Ask your classmates, friends and family members about their birthdays and animal signs, and then fill in the following table. Report your findings to the class next time.

	生日	属相（shǔxiàng, animal sign）
爸爸（bàba, father）		
妈妈（māma, mother）		
同学（tóngxué, classmate）_____		
朋友（péngyou, friend）_____		

文化点滴 | Cultural Note

十二属相
Shí'èr shǔxiàng
Animal Signs (Chinese Zodiac)

> 问属相，知年龄。
>
> Ask one's animal sign and you will know his/her age.

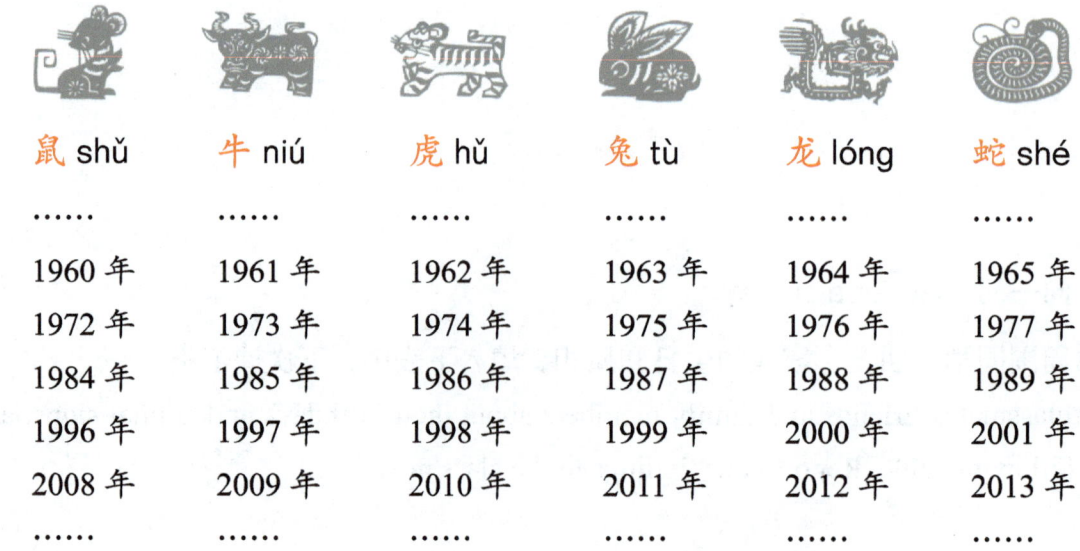

鼠 shǔ	牛 niú	虎 hǔ	兔 tù	龙 lóng	蛇 shé
……	……	……	……	……	……
1960 年	1961 年	1962 年	1963 年	1964 年	1965 年
1972 年	1973 年	1974 年	1975 年	1976 年	1977 年
1984 年	1985 年	1986 年	1987 年	1988 年	1989 年
1996 年	1997 年	1998 年	1999 年	2000 年	2001 年
2008 年	2009 年	2010 年	2011 年	2012 年	2013 年
……	……	……	……	……	……

第 15 课　你的生日是几月几号

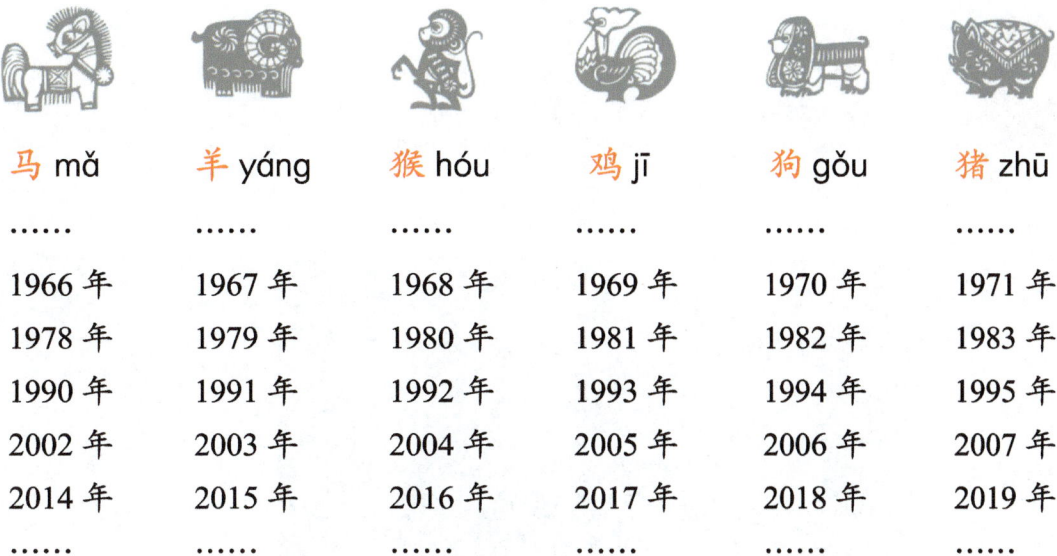

马 mǎ	羊 yáng	猴 hóu	鸡 jī	狗 gǒu	猪 zhū
……	……	……	……	……	……
1966 年	1967 年	1968 年	1969 年	1970 年	1971 年
1978 年	1979 年	1980 年	1981 年	1982 年	1983 年
1990 年	1991 年	1992 年	1993 年	1994 年	1995 年
2002 年	2003 年	2004 年	2005 年	2006 年	2007 年
2014 年	2015 年	2016 年	2017 年	2018 年	2019 年
……	……	……	……	……	……

圈一圈　Circle

1. 圈出你的属相。

    Circle your animal sign.

2. 圈出你爸爸、妈妈的属相。

    Circle your parents' animal signs.

3. 2000 年是什么年？今年是什么年？

    What is the animal sign for the year of 2000? How about this year?

16 咖啡多少钱一杯
How Much Is a Cup of Coffee

学习提示 Learning Tips

重点词 Key Words	钱　块　要　两　还　一共　给　您
重点句 Key Sentences	1. 咖啡 多少 钱 一杯? Kāfēi duōshao qián yì bēi? 2. 要 两 瓶 水、一杯 牛奶。 Yào liǎng píng shuǐ、yì bēi niúnǎi. 3. 还 要 什么? Hái yào shénme? 4. 蛋糕 六块 五一块，一共 十二 块 五。 Dàngāo liù kuài wǔ yí kuài, yígòng shí'èr kuài wǔ. 5. 给 您，十二 块 五。 Gěi nín, shí'èr kuài wǔ.
功能 Function	购物（1）　Shopping (1) 询问价钱　Asking for the price

第16课　咖啡多少钱一杯

课文　Text  16-01

杰克：服务员，水多少钱一瓶？
Jiékè: Fúwùyuán, shuǐ duōshao qián yì píng?

服务员：一块五一瓶。
Fúwùyuán: Yí kuài wǔ yì píng.

杰克：咖啡多少钱一杯？
Jiékè: Kāfēi duōshao qián yì bēi?

服务员：四块。
Fúwùyuán: Sì kuài.

杰克：牛奶呢？
Jiékè: Niúnǎi ne?

服务员：三块。
Fúwùyuán: Sān kuài.

杰克：要两[1]瓶水、一杯牛奶。
Jiékè: Yào liǎng píng shuǐ、yì bēi niúnǎi.

服务员：还[2]要什么？
Fúwùyuán: Hái yào shénme?

杰克：还要一块水果蛋糕。
Jiékè: Hái yào yí kuài shuǐguǒ dàngāo.

服务员：蛋糕六块五一块，一共十二块五。
Fúwùyuán: Dàngāo liù kuài wǔ yí kuài, yígòng shí'èr kuài wǔ.

杰克：给您[3]，十二块五。
Jiékè: Gěi nín, shí'èr kuài wǔ.

练一练　Exercises

1. 听课文，说说你听到了什么　Listen to the text and talk about what you hear.

2. 跟老师读课文　Read the text after the teacher.

3. 两人一组，分角色读　Work in pairs to play the roles and read the text.

4. 先回答问题，再根据课文内容互相提问

   Answer the questions and then ask each other questions based on the text.

   （1）杰克要水，还要什么？
   （2）两瓶水多少钱？
   ……

5. 两人一组，分角色表演　Work in pairs and play the roles.

6. 根据课文内容填表，两人一组互相问答

   Fill in the table based on the text and then ask questions and answer them in pairs.

	价钱 （jiàqian, price）	数量 （shùliàng, quantity）
水 （瓶）		
咖啡 （杯）		
牛奶 （杯）		
水果蛋糕 （块）		
一共多少钱		

生词　New words　16-02

序号 No.	词语 Word	拼音 Pinyin	词性 Word Class	英文释义 Meaning in English	例子 Example
1	服务员	fúwùyuán	N	waiter; waitress	一个服务员
	服务	fúwù	V	to serve	服务很好
2	水	shuǐ	N	water	买水
3	钱	qián	N	money	有钱　没钱　多少钱

第16课　咖啡多少钱一杯

4	瓶	píng	N	bottle	一瓶　几瓶　多少瓶 一瓶水
5	块	kuài	M	a unit of Chinese currency, equivalent to 10 mao; piece	一块钱　几块钱 三块蛋糕
6	咖啡	kāfēi	N	coffee	要咖啡　买咖啡
7	杯	bēi	N	glass	三杯　一杯咖啡
8	牛奶	niúnǎi	N	milk	一杯牛奶
9	要	yào	V	to want	要一瓶水 要电话号码
10	两	liǎng	Num	two	两个人　两瓶水
11	还	hái	Adv	in; addition; also	还有　还去
12	水果	shuǐguǒ	N	fruit	买水果
13	蛋糕	dàngāo	N	cake	一个蛋糕　一块蛋糕
14	一共	yígòng	Adv	in all; altogether	一共多少钱
15	给	gěi	V	to give	给你　给你钱
16	您	nín	Pr	you (the respectful form of "你")	您好　给您钱

注释　Notes

[1] "二"和"两"　"二" and "两"

		二	两
	数字 Cardinal number	二（2）　十二（12） 二十（20）　二百（200）	两百（200）　两千（2000） 两万（20000）
	序号 Ordinal number	第（dì）二	
	号码 Number	电话号码 13692013072 房间号码 202	
	与量词、名词搭配 Collocation with a measure word/noun		两+M+N / 两+N 两个人　两节课 两杯水　两天　两年

209

练一练　Exercises

读一读，在括号中写出"2"分别对应的是"二"还是"两"
Read and write "二" or "两" in the brackets for each "2".

（1）A：那是多少钱？
　　　B：那是251.52元。（　　）（　　）
（2）我的电话号码是13520731183。（　　）
（3）今年我28岁。（　　）
（4）你好，我买2杯咖啡。（　　）
（5）A：你一周有多少节课？
　　　B：我一周有20节课。（　　）

[2]　副词"还"　The adverb "还"

还，副词，放在动词前，表示增加或补充。
The adverb "还" is used before a verb to indicate "also" or "in addition".

（1）我有日本朋友，还有韩国朋友。
（2）我今天有课，明天有课，后天还有课。
（3）周六我打算游泳，还打算买东西。

练一练　Exercises

替换练习　Substitution drills.

我去图书馆、银行，　　　还去办公楼。

认识金大成、金在元	认识山口爱子
去买东西、游泳	去踢足球
要水、咖啡	要蛋糕

[3]　人称代词"您"　The personal pronoun "您"

汉语中常常用"您"表示对对方的尊称，但不用于复数。
The pronoun "您" is a respective term for the addressee and it cannot be used in the plural form.

练一练 Exercises

用"你"还是用"您"？ Choose "你" or "您" to fill in the blanks.

（1）老师，_____好！

（2）A：请问，_____今年多大岁数？
　　　B：我今年86岁。

（3）请问，_____喝什么？

（4）A：今天是我的18岁生日。
　　　B：祝_____生日快乐。

语法 | Grammar

❶ 人民币的单位及表述　The units of RMB and their Chinese expressions

人民币（Rénmínbì）是中国货币的总称，人民币的单位是：元（口语：块）、角（jiǎo，口语：毛 máo）、分。人民币的换算关系是：1元=10角，1角=10分。

Renminbi is a general term for the currency used in China. The units of RMB include "元" ("块" in oral Chinese), "角" (jiǎo, "毛" máo in oral Chinese) and "分". The conversion relation is "1元=10角" and "1角=10分".

纸币　Paper money
zhǐbì

100元　　　　　　　　50元　　　　　　　　20元

10元

5元

1元

5角

1角

硬币　Coins
yìngbì

1元

5角

1角

5分

2分

1分

9元	九块	jiǔ kuài
22元	二十二块	èrshí'èr kuài
100元	一百块	yìbǎi kuài
658元	六百五十八块	liùbǎiwǔshíbā kuài
8.6元	八块六（毛）	bā kuài liù (máo)

112.4 元	一百一十二块四（毛）	yìbǎiyīshí'èr kuài sì (máo)
1.05 元	一块零五（分）	yí kuài líng wǔ (fēn)
0.72 元	七毛二（分）	qī máo èr (fēn)

练一练　Exercises

读钱数　Read the following amounts of money.

0.02 元	0.12 元	1.85 元	3.67 元
5.92 元	10.06 元	11.99 元	98.52 元
105 元	147.34 元	260 元	874 元
1105 元	2000 元	10021 元	10221 元

2　量词　Measure words

在汉语中，数词和名词之间一般要加量词。每种事物都有相应的量词，比较常用的量词有"个""张（zhāng）""件（jiàn）""种（zhǒng）"等。例如：

A measure word is usually used between a numeral and a noun. Everything has its corresponding measure word. The frequently-used measure words include "个", "张（zhāng）", "件（jiàn）" and "种（zhǒng）", etc. For example,

一个人

一张（zhāng）床（chuáng）

一件（jiàn）衣服（yīfu, garment）

一种（zhǒng）动物（dòngwù, animal）

汉语中也常常把一些名词（多为容器）临时用作量词，如"杯""瓶""盒"等。

Some nouns (usually indicating containers) in Chinese are often temporarily used as measure words, for example, "杯", "瓶" and "盒", etc.

一杯果汁（guǒzhī, juice）

一瓶水

一盒（hé, box）巧克力（qiǎokèlì, chocolate）

练一练 Exercises

填量词（或用作量词的名词）

Fill in the measure words (or nouns temporarily used as measure words).

一（　）留学生　　一（　）老师　　一（　）电话　　一（　）足球

一（　）房间　　　一（　）课　　　一（　）外文书　一（　）商店

一（　）月　　　　一（　）咖啡　　一（　）牛奶　　一（　）水

情景交际 Communication

两三个同学一组，表演买东西。准备时间：3～5分钟。

Act as if you are shopping in groups of two or three. Preparation time: 3-5 minutes.

提示　Tips

饮料（yǐnliào, beverage）

文具（wénjù, stationery）

水果（shuǐguǒ, fruit）

钱　杯　要　瓶　给　个　还　一共　多少钱

写作 Writing

◆ **添句成段** Write more sentences to compose a paragraph

在所给句子前后加上两三句话，把它补充成一段完整的文字。

Write two or three sentences before or after the given sentence to make a complete passage.

还要一杯咖啡

_____

_____

_____

语音 Pronunciation

总复习 Review

1 听后填声母 Listen and fill in the initials  16-03

___à（爸）	___iā（家）	___īn（拼）	___ù（去）
___áng（忙）	___iǎng（想）	___èi（费）	___ōu（周）
___iàn（店）	___ī（吃）	___áng（堂）	___ēng（生）
___iú（留）	___è（热）	___ǎi（奶）	___ěn（怎）
___ǒu（狗）	___uàn（算）	___àn（看）	___óng（红）
___ì（次）	___ī（一）	___ǔ（五）	___ǔ（语）

___ín ___áng（银行）   ___áng ___íng（王明）   ___ǎn ___ang（晚上）

2 听后填韵母 Listen and fill in the finals  16-04

h_____（黑）	k_____（考）	c_____（从）	t_____（铁）
b_____（百）	g_____（跟）	j_____（叫）	d_____（大）
_____（儿）	p_____（婆）	l_____（楼）	zh_____（站）
ch_____（唱）	q_____（球）	f_____（风）	n_____（你）
x_____（下）	n_____（年）	j_____（今）	y_____（泳）

● 215

q _____（请）	k _____（快）	n _____（女）	l _____（两）
d _____（对）	ch _____（春）	y _____（远）	j _____（觉）
j _____（军）	h _____（换）	h _____（话）	z _____（租）
d _____（多）	w _____（王）	h _____（喝）	
l _____ Zh _____ g _____（来中国）		x _____ H _____ y _____（学汉语）	
x _____ sh _____ h _____（学说话）		t _____ l _____ y _____（听录音）	
x _____ H _____ z _____（写汉字）			

❸ 听后填声调　Listen and place the tonal marks to the *pinyin*　 16-05

mei（没）	guan（馆）	liu（六）	san（三）
jiu（九）	zuo（做）	gao（高）	nian（年）
pengyou（朋友）	qu le（去了）	mama（妈妈）	chang ge（唱歌）
laoshi（老师）	fanwan（饭碗）	bu kuai（不快）	benren（本人）

Ta meiyou qu, ta xiang mingtian qu.（他没有去，他想明天去。）

Wo qi che qu, ta zoulu lai.（我骑车去，他走路来。）

❹ 请标出变化后的实际声调　Mark the actual tones after the change　 16-06

yi ge（一个）	bu shì（不是）	wu bǎi（五百）
yi tiān（一天）	bu qù（不去）	ni hǎo（你好）

❺ 双音节连读　Practice the liaison of the disyllabic words　16-07

miànbāo	tǔdòu	jīdàn	báijiǔ
bread	potato	egg	spirit; liquor
píjiǔ	niú ròu	shūcài	nǎilào
beer	beef	vegetable	cheese

❻ 多音节连读　Practice the liaison of the polysyllabic words　 16-08

zhájiàngmiàn	sānmíngzhì	xīhóngshì
noodles with fried bean sauce	sandwich	tomato
húluóbo	pútaojiǔ	fāngbiànmiàn
carrot	wine	instant noodles

7 朗读 Read aloud 🔘 16-09

你要什么？	我要牛奶。
还要什么？	还要水果。
一共十五。	服务很好。

8 趣味朗读 Interesting reading materials 🔘 16-10

两 只 (a measure word for animals) 老虎 (tiger)
Liǎng zhī　　　　　　　　　　lǎohǔ

两 只 老虎, 两 只 老虎,
Liǎng zhī lǎohǔ, liǎng zhī lǎohǔ,

跑 (to run) 得 快 (fast), 跑 得 快。
pǎo　　　de kuài,　　pǎo de kuài.

一 只 没有 耳朵 (ear),
Yì zhī méiyǒu ěrduo,

一 只 没有 尾巴 (tail)。
yì zhī méiyǒu wěiba.

真 (really) 奇怪 (strange)! 真 奇怪!
Zhēn　　qíguài!　　　Zhēn qíguài!

汉字 | Characters

边学边练 Study and practice

1 汉字的部件（4） Components of Chinese characters (4)

女 nǚzìpáng female	好 good	女+子
	姓 surname	女+生
	她 she; her	女+也
	奶 grandma	女+乃

辶 zǒuzhīpáng to walk; road	这 this	文+辶
	远 far	元+辶
	过 to spend	寸+辶
	还 in addition; also	不+辶

2 认写基本汉字   Learn and write the basic Chinese characters

(1) 力   lì   power; strength

　　 ㇆ 力   2 strokes

(2) 非   fēi   not

　　 丨 𠂆 𡰣 ㇂ 非 非 非   8 strokes

(3) 贝   bèi   shellfish

　　 丨 冂 贝 贝   4 strokes

(4) 水   shuǐ   water

　　 丨 刀 水 水   4 strokes

(5) 并   bìng   and

　　 丶 丷 䒑 兰 羊 并   6 strokes

(6) 瓦   wǎ   tile

　　 一 𠂉 瓦 瓦   4 strokes

(7) 牛   niú   cattle

　　 丿 𠂉 二 牛   4 strokes

(8) 乃   nǎi   to be; therefore

　　 ㇇ 乃   2 strokes

(9) 两   liǎng   two

　　 一 厂 丌 丙 丙 两 两   7 strokes

(10) 羔   gāo   lamb

　　 丶 丷 䒑 兰 羊 羊 羊 羔 羔 羔   10 strokes

218

（11）共　gòng　altogether

一 十 卄 共 共 共　6 strokes

（12）合　hé　to close

丿 人 亼 合 合 合　6 strokes

3 认写本课汉字　Learn and write the Chinese characters in this lesson

(1) 咖啡　kāfēi　coffee

咖 → 口 + 加 + 口

啡 → 口 + 非

(2) 钱　qián　money

钱 → 钅 + 一 + 戈

(3) 杯　bēi　glass

杯 → 木 + 不

(4) 服务员　fúwùyuán　waiter; waitress

服 → 月 + 卩 + 又　to serve

务 → 夂 + 力　affair; business

员 → 口 + 贝　a person engaged in some field of activity

(5) 瓶　píng　bottle

瓶 → 并 + 瓦

(6) 块　kuài　*a unit of Chinese currency, equivalent to 10 mao; piece*

块 → 土 + 夬

(7) 牛奶　niúnǎi　milk

奶 → 女 + 乃　milk

(8) 要　yào　to want

要 → 西 + 女

（9）还　hái　in addition; also

　　还 → 不 + 辶

（10）蛋糕　dàngāo　cake

　　蛋 → 疋 + 虫　egg

　　糕 → 米 + 羔　cake

（11）给　gěi　to give

　　给 → 纟 + 合

（12）您　nín　you (*the respectful form of "你"*)

　　您 → 你 + 心

实践活动 | Activity

◆ **小调查**　Survey

调查下边这些饮料的价钱，给你喜欢喝的饮料画上√，下次课汇报。

Find out the prices of the following drinks and tick your favorite ones. Report your findings to the class next time.

饮料 （yǐnliào, beverage）	价钱 （jiàqian, price）	我喜欢（xǐhuan, to like） 喝（hē, to drink）
矿泉水 （kuàngquánshuǐ, mineral water）		
冰红茶 （bīnghóngchá, ice black tea）		
乌龙茶 （wūlóngchá, oolong tea）		
酸梅汤 （suānméitāng, plum juice）		
鲜橙多 （xiānchéngduō, orange juice）		

第16课　咖啡多少钱一杯

文化点滴 | Cultural Note

中国的民族
Zhōngguó de mínzú
Ethnic Groups in China

> 中国是一个多民族国家。
> China is a country with multiple ethnic groups.

答一答 Answer the questions

1. 你知道中国有多少个民族吗？中国人口最多的民族是哪个民族？

   Do you know how many ethnic groups China has? Which is the most populous ethnic group in China?

2. 你知道中国人口最多的少数民族是哪个民族吗？它主要分布在哪儿？请你在地图上圈出来。

   Do you know which minority group is the most populous? Where is its population mainly distributed? Please circle it in the map.

3. 你的中国朋友中有没有人是少数民族？他/她是哪个民族的？

   Do you have Chinese friends of a minority group? Which ethnic group is it?

学习后记 | Summary

词语 Vocabulary	语言点 Grammar

注释、语法：单元总结（二）（第 13 课～第 16 课）
Notes and Grammar: Unit Review 2 (Lesson 13 ~ Lesson 16)

课号 Lesson		注释 / 语法 Note / Grammar	页码 Page No.	例句 Example sentence	我的句子 My sentence
第13课	注释	用"呢"的省略式问句	162	下午呢？	
		用"……，好吗？"征求意见		我们三点去，好吗？	
	语法	"有"字句（表示领有、具有）	163	明天你有课吗？	
		钟点表示法		我八点半上课。	
		时间名词做状语		明天我去图书馆。	
		汉语的主要句子成分：状语		我明天上午有四节课。	
第14课	注释	星期的表达方式	178	我星期六学习，星期天休息。	
	语法	名词谓语句	179	后天星期天。	
		连动句（表示目的）		我上午去商店买东西。	
第15课	注释	"多大"	193	你今年多大？	
	语法	年、月、日的表示方法	195	我1994年9月29号出生。	
		数字的读法（2）		我十九岁。	
		汉语的主要句子成分：定语		今天是爱子的生日。	
第16课	注释	"二"和"两"	209	要两瓶水、一杯牛奶、一块水果蛋糕。一共十二块五。	
		副词"还"（表示增加或补充）		还要什么？	
		人称代词"您"		给您，十二块五。	
	语法	人民币的单位及表述	211	水一块五一瓶。	
		量词		蛋糕多少钱一块？	

● 223

生词表
Vocabulary Index

词语 Word / Phrase	拼音 Pinyin	词性 Word Class	英文释义 Meaning in English	课号 Lesson
B				
八	bā	Num	eight	13
吧	ba	Pt	*a modal particle*	8,12
办公楼	bàngōnglóu	N	office building	12
半	bàn	Num	half	13
杯	bēi	N	glass	16
不错	búcuò	A	not bad	2
不客气	bú kèqi		You're welcome.	4
不	bù	Adv	no; not	1,9
C				
层	céng	M	floor	6,12
茶	chá	N	tea	2
常	cháng	Adv	often; usually	3
吃饭	chīfàn	VO	to eat (a meal)	8
出生	chūshēng	V	to be born	15
D				
打电话	dǎ diànhuà		to make a phone call	3
打算	dǎsuan	V	to plan	14
大	dà	A	large; big	2
			old	15
蛋糕	dàngāo	N	cake	16
的	de	Pt	(*used after an attribute*) of	2,11
等	děng	V	to wait	6
点	diǎn	M	o'clock	13
电话	diànhuà	N	telephone	8,11
东西	dōngxi	N	thing; stuff	14
都	dōu	Adv	all; both	10

对不起	duìbuqǐ	V	I'm sorry.	4
多	duō	A	many	2,13
		Adv	how	15
多大	duō dà		how old	15
多少	duōshao	Pr	how many; how much	8,11

E

二	èr	Num	two	6

F

方便	fāngbiàn	A	convenient	11
房间	fángjiān	N	room	11
服务	fúwù	V	to serve	16
服务员	fúwùyuán	N	waiter; waitress	16

G

高兴	gāoxìng	A	glad; happy	10
个	gè	M	*a measure word of general use*	3,11
给	gěi	V	to give	16
狗	gǒu	N	dog	15
国	guó	N	country; nation	7,10
过	guò	V	to celebrate; to spend	15

H

还	hái	Adv	in addition; also	16
汉语	Hànyǔ	N	Chinese language	5
好	hǎo	A	good; fine; OK	1,9
号	hào	M	*used after a number to mark the order*	7,11
			date	15
号码	hàomǎ	N	number	11
很	hěn	Adv	very; quite	2,10
红	hóng	A	red	12
后天	hòutiān	N	the day after tomorrow	14

J

鸡	jī	N	chicken	15
几	jǐ	Pr	how many	11
见	jiàn	V	to see	4
叫	jiào	V	to be called	7,10

225

教室	jiàoshì	N	classroom	8
节	jié	M	a measure word for class hours	13
今年	jīnnián	N	this year	15
今天	jīntiān	N	today	15
就	jiù	Adv	just	12

K

咖啡	kāfēi	N	coffee	16
看	kàn	V	to look	12
课	kè	N	lesson	13
块	kuài	M	a unit of Chinese currency, equivalent to 10 mao; piece	16
快	kuài	A	fast; quick	6
快乐	kuàilè	A	happy	15

L

老师	lǎoshī	N	teacher	9
里	li	N	inside	12
两	liǎng	Num	two	16
留学生	liúxuéshēng	N	student studying abroad; international student	9
楼	lóu	N	building	7,11

M

吗	ma	Pt	an interrogative particle for questions expecting a yes-or-no answer	1,9
买	mǎi	V	to buy; to purchase	14
忙	máng	A	busy	1
没关系	méi guānxi		Never mind; It doesn't matter.	4
没有	méiyǒu	V/Adv	not to have, there is not	13
名字	míngzi	N	name	7,10
明天	míngtiān	N	tomorrow	4,13

N

哪	nǎ	Pr	which	7,10
哪儿	nǎr	Pr	where	6,11
那儿	nàr	Pr	there	12
那个	nàge/nèige	Pr	that	12
难	nán	A	difficult	5

呢	ne	Pt	*a modal particle used for elliptical questions*	9
你	nǐ	Pr	you	1,9
你们	nǐmen	Pr	you (*pl.*)	3,10
年	nián	N/M	year	15
您	nín	Pr	you (*the respectful form of "你"*)	16
牛奶	niúnǎi	N	milk	16

P

朋友	péngyou	N	friend	3
瓶	píng	N	bottle	16

Q

钱	qián	N	money	16
请问	qǐngwèn	V	may I ask...; Excuse me...	6,12
去	qù	V	to go	4,12

R

人	rén	N	person; people	2,10
认识	rènshi	V	to meet; to know	10

S

三	sān	Num	three	13
商店	shāngdiàn	N	store; shop	6,14
上课	shàngkè	VO	to go to class (both for students and teachers)	4,13
上午	shàngwǔ	N	morning	13
什么	shénme	Pr	what	5, 10
生日	shēngrì	N	birthday	15
十八	shíbā	Num	eighteen	15
十二	shí'èr	Num	twelve	13
十九	shíjiǔ	Num	nineteen	15
十四	shísì	Num	fourteen	7
是	shì	V	to be	7,9
书	shū	N	book	13
属	shǔ	V	to be born in the year of	15
水	shuǐ	N	water	16
水果	shuǐguǒ	N	fruit	16
四	sì	Num	four	13

| 宿舍 | sùshè | N | dormitory | 11 |
| 岁 | suì | M | age | 15 |

T

他	tā	Pr	he; him	3,10
她	tā	Pr	she; her	10
踢	tī	V	to kick; to play	14
天	tiān	M	day	14
图书馆	túshūguǎn	N	library	13

W

外文	wàiwén	N	foreign language	13
晚上	wǎnshang	N	evening	15
卫生间	wèishēngjiān	N	toilet	6
为什么	wèi shénme		why	5
问	wèn	V	to ask	3,12
问题	wèntí	N	question; problem	3
我	wǒ	Pr	I; me	3,9
我们	wǒmen	Pr	we; us	3,10

X

下课	xiàkè	VO	to dismiss the class	13
下午	xiàwǔ	N	afternoon	13
校内	xiàonèi	N	on campus	11
校外	xiàowài	N	off campus	11
谢谢	xièxie	V	to thank	4
星期	xīngqī	N	week	14
星期二	xīngqī'èr	N	Tuesday	14
星期六	xīngqīliù	N	Saturday	14
星期三	xīngqīsān	N	Wednesday	14
星期四	xīngqīsì	N	Thursday	14
星期天	xīngqītiān	N	Sunday	14
星期五	xīngqīwǔ	N	Friday	14
星期一	xīngqīyī	N	Monday	14
行	xíng	V	all right	12
姓	xìng	V/N	one's surname is… / surname	10
休息	xiūxi	V	to take a break; to rest	14

学	xué	V	to study; to learn	5
学生	xuésheng	N	student	9
学习	xuéxí	V	to study; to learn	14

Y

要	yào	V	to want	16
也	yě	Adv	too; also	4,9
一	yī	Num	one	3
一共	yígòng	Adv	in all; altogether	16
一会儿	yíhuìr		a little while	6
（一）点儿	(yì)diǎnr		a little; a few	6
一起	yìqǐ	Adv	together	8,12
因为	yīnwèi	Conj	because	5
银行	yínháng	N	bank	12
游泳	yóuyǒng	V	to swim	14
有	yǒu	V	to have	3,13
有用	yǒuyòng	A	useful	5
远	yuǎn	A	far	13
月	yuè	N	month	15

Z

再见	zàijiàn	V	to see you later	4
在	zài	V	to be (at; in; on); to be (here; there)	6,12
早上	zǎoshang	N	morning	2
这儿	zhèr	Pr	here	6,12
这个	zhège/zhèige	Pr	this	12
周末	zhōumò	N	weekend	14
主意	zhǔyi	N	idea	15
住	zhù	V	to live	7,11
祝	zhù	V	to wish	15
足球	zúqiú	N	soccer	14
昨天	zuótiān	N	yesterday	15
作业	zuòyè	N	homework	14
做	zuò	V	to do	14

专有名词表
Proper Noun Index

词语 Word / Phrase	拼音 Pinyin	英文释义 Meaning in English	课号 Lesson
A			
安娜	Ānnà	Anna, name of a girl student from Russia. Please refer to "Introduction to the Main Characters" for more details.	13
G			
故宫	Gùgōng	the Forbidden City	14
H			
韩国	Hánguó	Republic of Korea	10
J			
杰克	Jiékè	Jack, name of a boy student from the USA. Please refer to "Introduction to the Main Characters" for more details.	9
金大成	Jīn Dàchéng	Jin Daesung, name of a boy student from Republic of Korea. Please refer to "Introduction to the Main Characters" for more details.	10
金在元	Jīn Zàiyuán	Jin Jae-won, name of a boy student from Republic of Korea. Please refer to "Introduction to the Main Characters" for more details.	10
L			
李明	Lǐ Míng	Li Ming, name of a Chinese boy student. Please refer to "Introduction to the Main Characters" for more details.	9
R			
日本	Rìběn	Japan	7,10
S			
山口爱子	Shānkǒu Àizǐ	Yamaguchi Aiko, name of a girl student from Japan. Please refer to the "Introduction to the Main Characters" for more details.	7,10
W			
王	Wáng	*a family name*	15
Z			
张小英	Zhāng Xiǎoyīng	Zhang Xiaoying, name of a Chinese girl student. Please refer to "Introduction to the Main Characters" for more details.	12
中国	Zhōngguó	China	2

生字表
Index of New Characters

	A	
爱	ài	7,10
安	ān	13
	B	
八	bā	6,13
吧	ba	8,12
白	bái	11
百	bǎi	11
办	bàn	12
半	bàn	13
杯	bēi	16
贝	bèi	16
本	běn	7,10
便	biàn	11
并	bìng	16
不	bù	1,9
	C	
茶	chá	2
长	cháng	9
常	cháng	3
层	céng	6,12
成	chéng	10
吃	chī	8
虫	chóng	15
出	chū	15
寸	cùn	15
错	cuò	2
	D	
打	dǎ	3,14
大	dà	2,15

蛋	dàn	16
刀	dāo	9
的	de	2,11
等	děng	6
点	diǎn	6,13
电	diàn	3,11
店	diàn	6,14
丁	dīng	8
东	dōng	14
冬	dōng	13
都	dōu	10
对	duì	4
多	duō	2,11
	E	
儿	ér	6,11
尔	ěr	9
二	èr	6,13
	F	
饭	fàn	8
方	fāng	11
房	fáng	11
非	fēi	16
啡	fēi	16
服	fú	16
	G	
高	gāo	10
羔	gāo	16
糕	gāo	16
个	gè	3,11
给	gěi	16

更	gèng	11
工	gōng	12
公	gōng	12
宫	gōng	14
共	gòng	16
狗	gǒu	15
古	gǔ	14
故	gù	14
关	guān	4
官	guān	13
馆	guǎn	13
国	guó	2,10
果	guǒ	13,16
过	guò	15
	H	
还	hái	16
韩	hán	10
汉	hàn	5
行	háng	12
好	hǎo	1,9
号	hào	7,11
合	hé	16
很	hěn	2,10
红	hóng	12
后	hòu	14
户	hù	11
话	huà	3,11
会	huì	6
	J	
鸡	jī	15

几	jǐ	11
己	jǐ	12
间	jiān	6,11
见	jiàn	4
交	jiāo	11
叫	jiào	7,10
教	jiào	8
节	jié	13
杰	jié	9
巾	jīn	9
今	jīn	15
金	jīn	10
京	jīng	12
九	jiǔ	9
就	jiù	12
	K	
咖	kā	16
看	kàn	12
克	kè	9
客	kè	4
课	kè	4,13
口	kǒu	7,8
块	kuài	16
快	kuài	6,15
	L	
老	lǎo	9
乐	lè	15
李	lǐ	9
力	lì	16
立	lì	15

231

里	li	12	鸟	niǎo	15	师	shī	9	午	wǔ	13
两	liǎng	16	您	nín	16	十	shí	6,13	勿	wù	14
留	liú	9	牛	niú	16	石	shí	11	务	wù	16
六	liù	6,14	女	nǚ	8	识	shí	10			

M
楼	lóu	7,11

P
朋	péng	3
瓶	píng	16

Q
七	qī	8
期	qī	14
其	qí	14
起	qǐ	4,12
钱	qián	16
青	qīng	12
请	qǐng	6,12
求	qiú	14
球	qiú	14
去	qù	4,9

R
人	rén	2,6,10
认	rèn	10
日	rì	8

S
三	sān	6,13
山	shān	9
商	shāng	6,14
上	shàng	2,13
勺	sháo	11
少	shǎo	8,11
舌	shé	11
舍	shè	11
什	shén	5,10
生	shēng	6,9
尸	shī	12

是 shì 7,9
室 shì 8
书 shū 13
属 shǔ 15
水 shuǐ 16
四 sì 13
宿 sù 11
算 suàn 14
岁 suì 15

T
他 tā 3,10
她 tā 10
踢 tī 14
题 tí 3
天 tiān 4,13
田 tián 9
头 tóu 14
图 tú 13
土 tǔ 6

W
瓦 wǎ 16
外 wài 11
晚 wǎn 15
王 wáng 14
为 wèi 5
卫 wèi 6
文 wén 12,13
问 wèn 3,12
我 wǒ 3,9
五 wǔ 8,16

X
夕 xī 10
西 xī 14
息 xī 14
习 xí 14
系 xì 4
下 xià 13
小 xiǎo 8,12
校 xiào 11
谢 xiè 4
心 xīn 14
星 xīng 14
行 xíng 12
兴 xìng 10
姓 xìng 10
休 xiū 14
学 xué 5,9

Y
要 yào 16
也 yě 4,9
业 yè 14
一 yī 3,6,11
意 yì 15
因 yīn 5
银 yín 12
英 yīng 12
永 yǒng 14
泳 yǒng 14
用 yòng 5
尤 yóu 12
游 yóu 14

马 mǎ 9
码 mǎ 11
吗 ma 1,9
买 mǎi 14
忙 máng 1
么 me 5,10
没 méi 4,13
门 mén 8
们 men 3,10
米 mǐ 11
免 miǎn 15
名 míng 7,10
明 míng 4,13
末 mò 14
木 mù 6
目 mù 12

N
哪 nǎ 6,10
那 nà/nèi 12
娜 nà 13
乃 nǎi 16
奶 nǎi 16
难 nán 5
呢 ne 9
内 nèi 11
尼 ní 9
你 nǐ 1,9
年 nián 15

生字表

友	yǒu	3	云	yún	12	这	zhè/zhèi	6,9	字	zì	7,10
有	yǒu	3,13	**Z**			只	zhǐ	10	走	zǒu	12
又	yòu	8	再	zài	4	中	zhōng	2	足	zú	14
语	yǔ	5	在	zài	6,10,12	周	zhōu	14	昨	zuó	15
玉	yù	10	早	zǎo	2	主	zhǔ	11	作	zuò	14
元	yuán	10,13	乍	zhà	14	住	zhù	7,11	做	zuò	14
员	yuán	16	占	zhàn	13	祝	zhù	15			
远	yuǎn	13	张	zhāng	12	子	zǐ	7,9			
月	yuè	8,15	者	zhě	10	自	zì	14			

233

本册单音节声调表
Tones of Monosyllables in This Book

声调 Tone	例字 Example character
ˉ	都　他　她　八　多　三　天　踢　鸡　杯　吃　东　西
ˊ	国　人　楼　红　层　行　节　年　钱　瓶　还　您
ˇ	你　好　我　也　哪　很　几　里　有　点　远　买　属 狗　水　两　给
ˋ	是　不　叫　姓　住　个　号　在　看　那　这　就　去 课　四　半　做　月　祝　大　岁　过　块　要
˚	吗　呢　的　吧

本册双音节声调组合表
Tones of Disyllables in This Book

- -	- ˊ	- ˇ	- ˋ	- ˚
星期　今天 出生　咖啡	今年		高兴　方便 周末　商店 多大	他们　多少 东西　休息
ˊ -	ˊ ˊ	ˊ ˇ	ˊ ˋ	ˊ ˚
房间　明天 昨天　十八	银行　学习 足球	没有　游泳 十九　牛奶	十二　服务 一共	学生　什么 名字
ˇ -	ˇ ˊ	ˇ ˇ	ˇ ˋ	ˇ ˚
老师		水果	请问	你们　我们 打算　晚上 主意
ˋ -	ˋ ˊ	ˋ ˇ	ˋ ˋ	ˋ ˚
后天　蛋糕		号码　一起 上午　下午	宿舍　校外 电话　校内 上课　下课 作业　快乐	认识

本册多音节声调组合表
Tones of Polysyllables in This Book

ˉ ˉ	ˉ ˊ	ˉ ˉ	ˉ ˇ	ˉ ˋ	ˉ ˋ	ˉ ˋ
星期一	星期三	星期天	星期五	星期二	星期六	星期四

ˊ ˉ ˇ	ˊ ˊ ˉ	ˊ ˋ ˊ
图书馆	留学生	服务员

ˋ ˉ ˊ	ˋ ˊ ˉ
办公楼	外文书

汉字常用部件表
Frequently-Used Components of Chinese Characters

序号 No.	部件 Component		义类 Meaning	例字 Example Character	
1	亻	dānrénpáng	person	你 (you) nǐ	住 (to live) zhù
2	彳	shuāngrénpáng	two persons	行 (to walk) xíng	往 (to go) wǎng
3	冫	liǎngdiǎnshuǐ	ice	冷 (cold) lěng	冰 (ice) bīng
4	氵	sāndiǎnshuǐ	water	海 (sea) hǎi	洗 (to wash) xǐ
5	彡	sānpiěr	ornament	彩 (color) cǎi	须 (beard) xū
6	口	kǒuzìpáng	mouth	吃 (to eat) chī	叫 (to shout) jiào
7	讠	yánzìpáng	speech	语 (language) yǔ	说 (to speak) shuō
8	禾	hézìpáng	cereal	秋 (autumn) qiū	种 (to plant) zhòng
9	木	mùzìpáng	wood	林 (forest) lín	楼 (building) lóu
10	米	mǐzìpáng	rice	糖 (sugar) táng	糕 (cake) gāo
11	扌	tíshǒupáng	hand	打 (to hit) dǎ	找 (to find) zhǎo
12	日	rìzìpáng	sun; time	明 (bright) míng	星 (star) xīng
13	月	yuèzìpáng	time; light; flesh	胖 (fat) pàng	期 (period) qī
14	目	mùzìpáng	eye	眼 (eye) yǎn	睡 (to sleep) shuì

15	田	tiánzìtóu	field; farm	男 (male) nán	累 (tired) lèi
16	火	huǒzìpáng	fire	灯 (light) dēng	烤 (to bake) kǎo
17	灬	sìdiǎndǐ	fire	点 (to burn) diǎn	热 (hot) rè
18	心	xīnzìdǐ	thinking; feeling	您 (you, *the respectful form of "你"*) nín	想 (to think) xiǎng
19	忄	shùxīnpáng	heart	怕 (to fear) pà	怪 (strange) guài
20	礻	shìzìpáng	to pray; to bless	祝 (to wish) zhù	福 (happiness) fú
21	衤	yīzìpáng	clothes	裤 (trousers) kù	衫 (shirt) shān
22	艹	cǎozìtóu	grass	花 (flower) huā	茶 (tea) chá
23	竹	zhúzìtóu	bamboo	笔 (pen) bǐ	简 (simple) jiǎn
24	广	guǎngzìpáng	room	床 (bed) chuáng	店 (store) diàn
25	疒	bìngzìpáng	illness	疼 (painful) téng	病 (illness) bìng
26	纟	jiǎosīpáng	silk	绣 (to embroider) xiù	绳 (rope) shéng
27	钅	jīnzìpáng	metal	钱 (money) qián	银 (silver) yín
28	宀	bǎogàitóu	roof	家 (home) jiā	宿 (to stay overnight) sù
29	穴	xuézìtóu	cave	窗 (window) chuāng	空 (empty) kōng
30	廴	jiànzhīpáng	to build	延 (to extend) yán	建 (to build) jiàn

31	辶	zǒuzhīpáng	to walk; road	过 (to pass) guò	进 (to enter) jìn
32	走	zǒuzìpáng	running	越 (to exceed) yuè	赶 (to catch up with) gǎn
33	卩	dān'ěrdāo	sb. on his knees	却 (but) què	印 (to print) yìn
34	阝	shuāng'ěrdāo	fence; city	院 (courtyard) yuàn	都 (all; both) dōu
35	耳	ěrzìpáng	ear; to listen	聊 (to chat) liáo	聪 (smart) cōng
36	其	qízìpáng	other	期 (period) qī	基 (base) jī
37	女	nǚzìpáng	female	她 (she; her) tā	妈 (mother) mā
38	方	fāngzìpáng	place	放 (to put) fàng	旁 (side) páng
39	尸	shīzìtóu	room; body	屋 (room) wū	居 (to live) jū
40	户	hùzìtóu	door	房 (house) fáng	扇 (fan) shàn
41	欠	qiànzìpáng	mouth; mood	歌 (song) gē	歉 (apology) qiàn
42	攵	fǎnwénpáng	action	教 (to teach) jiāo	数 (to count) shǔ
43	又	yòuzìpáng	again	对 (right) duì	双 (double) shuāng
44	饣	shízìpáng	food	饭 (meal) fàn	饱 (full) bǎo
45	王	wángzìpáng	jade	球 (ball) qiú	理 (veins) lǐ
46	土	tǔzìpáng	soil	地 (ground) dì	场 (field) chǎng
47	工	gōngzìpáng	work	功 (work) gōng	差 (bad) chà

48	舌	shézìpáng	tongue	乱 (random) luàn	甜 (sweet) tián
49	足	zúzìpáng	foot	跳 (to jump) tiào	跑 (to run) pǎo
50	石	shízìpáng	stone	碗 (bowl) wǎn	破 (broken) pò
51	犭	fǎnquǎnpáng	animal	狗 (dog) gǒu	猫 (cat) māo
52	牛	niúzìpáng	ox	物 (object) wù	牲 (animal sacrifice) shēng
53	虫	chóngzìpáng	insect	虾 (shrimp) xiā	蛋 (egg) dàn
54	马	mǎzìpáng	horse	骑 (to ride) qí	驾 (to drive) jià
55	见	jiànzìpáng	to see	观 (to observe) guān	视 (to watch) shì
56	贝	bèizìpáng	money	账 (account) zhàng	贵 (expensive) guì
57	页	yèzìpáng	head	预 (beforehand) yù	颜 (face) yán
58	巾	jīnzìpáng	cloth	带 (belt) dài	帽 (hat) mào
59	舟	zhōuzìpáng	boat	船 (boat) chuán	航 (to navigate) háng
60	车	chēzìpáng	vehicle	辆 (a measure word) liàng	输 (to convey) shū
61	弓	gōngzìpáng	bow	张 (a measure word) zhāng	弹 (bomb) dàn
62	矢	shǐzìpáng	arrow	短 (short) duǎn	知 (knowledge) zhī
63	力	lìzìpáng	strength	加 (to add) jiā	动 (to move) dòng
64	刀	dāozìpáng	knife	分 (to divide) fēn	切 (to chop) qiē

65	刂	lìdāopáng	knife	刻 (to engrave) kè	别 (to part) bié
66	门	ménzìkuàng	door	间 (*a measure word*) jiān	问 (to ask) wèn
67	鸟	niǎozìpáng	bird	鸡 (chicken) jī	鸭 (duck) yā
68	鱼	yúzìpáng	fish	鲜 (fresh) xiān	鲤 (carp) lǐ

本册注释、语法总结
Summary of Notes and Grammar in This Book

课号 Lesson	注释 Note	页码 Page No.	例句 Example sentence	我的句子 My sentence
第9课	副词"也"	96	我也是学生。	
第10课	后缀"们"	111	你们是留学生吗?	
	副词"都"		我们都是韩国人。	
	动词"叫"		我叫金大成。	
第11课	"……号码是多少?"	130	你的电话号码是多少?	
第12课	"请问,……?"	146	请问,银行在哪儿?	
	副词"就"(表示强调)		那个红楼就是。	
第13课	用"呢"的省略式问句	162	下午呢?	
	用"……,好吗?"征求意见		我们三点去,好吗?	
第14课	星期的表达方式	178	我星期六学习,星期天休息。	
第15课	"多大"	193	你今年多大?	
第16课	"二"和"两"	209	要两瓶水、一杯牛奶、一块水果蛋糕。一共十二块五。	
	副词"还"（表示增加或补充）		还要什么?	
	人称代词"您"		给您,十二块五。	

本册注释、语法总结

课号 Lesson	语法 Grammar	页码 Page No.	例句 Example sentence	我的句子 My sentence
第9课	"是"字句（表示判断）	97	我不是留学生。	
	用"吗"的是非疑问句		你是老师吗？	
	汉语的语序及主要句子成分：主语、谓语、宾语		我不是老师。	
第10课	动词谓语句	114	我叫爱子。	
	形容词谓语句		我很高兴。	
	疑问代词"哪"		你是哪国人？	
	疑问代词"什么"		你叫什么名字？	
第11课	数字的读法（1）	130	我住8号楼401房间。	
	疑问代词"哪儿"		你住哪儿？	
	疑问代词"几"		几个人住？	
	结构助词"的"		我的电话号码是13801057259。	
第12课	方位词"里"和"外"	147	银行在办公楼里。	
	语气助词"吧"		我也去银行，一起去吧。	
第13课	"有"字句（表示领有、具有）	163	明天你有课吗？	
	钟点表示法		我八点半上课。	
	时间名词做状语		明天我去图书馆。	
	汉语的主要句子成分：状语		我明天上午有四节课。	
第14课	名词谓语句	179	后天星期天。	
	连动句（表示目的）		我上午去商店买东西。	
第15课	年、月、日的表示方法	195	我1994年9月29号出生。	
	数字的读法（2）		我十九岁。	
	汉语的主要句子成分：定语		今天是爱子的生日。	
第16课	人民币的单位及表述	211	水一块五一瓶。	
	量词		蛋糕多少钱一块？	

243

"十二五"国家重点出版物出版规划项目

汉语言专业本科系列教材·综合类

BASIC CHINESE: COMPREHENSIVE COURSE（I）
基础汉语综合教程

上

本册主编：全　军
编　　者：全　军　徐京梅　柯润兰　李靖华
翻　　译：何　洁

Worksheets 练习活页

ERYA CHINESE

北京语言大学出版社
BEIJING LANGUAGE AND CULTURE
UNIVERSITY PRESS

编写说明

一、总体介绍

练习活页与《尔雅中文·基础汉语综合教程》课本配套使用，可作为课后作业布置给学生完成。在练习的设计和编写上注重针对性、实用性、科学性、趣味性的原则，题量丰富，题型新颖。语音阶段练习重在辨音和诵读，语法阶段的练习从字到词、短语、句、句群、段落，层层推进，由易到难、由浅入深、由固定到开放，层次鲜明。练习设计从复习巩固所学的基本知识入手，到训练学生对所学知识进行综合掌握，最后使学生熟练自如地生成正确的语句，目的在于让学生全面复习和巩固本课所学的汉字、词汇、语法、课文。

二、练习形式

1. 语音阶段

包括"辨音""双音节连读""声调组合"等。

2. 语法阶段

包括"读一读，记一记""写汉字，先描后写""写生词""组词""朗读与书写（短语、句子）""选词填空""给括号中的词选择适当的位置""组句""完成对话""根据实际情况回答问题""综合填空"等。

三、特色练习

1. 朗读与书写（短语、句子）

这一练习形式不仅好学易用，而且使学习者无形中习得了许多能产的结构，从而增强了话语生成的能力。另一方面，它还弥补了不适合放在语法注释之内的语法延伸形式的学习空白，方便学生更加灵活地使用。

同时，为了帮助学生更深入、更灵活地掌握课文，编者还根据课文内容重新组合了若干个句子，并保证每一项都包括两个有语义逻辑关系的分句，构成一个相对独立的语段表达，增强学习者正确掌握汉语语意连贯和衔接的能力，并使学习者从中学到一些灵活的语法延伸形式。

2. 根据实际情况回答问题

这一练习贴近学生（多数学习者）的生活，问题涉及面广而且幽默有趣，话题现实，使学生有话可说，能增强学生的表达欲望。

3. 其他

本册的练习都注意将"语境"巧妙融入其中，利用"语境"的规定加强学生对词语的理解和正确使用。

四、使用说明

1到8课是语音阶段，集中学习拼音，重点练习发音以及汉语拼音的书写，学习和考查过程主要在课上进行，因此作业中只设有拼音认读，供学生课后复习时作为口头练习使用，同时也可供教师检查学生复习情况时使用。为了突出重点，也为了不给学生过重的负担，前8课只让学生接触一些汉字的笔画和简单的汉字，课文中的汉字只要求认读，书写不作为这一部分的考核内容，因此，前8课作业不设相关的汉字练习。

从第9课开始，正式要求学生掌握每一课的汉字书写，因此作业中设有较多的汉字书写练习，练习一、二、三可供所有学生课前预习时使用；练习四、五根据学生的具体情况可在预习或者学习之后完成；从第六项练习开始都是学完本课复习时使用。每课作业在学习完该课之后一次性提交。作业题目的设置顺序原则上是由易到难、由固定到开放、由记忆到生成，循序渐进。为了考查学生的学习效果，从第9课之后每4课设一次单元练习，也可作为单元测试使用。每次单元练习要求两课时之内完成。因此，教师应在授课之初就请学生抽出所有单元练习（上册两套、下册四套）以备其后使用。

所有练习均采取活页形式，便于教师收取和批改。

五、鸣谢

本书为北京语言大学本科系列教材项目的一部分。感谢本套系列教材的编委会成员和北京语言大学出版社的编辑组成员，感谢他们为本书的出版所作的一切支持和努力。同时，恳请各位教材使用者提出批评、建议和指正，使得本书不断完善。

编　者

2013年3月

A Guide to the Use of the Worksheets

I. Introduction

The worksheets are designed to be used together with the textbook *Basic Chinese: Comprehensive Course*, which can be used as students' after-class assignments. In writing and designing the exercises, the authors observe such principles as pertinence, practicability, scientific soundness and interestingness. The exercises of the phonetic part focus on sound discrimination and reading aloud, while those of the grammar part proceed from characters to words, phrases, sentences, sentence clusters and paragraphs, demonstrating a step-by-step increase in difficulty, depth and flexibility. The exercises are designed to help students review and reinforce the basic knowledge they've learned first, then improve their integrated mastery of the knowledge learned and finally enable them to generate correct expressions and sentences fluently without difficulty. In this way, students will have a comprehensive review and reinforcement of the characters, vocabulary, grammar and text taught in each lesson.

II. Forms of Exercises

(A) Phonetics:

Including "Distinguish the syllables", "Practice the liaison of the disyllabic words" and "Combination of tones", etc.

(B) Grammar:

Including "Read and memorize", "Write the characters after tracing them", "Write the new words", "Use the characters provided to make up words or phrases", "Read aloud and write (the phrases and sentences)", "Choose the words to fill in the blanks", "Put the words in the brackets in the right positions", "Make sentences", "Complete the following dialogue", "Answer the questions based on the actual situations" and "Cloze", etc.

III. Highlights of Exercises

1. Read aloud and write (the phrases and sentences)

This form of exercise is not only easy to learn and use, but also enables learners to learn many productive structures unconsciously, thereby enhancing their ability to generate discourses. Besides, it fills a gap by adding some extended grammatical forms which are not suitable to be included in grammar notes, thus enabling students to use the structures more flexibly.

In order to help students have a better and more flexible understanding of the text, sentences are rearranged in this exercise according to the content of the text so that two clauses which are semantically and logically related are included in every independent discourse. This enhances learners' ability to correctly grasp the semantic coherence and cohesion in Chinese discourses and enables them to learn some flexible and extended grammatical forms.

2. Answer the questions based on the actual situations

This form of exercise is close to students' (the majority of them) real life, involving a wide range of humorous and interesting questions and practical topics. It triggers students' flow of thoughts and enhances their desire to express themselves.

3. Others

Contexts are provided in most of the exercises. The employment of "context" helps students better understand the words and use them correctly.

IV. Instructions for Users

Lessons 1-8, the phonetic part, focus on pronunciation practice and the writing of *pinyin*. The study and check-out are mainly carried out in class. Only reading and sound discriminating exercises are designed for students to do oral practice after class or for teachers to test their students. With phonetics being the focus, and to lighten the burden on students, the first eight lessons only teach a few strokes of Chinese characters and simple Chinese characters. Students are only required to know how to read the characters in the text. Character writing is not a requirement in this part. Therefore, there are no exercises on Chinese characters in the first eight lessons.

From Lesson 9 onwards, students are required to write characters and therefore character writing exercises are included. Exercises 1, 2 and 3 are designed for preview and Exercises 4 and 5 for either preview or review according to students' individual needs; Exercise 6 and the exercises following it are for review use after the whole lesson is finished and the homework is required to be submitted after each lesson. Basically the exercises are arranged in a progressive order, from easy to difficult, from fixed to open, from memorizing learned knowledge to generating new expressions. In order to examine students' learning progress, exercises for every unit (or every four lessons) are available starting Lesson 9, which are also used as a unit test. The exercises are supposed to be completed within two class hours. Therefore, teachers should collect all the exercises for the units (2 sets for Volume 1 and 4 sets for Volume 2) at the beginning of the semester for future use.

For convenience purposes, all exercises are put in loose-leaf sheets.

V. Acknowledgements

This book is part of the project of undergraduate textbook series developed by Beijing Language and Culture University. Thanks go to the members of the authors' committee of this textbook series and the editors in Beijing Language and Culture University Press for their support and hard work. Any criticism and suggestions from our readers will be highly appreciated.

The authors

March, 2013

目录 Contents

第 1 课　你好 1
　　　　　Hello

第 2 课　早上好 3
　　　　　Good Morning

第 3 课　打电话 5
　　　　　Making a Phone Call

第 4 课　对不起 7
　　　　　I'm Sorry

第 5 课　汉语不难 9
　　　　　Chinese Is Not Difficult

第 6 课　快点儿 11
　　　　　Hurry up

第 7 课　你叫什么名字 13
　　　　　What Is Your Name

第 8 课　你的电话是多少 15
　　　　　What Is Your Telephone Number

第 9 课　你是留学生吗 17
　　　　　Are You an International Student

第 10 课　你是哪国人 ·· 23
　　　　　Which Country Are You from

第 11 课　你住哪儿 ·· 31
　　　　　Where Do You Live

第 12 课　银行在哪儿 ·· 39
　　　　　Where Is the Bank

单元练习（一）(第 9 课～第 12 课) ··· 47
Exercises for Unit 1 (Lesson 9 ~ Lesson 12)

第 13 课　明天你有课吗 ·· 55
　　　　　Will You Have Classes Tomorrow

第 14 课　周末你做什么 ·· 63
　　　　　What Do You Do on Weekends

第 15 课　你的生日是几月几号 ·· 73
　　　　　When Is Your Birthday

第 16 课　咖啡多少钱一杯 ··· 81
　　　　　How Much Is a Cup of Coffee

单元练习（二）(第 13 课～第 16 课) ··· 91
Exercises for Unit 2 (Lesson 13 ~ Lesson16)

1 你好
Hello

Name: _____

一、辨音 Distinguish the syllables

| bù — pù | bǎo — pǎo | páng — fáng | pán — fán |
| cloth plank bed | full to run | side house | plate annoyed |

| miàn — niàn | mǐ — nǐ | dǐng — tǐng | dù — tù |
| noodle to read | rice you | peak; top quite | belly rabbit |

| lián — nián | liǎo — niǎo | gāi — kāi | gàn — kàn |
| curtain year | to finish bird | should to open | to do to see |

二、双音节连读 Practice the liaison of the disyllabic words

| fāngfǎ | tiāotì | huàidàn | hàipà |
| method | to find fault | bad person | to fear; to be afraid of |

| nóngmín | kōngtiáo | bāokuò | huǎnghuà |
| farmer | air conditioner | to include | lie |

| lóutī | gǎnlǎn | mǐfàn | bǎohù |
| stairs | olive | cooked rice | to protect |

| diànhuà | guǎnlǐ | míngliàng | gùtǐ |
| telephone | to administer | bright | solid |

三、声调组合　Combination of tones

ˉ ˉ	ˉ ´	ˉ ˇ	ˉ `
kāihuā to bloom	pāomáo to break down	tōulǎn to be lazy	tōukàn to peep
´ ˉ	**´ ´**	**´ ˇ**	**´ `**
lán bāo blue bag	tóulán to shoot at the basket	máobǐ Chinese writing brush	mílù to lose one's way
ˇ ˉ	**ˇ ´**	**ˇ ˇ**	**ˇ `**
dǎgōng to do a part-time job	lǎngdú to read aloud	nǐ hǎo hello	lǐmào polite
` ˉ	**` ´**	**` ˇ**	**` `**
dàdōu mostly	Tàiguó Thailand	lùkǒu crossing	dàolù avenue

2 早上好
Good Morning

Name: _____

一、辨音 Distinguish the syllables

1. zh — ch — sh

   zhōu — chōu — shōu   zhè — chè — shè
   porridge to whip to collect   this to withdraw to shoot; to fire

   zhèng — chèng — shèng   zhú — chú — shú
   certificate steelyard to be left over   bamboo except; besides familiar

2. z — c

   zǎn — cǎn   zèng — cèng
   to save (money) miserable   to give...as a present to scrape

   zuān — cuān   zòu — còu
   to go through to flee   to beat to gather

3. z — zh

   zǎo — zhǎo   zàn — zhàn
   early to look for   to praise to stand

   zuō — zhuō   zuàn — zhuàn
   to suck table; desk   drill to revolve

4. c — ch

   cāi — chāi   cuān — chuān
   to guess to tear...open   to flee to wear

   cuò — chuò   cán — chán
   wrong to sip   silkworm gluttonous

5. s — sh

suàn — shuàn	sè — shè
garlic to rinse	colour to shoot; to fire

suō — shuō	sǎng — shǎng
to suck to say	throat to reward

6. r — l

róu — lóu	ràng — làng
to rub building	to let wave

rào — lào	rè — lè
to make a detour to bake in a pan	hot to laugh

二、双音节连读 Practice the liaison of the disyllabic words

Déguó	zhànzhēng	zuòmèng	shānghén
Germany	war	to dream	scar
shēnkè	rénmín	chènshān	mēnrè
deep	people	shirt; blouse	sultry
rěnshòu	réngrán	zhèngmíng	zhēnlǐ
to bear; to endure	still; yet	to prove; to testify	truth

三、轻声练习 Practice the neutral tone

rénmen	zǎochen	gūniang	bàba
people	morning	(unmarried) girl	father
gēge	tóufa	dòufu	bǐfang
elder brother	hair	tofu	for example
shāngliang	chuānghu	dǎting	àiren
to consult	window	to ask about	spouse

3 打电话
Making a Phone Call

Name: _____

一、读一读 Read the following syllables

yāo	yìn	yě	yǎn
waist	seal	also; too	eye

wǎng	wěn	wù	wò
net	to kiss	fog	to hold

yǒu	yī	yìng	yòng
to have	one	hard; stiff	to use

二、双音节连读 Practice the liaison of the disyllabic words

dāying	gèbié	yěcān	wùlǐ
to respond	very few	picnic	physics

yǒuyòng	yǒngbié	méiyǒu	wèiwèn
useful	to part forever	not to have	to convey greetings to

yǒu kòng	gōngyòng	bèiyòng	wòshǒu
to have time	for public use	to reserve; spare	to shake hands

4 对不起
I'm Sorry

Name: _____

一、辨音   Distinguish the syllables

1. 单音节辨音   Distinguish the monosyllables

jǐng — qǐng — xǐng		jiāo — qiāo — xiāo
well to invite to wake up		to teach to knock to peel with a knife
jiān — qiān — xiān		jì — qì — xì
pointed thousand first		to post gas thin; slender
jǔ — qǔ — xǔ		juǎn — quǎn — xuǎn
to lift to fetch *a surname*		to roll up dog to choose
jué — qué — xué		jūn — qūn — xūn
unique; superb to be lame to learn		army; troops granary to fumigate
yù — yuàn — yùn — yuè		
jade institute to transport month		

2. 双音节辨音   Distinguish the disyllables

jí zǎo   —   qǐzǎo   —   xǐzǎo
at an early date   to get up early   to take a bath

jiàomén   —   qiàomén   —   xiàomén
to knock at the door   know-how   school gate

jíshǒu   —   qíshǒu   —   xǐ shǒu
difficult to handle   chess player   to wash one's hands

7

二、双音节连读   Practice the liaison of the disyllabic words

wěiqu	nǚ de	xuéwèi	yóujiàn
to feel wronged	female	academic degree	mail
yíqiè	yuánmǎn	yǒuqù	jǔxíng
everything	perfect	interesting	to hold
quànshuō	bìxū	cháng qún	zhéxué
to persuade	must	long skirt	philosophy
xuānchuán	qúnzhòng	píjuàn	xìjūn
to propagate	the masses	weary; tired	bacterium
juéxīn	shěnglüè	wéijīn	xùnqíng
determination	to omit	scarf	to commit suicide for love
diàoyú	yuányīn	yùxí	yǔyán
to go fishing	reason	to preview	language

5 汉语不难
Chinese Is Not Difficult

Name: _____

一、辨音 Distinguish the syllables

zuì — zhuì	duī — tuī	cuī — chuī	suì — shuì
drunk to fall	to pile up to push	to urge to blow	age to sleep

niú — liú	jiǔ — jiǒng	qiú — qióng	
cattle to flow	nine embarrassed	ball poor	

wèn — wèi	ròu — ruò	rù — rùn	
to ask to feed	meat weak	to enter moist	

二、双音节连读 Practice the liaison of the disyllabic words

cūnzhuāng	chūnqiū	zūnshǒu	diūrén
village	spring and autumn	to abide by	to lose face

shūguì	suíbiàn	jiūzhèng	huīsè
bookcase	casually	to correct	grey

chángxiù	liúlì	jiéhūn	yúchǔn
long sleeve	fluent	to marry	stupid

zhǔnquè	tuìxué		
accurate	to drop out of school		

6 快点儿
Hurry up

Name: _____

一、辨音 Distinguish the syllables

| bàn — bànr | zhāo — zhāor | pí — pír | xiàn — xiànr |
| companion | trick | skin | filling; stuffing |

| jiān — jiānr | dǐ — dǐr | gǎn — gǎnr | sháo — sháor |
| point; tip | bottom | rod | spoon |

| diào — diàor | bà — bàr | mén — ménr | tuǐ — tuǐr |
| tune; melody | grip; handle | door | leg or sth. like one's leg |

| gùn — gùnr | wǎn — wǎnr | niǎo — niǎor | yàng — yàngr |
| stick | bowl | bird | appearance; shape; type |

| dài — dàir | dǐng — dǐngr | tào — tàor | pǔ — pǔr |
| belt; ribbon | top | trap; trick | sth. to count on |

二、双音节连读 Practice the liaison of the disyllabic words

| méi kòngr | tōulǎnr | báimiànr | lǎobànr |
| to have no time | to be lazy | heroin | (of old married couple) husband or wife |

| yíhuìr | liáotiānr | kāitóur | chōujīnr |
| a little while | to chat | beginning | to cramp |

| zǒudiàor | dǎzár | méiqùr | guōguor |
| out of tune | to do odds and ends | to feel put out | katydid |

| shǒuwànr | miàntiáor | sǎngménr | chòuwèir |
| finesse | noodles | voice | stink |

7 你叫什么名字
What Is Your Name

Name: _____

一、三声变调 The third tone sandhi

lǎohǔ	guǎngchǎng	hǎishuǐ	lǎnsǎn
tiger	square; plaza	sea water	sluggish
gǎnxiǎng	lǐjiě	zǔzhǐ	guǎnlǐ
impressions	to understand	to stop	to manage

二、双音节连读 Practice the liaison of the disyllabic words

zìdiǎn	zhuōzi	shīzi	zhízi
dictionary	table	lion	nephew
shìjì	chìzì	rìzhì	zhìshāng
century	deficit	journal	IQ
xiǎochī	chìluǒ	lǚcì	zhìsǐ
snack	naked	time and again	to lead to sb.'s death

三、声调组合　Combination of tones

- -	- ˊ	- ˇ	- ˋ	- ˚
sījī driver	chuīniú to boast	shēntǐ body	jiāwù housework	zhīdao to know
ˊ -	**ˊ ˊ**	**ˊ ˇ**	**ˊ ˋ**	**ˊ ˚**
Cháng Jiāng the Yangtze River	zúqiú football	rénkǒu population	chídào to be late	háizi child
ˇ -	**ˇ ˊ**	**ˇ ˇ**	**ˇ ˋ**	**ˇ ˚**
huǒchē train	yǔyán language	xuǎnjǔ to elect	chǎocài to make a stir-fry	mǔqin mother
ˋ -	**ˋ ˊ**	**ˋ ˇ**	**ˋ ˋ**	**ˋ ˚**
jùshuō it is said	zìrán nature	jièkǒu excuse	shuìjiào to sleep	dìfang place

8 你的电话是多少
What Is Your Telephone Number

Name: _____

一、读一读，注意声母的发音

Read the following syllables and pay attention to the pronunciation of the initials

bái — pái	dā — tā	fàn — pàn	gǔ — kǔ
white row	to put up to collapse	food to long for	drum bitter

jiā — zhā	qiáng — cháng	xiàng — shàng	jiǎn — qiǎn
home to prick	wall often	to be like upper	to pick up shallow

二、读一读，注意"a"的发音

Read the following syllables and pay attention to the pronunciation of a

qiān — suān	jiǎn — yǎn	liàn — luàn
thousand sour	to cut eye	to practice in a mess

kuài — kàn	lán — lái	chuān — quān
quick; fast to look	blue to come	to wear circle

bāngmáng	liánxiǎng	duànliàn
to help	to associate	to have physical training

三、读一读，注意"o"的发音

Read the following syllables and pay attention to the pronunciation of o

bóbo	pópo	xǔduō	fófǎ
uncle	husband's mother	many	Buddhist doctrine

zuòcuò	bómó	mòluò	mōsuǒ
to do wrong	thin film	to decline	to grope

四、读一读，注意"e"的发音
Read the following syllables and pay attention to the pronunciation of e

| lěng fēng | jiějie | xièjué |
| cold wind | elder sister | to refuse; to decline |

| quē qián | chéngrén | zhèngquè |
| short in money | adult | correct |

| zhège | mèimei | biérén |
| this | younger sister | other people |

你是留学生吗
Are You an International Student

Name: _____

一、读一读，记一记 Read and memorize

你	nǐ	you
是	shì	to be
留	liú	to study abroad
学	xué	to study
生	shēng	student
吗	ma	*an interrogative particle for questions expecting a yes-or-no answer*
好	hǎo	good; fine; OK
我	wǒ	I; me
呢	ne	*a modal particle used for elliptical questions*
不	bù	no; not
老	lǎo	old
师	shī	teacher
也	yě	too; also

二、写汉字，先描后写 Write the characters after tracing them

你 ノ 亻 亻 亻 佮 佮 你
你 你 你

17

是 丶 冂 日 日 旦 早 early 昰 是
是 是 是

留 丿 ㄣ ㄨ ㄣ ㄣ 卯 卯 留 留 留
留 留 留

学 丶 丷 丷 ⺍ 兴 学 学
学 学 学

生 丿 ㅏ 匕 牛 生
生 生 生

吗 丨 冂 口 叮 吗 吗
吗 吗 吗

好 ㄑ 乂 女 妇 好 好
好 好 好

我 丿 一 于 手 我 我 我
我 我 我

呢 丨 冂 口 叮 叩 呎 呢 呢
呢 呢 呢

第 9 课　你是留学生吗

不　一 ナ 不 不
不 不 不

老　一 十 土 耂 耂 老
老 老 老

师　丿 丿 亻 丆 师 师
师 师 师

也　丁 力 也
也 也 也

三、写生词　**Write the new words**

留 学 生
老 师

四、组词　**Use the characters provided to make up words or phrases**

你：_____　　学：_____　　老：_____

五、朗读与书写　**Read aloud and write**

1. 朗读并抄写句子

   Read aloud the sentences and copy them

   你是 学生 吗?　_____
   Nǐ shì xuésheng ma?

   你是 老师 吗?　_____
   Nǐ shì lǎoshī ma?

19

你 是 杰克 吗? _____
Nǐ shì Jiékè ma?

我 不是 学生。 _____
Wǒ bú shì xuésheng.

我 不是 老师。 _____
Wǒ bú shì lǎoshī.

我 不是 杰克。 _____
Wǒ bú shì Jiékè.

他也是 学生。 _____
Tā yě shì xuésheng.

她也是 老师。 _____
Tā yě shì lǎoshī.

他也是 留学生。 _____
Tā yě shì liúxuéshēng.

2. 在汉字上方标出调号，朗读并抄写句子

Place the tonal mark above each character. Read aloud the sentences and copy them

（1）你 好! 你 是 留学生 吗?
　　 Nǐ hǎo! Nǐ shì liúxuéshēng ma?

_____

（2）我 是 留学生，你 呢?
　　 Wǒ shì liúxuéshēng, nǐ ne?

_____

（3）我 是老师，不 是 学生。
　　 Wǒ shì lǎoshī, bú shì xuésheng.

_____

六、选词填空 Choose the words to fill in the blanks

1. A：我是留学生。

   B：我_____是留学生，我是老师。（也　不）

2. A：你是老师吗？

   B：我_____是老师，我是留学生。（也　不）

   A：我_____不是老师，我_____是留学生。（也　不）

七、填空 Fill in the blanks

1. _____是留学生。_____呢？

2. 我_____老师，我_____学生。

3. 你是留学生_____？

八、组句 Make sentences

1. 好　你

   _____

2. 我　留学生　是

   _____

3. 不　老师　是　我

   _____

4. 也　是　学生　你　吗

   _____

九、完成对话 Complete the following dialogue

A：_____？

B：我是留学生，你呢？你也是留学生吗？

A：_____。

十、根据实际情况回答问题　Answer the questions based on the actual situations

1. 你是留学生吗?

2. 你是老师吗?

10 你是哪国人
Which Country Are You from

Name: _____

一、读一读，记一记　Read and memorize

哪	nǎ	which
国	guó	country
人	rén	person; people
们	men	*used after a personal pronoun or a noun referring to a person to form a plural*
都	dōu	all; both
叫	jiào	to be called
什	shén	*an interrogative particle for a special question*
么	me	*an interrogative particle for a special question*
名	míng	name
字	zì	character
姓	xìng	one's surname is...; surname
他	tā	he; him
她	tā	she; her
认	rèn	to recognize
识	shí	to know
很	hěn	very; quite
高	gāo	high
兴	xìng	mood; excitement

二、写汉字，先描后写　Write the characters after tracing them

哪　丨 口 口 叨 叨 叨 哪 哪 哪 哪
哪 哪 哪

国　丨 冂 冂 冂 月 用 国 国
国 国 国

人　ノ 人
人 人 人

们　ノ 亻 亻 亻 们
们 们 们

都　一 十 土 耂 耂 者 者 者 者 都
都 都 都

叫　丨 口 口 叫 叫
叫 叫 叫

什　ノ 亻 亻 什
什 什 什

么　ノ 厶 么
么 么 么

第10课　你是哪国人

名 ノ ク タ 夕 名 名
| 名 | 名 | 名 | | | | | | | | | | | |

字 丶 丶 宀 宀 宁 字
| 字 | 字 | 字 | | | | | | | | | | | |

姓 ㄑ 夕 女 女＇ 女＋ 妙 姓 姓
| 姓 | 姓 | 姓 | | | | | | | | | | | |

他 ノ 亻 亻 亻 他
| 他 | 他 | 他 | | | | | | | | | | | |

她 ㄑ 夕 女 如 如 她
| 她 | 她 | 她 | | | | | | | | | | | |

认 丶 讠 认 认
| 认 | 认 | 认 | | | | | | | | | | | |

识 丶 讠 讠 汛 识 识 识
| 识 | 识 | 识 | | | | | | | | | | | |

很 ノ ク 亻 亻 亻 亻 很 很 很
| 很 | 很 | 很 | | | | | | | | | | | |

高 丶 一 亠 宀 宁 亨 亨 高 高 高 高
高 高 高

兴 丶 丶 ソ 平 兴 兴
兴 兴 兴

三、写生词 Write the new words

你	们
我	们
什	么
名	字
认	识
高	兴

四、组词 Use the characters provided to make up words or phrases

们：_____   我：_____   认：_____

什：_____   名：_____   高：_____

五、朗读与书写 Read and write

1. 朗读并抄写句子

   Read aloud the sentences and copy them

   你是哪国人？   _____
   Nǐ shì nǎ guó rén?

   他是哪国人？   _____
   Tā shì nǎ guó rén?

她 是 哪 国 人?
Tā shì nǎ guó rén?

我 也 是 留学生。
Wǒ yě shì liúxuéshēng.

他 也 是 日本 人。
Tā yě shì Rìběn rén.

我们 也是 韩国 人。
Wǒmen yě shì Hánguó rén.

我 叫 金 大成。
Wǒ jiào Jīn Dàchéng.

他 叫 金 在元。
Tā jiào Jīn Zàiyuán.

她 叫 山口 爱子。
Tā jiào Shānkǒu Àizǐ.

我们 都 是 留学生。
Wǒmen dōu shì liúxuéshēng.

他们 都 是 韩国 人。
Tāmen dōu shì Hánguó rén.

他们 都 姓 金。
Tāmen dōu xìng Jīn.

2. 在汉字上方标出调号，朗读并抄写句子

  Place the tonal mark above each character. Read aloud the sentences and copy them

  （1）我 是 日本 人，你们 是 哪 国 人?
    Wǒ shì Rìběn rén, nǐmen shì nǎ guó rén?

（2）我们 都是 韩国人。我叫 金 大成，他叫 金 在元。
Wǒmen dōu shì Hánguó rén. Wǒ jiào Jīn Dàchéng, tā jiào Jīn Zàiyuán.

_____

（3）认识 你 很 高兴。
Rènshi nǐ hěn gāoxìng.

_____

（4）我 也 是。
Wǒ yě shì.

_____

六、选词填空 Choose the words to fill in the blanks

1. 你是日本人_____? （呢　吗）

2. 你_____什么名字? （姓　叫）

3. 你是_____国人? （什么　哪）

七、给括号中的词选择适当的位置 Put the words in the brackets in the right positions

1. ___A___你们___B___留学生___C___吗? （是）

2. 你___A___是___B___国___C___人? （哪）

3. ___A___他___B___叫___C___名字? （什么）

4. 认识___A___你们___B___我___C___高兴。（很）

八、组句 Make sentences

1. 你　什么　叫　名字

_____

2. 人　是　国　你　哪

3. 是 也 人 我 日本

   _____

4. 高兴 认识 很 你

   _____

九、完成对话　Complete the following dialogue

A：_____？

B：我叫爱子，你呢？

A：我叫金大成。

B：_____？

A：不，我是韩国人。

B：_____。

A：认识你我也很高兴。

十、根据实际情况回答问题　Answer the questions based on the actual situations

1. 你叫什么名字？

2. 你姓什么？

3. 你是哪国人？

十一、综合填空　Cloze

我（1）_____山口爱子，我（2）_____日本人。金大成是韩国（3）_____，金在元（4）_____是韩国人，他们都（5）_____金。我们（6）_____是留学生。（7）_____他们我很高兴。

11 你住哪儿
Where Do You Live

Name: _____

一、读一读，记一记　Read and memorize

住	zhù	to live
儿	ér	son
宿	sù	to stay overnight
舍	shè	house; shed
几	jǐ	how many
个	gè	*a measure word of general use*
校	xiào	school
外	wài	outside
号	hào	*used after the number to mark the order*
楼	lóu	building
房	fáng	house
间	jiān	room
的	de	of
电	diàn	electric; electricity
话	huà	word; talk
码	mǎ	sign or thing indicating the number
多	duō	many; much
少	shǎo	few; little

内	nèi	inside
方	fāng	method; way
便	biàn	convenient

二、写汉字，先描后写 Write the characters after tracing them

住 ノ 亻 亻 亻 住 住 住
住 住 住

儿 ノ 儿
儿 儿 儿

宿 丶 丶 宀 宀 宀 宀 宀 宿 宿 宿
宿 宿 宿

舍 ノ 人 今 今 全 全 舍 舍
舍 舍 舍

几 ノ 几
几 几 几

个 ノ 人 个
个 个 个

第 11 课 你住哪儿

校 一 十 十 才 木 术 栌 栌 柠 柠 校
校 校 校

外 ノ ク タ 夘 外
外 外 外

号 丶 口 口 므 号
号 号 号

楼 一 十 十 才 木 术 栌 栌 桦 桦 棬 楼 楼
楼 楼 楼

房 丶 ㇇ 亠 户 户 户 房 房
房 房 房

间 丶 丨 门 门 门 问 问 间
间 间 间

的 ノ 亻 白 白 白 白 的 的
的 的 的

电 丨 口 口 日 电
电 电 电

基础汉语综合教程（上）练习活页

话　丶 讠 讠 讠 扩 许 话 话
话 话 话

码　一 丆 ア 石 石 石′ 码 码
码 码 码

多　丿 ク タ タ 多 多
多 多 多

少　丨 丩 小 少
少 少 少

内　丨 冂 内 内
内 内 内

方　丶 一 亠 方
方 方 方

便　丿 亻 亻 亻 佢 佢 佢 便 便
便 便 便

三、写生词　　Write the new words

哪儿
宿舍

34

外	校										
间	房										
话	电										
码	号										
少	多										
内	校										
便	方										

四、组词 Use the characters provided to make up words or phrases

儿：_____   校：_____   号：_____   多：_____

房：_____   电：_____   方：_____   宿：_____

五、朗读与书写 Read aloud and write

1. 朗读并抄写句子

   Read aloud the sentences and copy them

   我　住　校内。   _____
   Wǒ zhù xiàonèi.

   他　住　校外。   _____
   Tā zhù xiàowài.

   她　住　留学生　宿舍。   _____
   Tā zhù liúxuéshēng sùshè.

   你的　电话　号码　是　多少？   _____
   Nǐ de diànhuà hàomǎ shì duōshao?

你的 房间 号 是 多少？
Nǐ de fángjiān hào shì duōshao?

你的 手机（cellphone） 号 是 多少？
Nǐ de shǒujī hào shì duōshao?

住 校内 很 方便。
Zhù xiàonèi hěn fāngbiàn.

住 宿舍 很 方便。
Zhù sùshè hěn fāngbiàn.

一个 人 住 很 方便。
Yí ge rén zhù hěn fāngbiàn.

2. 在汉字上方标出调号，朗读并抄写句子

Place the tonal mark above each character. Read aloud the sentences and copy them

（1）我 住 校内 宿舍，你 住 哪儿？
Wǒ zhù xiàonèi sùshè, nǐ zhù nǎr?

（2）你 住 几 号 楼？我 住 8 号 楼 126 房间。
Nǐ zhù jǐ hào lóu? Wǒ zhù bā hào lóu yāo èr liù fángjiān.

（3）住 校内 方便 吗？很 方便。
Zhù xiàonèi fāngbiàn ma? Hěn fāngbiàn.

六、选词填空 Choose the words to fill in the blanks

1. 你住_____？（哪 哪儿）

2. 你的电话号码是_____？（几 多少）

3. 我住校外，你_____？（呢 吗）

七、给括号中的词选择适当的位置 Put the words in the brackets in the right positions

1. 我___A___7号楼___B___501房间___C___。（住）

2. ___A___你们___B___的房间号___C___是___D___？（多少）

3. ___A___住___B___留学生宿舍___C___方便。（很）

八、组句 Make sentences

1. 校外　住　我

   _____

2. 号　是　房间　的　多少　你

   _____

3. 号码　82304011　的　电话　我　是

   _____

4. 方便　校内　很　住

   _____

5. 几　楼　号　你　住

   _____

6. 住　房间　3　楼　号　501　我

   _____

九、问答练习 Ask questions and answer them

A：他住哪儿？

B：他住……

北京　（Běijīng, Beijing）	日本
美国　（Měiguó, America）	韩国
英国　（Yīngguó, England）	法国　（Fǎguó, France）

十、完成对话 Complete the following dialogue

A：_____？

B：我住校外，你呢？

A：_____。

B：_____？

A：很方便。

B：_____？

A：我的电话号码是 62328210。

十一、根据实际情况回答问题 Answer the questions based on the actual situations

1. 你住哪儿？

2. 你住几号楼几号房间？

3. 你的电话号码是多少？

十二、综合填空 Cloze

我（1）_____爱子，我（2）_____日本人。我（3）_____留学生宿舍17（4）_____楼401房间。住校内（5）_____方便。我的电话号码（6）_____62318015。

12 银行在哪儿
Where Is the Bank

Name: _____

一、读一读，记一记 **Read and memorize**

银	yín	silver
行	háng	business firm
在	zài	to be (at; in; on); to be (here; there)
请	qǐng	please
问	wèn	to ask
办	bàn	to do; to handle
公	gōng	public business
里	li	inside; inner
那	nà/nèi	that
这	zhè/zhèi	this
看	kàn	to look
红	hóng	red
就	jiù	just
层	céng	floor
去	qù	to go
起	qǐ	together
吧	ba	*a modal particle*

二、写汉字，先描后写 Write the characters after tracing them

银 ノ ヶ ╘ ┗ 钅 钅 钅 钅 银 银 银
银 银 银

行 ノ ノ 彳 彳 行 行
行 行 行

在 一 ナ オ 才 在 在
在 在 在

请 丶 讠 讠 讠 讠 诗 诗 请 请 请
请 请 请

问 丶 丨 门 门 问 问
问 问 问

办 フ 力 办 办
办 办 办

公 ノ 八 公 公
公 公 公

里 丨 口 日 曰 甲 甲 里
里 里 里

40

第 12 课　银行在哪儿

那　丁 ヨ ヨ 月 那 那
那 那 那

这　丶 亠 ㄨ 文 文 这 这
这 这 这

看　一 二 三 手 看 看 看 看
看 看 看

红　乚 幺 纟 纟 红 红
红 红 红

就　丶 亠 亠 古 古 亨 京 京 京' 京' 就 就
就 就 就

层　一 コ 尸 尸 层 层 层
层 层 层

去　一 十 土 去 去
去 去 去

起　一 十 土 卡 卡 走 走 起 起 起
起 起 起

吧　丨 ㄇ ㄇ ㄇㄱ ㄇㄇ ㄇㄩ 吧

| 吧 | 吧 | 吧 | | | | | | | | | | | | |

三、写生词　Write the new words

银	行												
请	问												
办	公	楼											
这	儿												
那	儿												
一	起												

四、组词　Use the characters provided to make up words or phrases

问：_____　　行：_____　　楼：_____　　那：_____

红：_____　　三：_____　　起：_____　　办：_____

五、朗读与书写　Read aloud and write

1. 朗读并抄写句子

　　Read aloud the sentences and copy them

　　请问，　办公室 (office) 在 哪儿？　_____
　　Qǐngwèn, bàngōngshì zài nǎr?

　　请问，　银行 在 哪儿？　_____
　　Qǐngwèn, yínháng zài nǎr?

　　请问，　宿舍 在 哪儿？　_____
　　Qǐngwèn, sùshè zài nǎr?

你看，那个人就是。
Nǐ kàn, nàge rén jiù shì.

你看，那个楼就是。
Nǐ kàn, nàge lóu jiù shì.

你看，那个房间就是。
Nǐ kàn, nàge fángjiān jiù shì.

那个银行在几层？
Nàge yínháng zài jǐ céng?

留学生办公室在几层？
Liúxuéshēng bàngōngshì zài jǐ céng?

你们的教室(classroom)在几层？
Nǐmen de jiàoshì zài jǐ céng?

2. 在汉字上方标出调号，朗读并抄写句子

   Place the tonal mark above each character. Read aloud the sentences and copy them

   （1）请问，留学生宿舍楼在哪儿？
   Qǐngwèn, liúxuéshēng sùshèlóu zài nǎr?

   （2）你看，就在那儿。那个白(white)楼就是。
   Nǐ kàn, jiù zài nàr. Nàge bái lóu jiù shì.

   （3）请问，留学生办公室在几层？
   Qǐngwèn, liúxuéshēng bàngōngshì zài jǐ céng?

   （4）银行就在一层。我们一起去吧。
   Yínháng jiù zài yī céng. Wǒmen yìqǐ qù ba.

六、选词填空 Choose the words to fill in the blanks

1. 你看，银行在_____。（那　那儿）

2. 我们一起去办公楼_____。（吧　吗）

3. 你的宿舍_____哪儿？（是　在）

七、给括号中的词选择适当的位置 Put the words in the brackets in the right positions

1. __A__我们__B__去__C__银行__D__吧。（一起）

2. __A__那个__B__红楼__C__是宿舍楼__D__。（就）

3. __A__银行__B__在__C__办公楼__D__。（里）

八、组句 Make sentences

1. 哪儿　楼　号　9　在

_____

2. 办公楼　在　里　银行

_____

3. 那　办公楼　就　是

_____

4. 我　那个　银行　也　去　，　吧　去　一起

_____

九、完成对话 Complete the following dialogue

A：请问，_____？

B：在办公楼里。

A：办公楼在哪儿？

B：_____。

A：是那个红楼吗?

B：_____。

十、根据实际情况回答问题 Answer the questions based on the actual situations

1. 你的宿舍在哪儿?

2. 你的宿舍在几层?

十一、综合填空 Cloze

银行（1）_____办公楼里，办公楼（2）_____是那个红楼。你看，就在（3）_____。我（4）_____去银行，（5）_____去吧。

单元练习（一）（第9课~第12课）
Exercises for Unit 1 (Lesson 9 ~ Lesson 12)

Name: _____ Score: _____

一、听写句子（每句2分，共10分）

Dictate the sentences (with 2 points for each and altogether 10 points)

1. _____

2. _____

3. _____

4. _____

5. _____

二、组词（每空1分，共10分）

Use the characters provided to make up words or phrases (with 1 point for each and altogether 10 points)

师：_____ 名：_____ 们：_____ 认：_____

高：_____ 便：_____ 宿：_____ 电：_____

银：_____ 间：_____

47

三、给括号中的词选择适当的位置（每题1分，共10分）

Put the words in the brackets in the right positions (with 1 point for each and altogether 10 points)

1. 他＿A＿是＿B＿留学生＿C＿吗＿D＿？（也）

2. 我是＿A＿韩国人，＿B＿是＿C＿日本人＿D＿。（不）

3. ＿A＿我们＿B＿住＿C＿校内，＿D＿你呢？（都）

4. 你＿A＿电话＿B＿号码＿C＿是多少＿D＿？（的）

5. 银行＿A＿办公楼＿B＿一层＿C＿104房间＿D＿。（在）

6. 我＿A＿也＿B＿去办公楼，＿C＿我们＿D＿去吧。（一起）

7. ＿A＿那个＿B＿红楼＿C＿是＿D＿我们的留学生宿舍。（就）

8. ＿A＿认识＿B＿你们我＿C＿也＿D＿高兴。（很）

9. ＿A＿你＿B＿的＿C＿名字叫＿D＿？（什么）

10. ＿A＿你的宿舍＿B＿个＿C＿人住＿D＿？（几）

四、选词填空（每空1分，共10分）

Choose the words to fill in the blanks (with 1 point for each and altogether 10 points)

1. 我是韩国人，他也是韩国人，我们＿＿＿＿＿＿＿是韩国人。（也 都）

2. 你的电话号码是＿＿＿＿＿＿＿？（几 多少）

3. 你好，我姓金，＿＿＿＿＿＿＿金大成。（是 叫）

4. 我住留学生宿舍，你住＿＿＿＿＿＿＿？（哪儿 那儿）

5. 爱子，你住＿＿＿＿＿＿＿号房间？（多少 几）

6. 办公楼在＿＿＿＿＿＿＿，那个红楼就是。（这儿 那儿）

7. 我是日本人，你＿＿＿＿＿＿＿？（吧 呢）

8. 你们都是日本留学生＿＿＿＿＿＿＿？（吗 呢）

9. 银行＿＿＿＿＿＿＿办公楼里。（在 是）

10. 你好，金大成，我＿＿＿＿＿＿＿爱子，你在宿舍吗？（叫 是）

五、用括号中的词语完成句子（每句 1 分，共 10 分）

Complete the following sentences using the words in the brackets (with 1 point for each and altogether 10 points)

1. A：_____？（哪国）

   B：我是日本人。

2. A：_____？（什么）

   B：我叫山口爱子。

3. A：_____。（高兴）

   B：认识你我也很高兴。

4. A：_____？（哪儿）

   B：我住留学生宿舍，你呢？

5. A：_____？（几）

   B：我住留学生宿舍 3 号楼。

6. A：_____？（多少）

   B：我的电话是 15904217568。

7. A：_____？（吗）

   B：我不是日本人，我是韩国人。

8. A：_____？（请问）

   B：银行在那个红楼的一层。

9. A：你们都是留学生吗？

   B：是，_____。（都是）

10. A：我不是中国人，爱子呢？

    B：_____。（也）

六、组句（每句1分，10分）
Make sentences (with 1 point for each and altogether 10 points)

1. 都　留学生　他们　是　韩国

   _____

2. 吗　留学生　你们　是

   _____

3. 名字　他　什么　叫

   _____

4. 我　高兴　认识　也　你们　很

   _____

5. 楼　他　8号　校内　住

   _____

6. 是　的　多少　号码　你　电话

   _____

7. 办公楼　里　在　银行

   _____

8. 宿舍　一起　吧　他　我们　的　去

   _____

9. 老师　都　我们　的　中国人　是

   _____

10. 方便　宿舍　住　留学生　很

    _____

七、完成对话（每句2分，共20分）
Complete the following dialogues (with 2 points for each and altogether 20 points)

1. A：你好，_____？

   B：是，你呢？

A：我也是留学生。

B：_____？

A：我是日本人。

B：我是韩国人。_____？

A：我叫山口爱子，你叫什么名字?

B：我叫金在元。

A：_____。

B：认识你我也很高兴。

2. A：杰克，_____？

B：我去银行。

A：银行在哪儿?

B：_____。

A：办公楼在哪儿?

B：就是那个红楼。

A：我也去银行，_____。

B：好，一起去。

A：我住校内，_____？

B：我住校外。_____？

A：很方便。

B：_____？

A：62935432。

八、综合填空（每空1分，共10分）

Cloze (with 1 point for each and altogether 10 points)

我叫山口爱子，我（1）_____日本留学生。我（2）_____校内8（3）_____楼401房间，我的（4）_____是62318015。我觉得（juéde, to think）住校内很（5）_____。他们是我的朋友（péngyou, friend）金大成、金在元，他们（6）_____是韩国人。我（7）_____银行，他们（8）_____去，银行（9）_____办公楼一层，办公楼（10）_____那个红楼。

九、根据题目写一段话（10分，可任选一题，60～80字）

Write a composition (with 10 points; choose one of the following topics to write a composition of 60-80 characters)

1. 介绍（jièshào）自己（zìjǐ） Introduce Yourself
2. 我的朋友（péngyou） My Friend

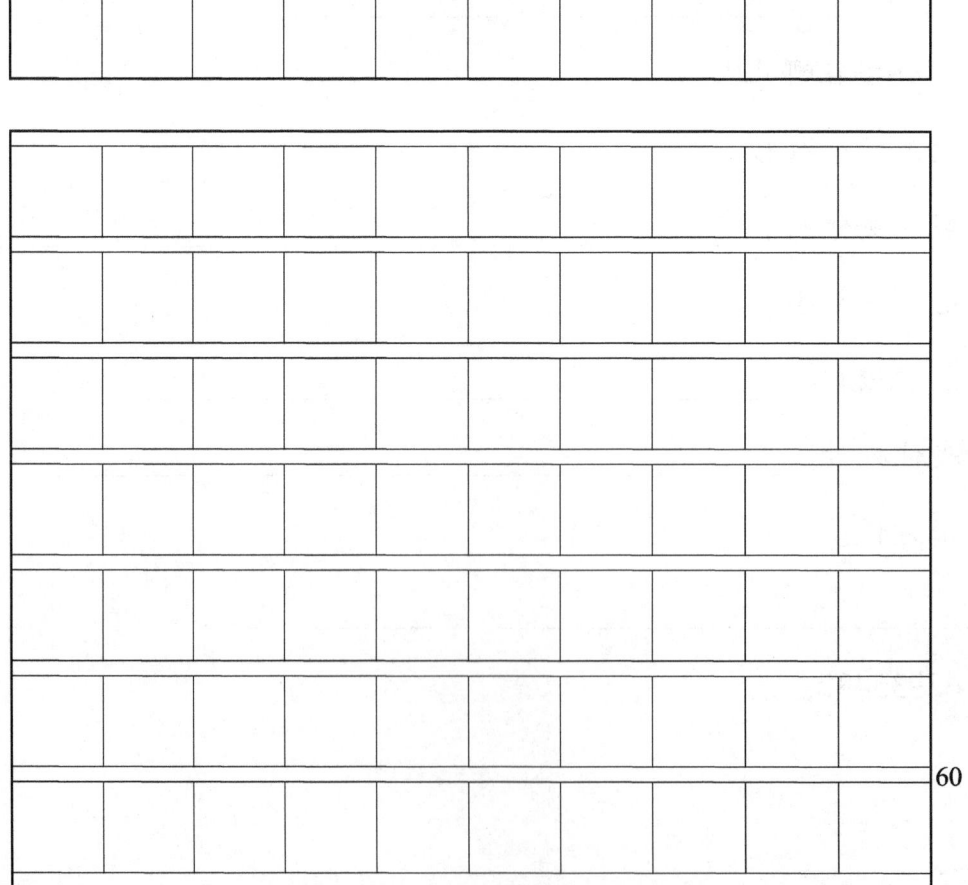

80

13 明天你有课吗
Will You Have Classes Tomorrow

Name: _____

一、读一读，记一记 Read and memorize

明	míng	bright
天	tiān	day
有	yǒu	to have
课	kè	lesson; class
上	shàng	upper; up
午	wǔ	noon
四	sì	four
节	jié	*a measure word for class hours*
八	bā	eight
点	diǎn	o'clock
半	bàn	half
十	shí	ten
二	èr	two
下	xià	below; down
没	méi	not to have
图	tú	picture
书	shū	book
馆	guǎn	a place for cultural activities; shop

文	wén	language
远	yuǎn	far
三	sān	three

二、写汉字，先描后写 Write the characters after tracing them

明 丨 冂 月 日 旫 明 明 明
明 明 明

天 一 二 于 天
天 天 天

有 一 ナ 才 有 有 有
有 有 有

课 丶 讠 讠 订 讱 诏 评 课 课
课 课 课

上 丨 卜 上
上 上 上

午 丿 ㇏ 二 午
午 午 午

四 丨 冂 四 四 四
四 四 四

节 一 艹 艹 芍 节

八 丿 八

点 丨 卜 占 占 占 点 点

半 丶 丶 丷 丷 半

十 一 十

二 一 二

下 一 丅 下

没 丶 丶 冫 冫 沪 沢 没

图 丨 冂 冂 冈 冈 图 图
图 图 图

书 乛 ㇇ 书 书
书 书 书

馆 丿 ㇏ 饣 饣 饣 饣 饣 馆 馆 馆
馆 馆 馆

文 丶 一 ナ 文
文 文 文

远 一 二 テ 元 沅 远 远
远 远 远

三 一 二 三
三 三 三

三、写生词　Write the new words

明	天							
上	午							
上	课							
十	二							

下	课											
图	书	馆										
外	文	书										

四、组词 Use the characters provided to make up words or phrases

明：_____　　有：_____　　午：_____　　图：_____

外：_____　　课：_____　　远：_____　　没：_____

五、朗读与书写 Read aloud and write

1. 朗读并抄写短语

　　Read aloud the phrases and copy them

今天　上午　_____
jīntiān shàngwǔ

明天　下午　_____
míngtiān xiàwǔ

后天　晚上　_____
hòutiān wǎnshang

去　图书馆　_____
qù túshūguǎn

去　银行　_____
qù yínháng

去　办公楼　_____
qù bàngōnglóu

四节课　_____
sì jié kè

五 个 人　_____
wǔ ge rén

八 层 楼　_____
bā céng lóu

2. 在汉字上方标出调号，朗读并抄写句子

Place the tonal mark above each character. Read aloud the sentences and copy them

（1）明天　你有课吗？我　明天　上午　有 四 节 课。
Míngtiān nǐ yǒu kè ma? Wǒ míngtiān shàngwǔ yǒu sì jié kè.

_____

（2）明天　我 去 图书馆，那儿 有 很 多 外 文 书。
Míngtiān wǒ qù túshūguǎn, nàr yǒu hěn duō wàiwén shū.

_____

（3）图书馆　远 吗？不 远。
Túshūguǎn yuǎn ma? Bù yuǎn.

_____

（4）我们　三 点 去 图书馆，好 吗？
Wǒmen sān diǎn qù túshūguǎn, hǎo ma?

_____

六、选词填空　Choose the words to fill in the blanks

1. 我明天上午_____四节课。（有　是）

2. 那个图书馆_____外文书。（没有　不是）

3. 图书馆的外文书很_____。（多　远）

七、给括号中的词选择适当的位置　Put the words in the brackets in the right positions

1. __A__我__B__明天__C__下午__D__课。（没有）

2. __A__图书馆__B__有__C__多__D__外文书。（很）

3. ___A___ 我下午三点 ___B___ 去 ___C___ 办公楼。（也）

八、组句　Make sentences

1. 图书馆　去　我　明天

   _____

2. 上午　明天　我　节　有　四　课

   _____

3. 人　有　银行　很多

   _____

4. 宿舍　远　我　不　的

   _____

九、完成对话　Complete the following dialogue

A：_____？

B：有，你呢？

A：_____。

B：你有几节课？

A：_____。

B：四节课不多。我们下午去图书馆吧。

A：_____。

十、根据实际情况回答问题　Answer the questions based on the actual situations

1. 你明天有课吗？有几节课？

2. 你明天几点上课？几点下课？

3. 你们学校（xuéxiào, school）有图书馆吗？

4. 图书馆有外文书吗？

十一、综合填空 Cloze

明天我（1）_____很多课，上午有课，下午（2）_____有课。上午有四（3）_____课，下午有两（liǎng, two）节（4）_____。下午四（5）_____下课。我五点（6）_____图书馆。图书馆不远，（7）_____有很（8）_____外文书。

14 周末你做什么
What Do You Do on Weekends

Name: _____

一、读一读，记一记 Read and memorize

周	zhōu	week
末	mò	end
做	zuò	to do
星	xīng	star
期	qī	phase
六	liù	six
打	dǎ	to work out
算	suàn	to plan
习	xí	to practice
休	xiū	to rest
息	xī	to rest
后	hòu	after
商	shāng	trade
店	diàn	shop
买	mǎi	to buy; to purchase
东	dōng	east
西	xī	west
游	yóu	to swim

泳	yǒng	to swim
作	zuò	task
业	yè	job
踢	tī	to kick; to play
足	zú	foot
球	qiú	ball

二、写汉字，先描后写　Write the characters after tracing them

周　丿 冂 刌 冃 用 周 周

周 周 周

末　一 二 丰 才 末

末 末 末

做　丿 亻 亻 什 什 估 估 伆 做 做 做

做 做 做

星　丶 冂 冂 日 尸 尸 早 星 星

星 星 星

期　一 十 廾 甘 甘 其 其 其 期 期 期 期

期 期 期

六　丶 亠 六 六

六 六 六

第14课 周末你做什么

打 一 十 扌 打 打
打 打 打

算 ノ ⺮ ⺮ ⺮ ⺮ ⺮ 竹 竹 笃 笪 笪 算 算 算
算 算 算

习 フ 刁 习
习 习 习

休 ノ 亻 亻 什 什 休
休 休 休

息 ノ 亻 冂 甪 甪 自 自 息 息 息
息 息 息

后 丿 厂 厂 斤 后 后
后 后 后

商 丶 亠 亠 亠 产 产 产 商 商 商
商 商 商

店 丶 亠 广 广 广 店 店 店
店 店 店

买 乛 亠 ㆇ 乥 买 买

东 一 七 冇 东 东

西 一 丆 襾 襾 西 西

游 丶 丶 氵 氵 氵 沽 汸 汸 浡 游 游 游

泳 丶 丶 氵 氵 汀 汈 泳 泳

作 丿 亻 亻 竹 竹 作 作

业 丨 亅 丬 业 业 业

踢 丨 口 口 口 甲 甲 旲 趴 趴 跙 跙 跙 踢 踢 踢

足 丶 ㄇ ㅁ 甲 甲 足 足

足 足 足

球 一 ニ ㇒ 干 王 王ˊ 玎 玎 玎 球 球 球

球 球 球

三、写生词　Write the new words

周	末		
星	期		
星	期	六	
星	期	天	
星	期	一	
星	期	二	
星	期	三	
星	期	四	
星	期	五	
打	算		
学	习		
休	息		
后	天		

商	店											
东	西											
游	泳											
作	业											
足	球											

四、组词 Use the characters provided to make up words or phrases

周：_____   星：_____   算：_____   习：_____

买：_____   东：_____   休：_____   踢：_____

后：_____   商：_____   游：_____   做：_____

五、朗读与书写 Read aloud and write

1. 朗读并抄写短语和句子

   Read aloud the phrases and sentences and copy them

   上午　学习　_____
   shàngwǔ xuéxí

   下午　休息　_____
   xiàwǔ xiūxi

   星期六　游泳　_____
   xīngqīliù yóuyǒng

   昨天　星期四。_____
   Zuótiān xīngqīsì.

   今天　星期五。_____
   Jīntiān xīngqīwǔ.

后天　星期天。　　　　＿＿＿＿＿＿＿＿＿＿＿＿＿＿＿
Hòutiān xīngqītiān.

一 天 学习，一 天 休息。　＿＿＿＿＿＿＿＿＿＿＿＿＿＿＿
Yì tiān xuéxí, yì tiān xiūxi.

一 天 休息，一 天 上课。　＿＿＿＿＿＿＿＿＿＿＿＿＿＿＿
Yì tiān xiūxi, yì tiān shàngkè.

一 天 买 东西，一 天 做 作业。　＿＿＿＿＿＿＿＿＿＿＿＿＿
Yì tiān mǎi dōngxi, yì tiān zuò zuòyè.

2. 在汉字上方标出调号，朗读并抄写句子

   Place the tonal mark above each character. Read aloud the sentences and copy them

   （1）我　星期六　打算　去　故宫，你呢？
   　　Wǒ xīngqīliù dǎsuan qù Gùgōng, nǐ ne?

   　　＿＿＿＿＿＿＿＿＿＿＿＿＿＿＿＿＿＿＿＿＿＿＿＿＿＿＿＿＿＿

   （2）我　一 天　学习，一 天　休息。星期六　学习，星期天　休息。
   　　Wǒ yì tiān xuéxí, yì tiān xiūxi. Xīngqīliù xuéxí, xīngqītiān xiūxi.

   　　＿＿＿＿＿＿＿＿＿＿＿＿＿＿＿＿＿＿＿＿＿＿＿＿＿＿＿＿＿＿

   （3）我　上午　买　东西，下午　游泳，你呢？
   　　Wǒ shàngwǔ mǎi dōngxi, xiàwǔ yóuyǒng, nǐ ne?

   　　＿＿＿＿＿＿＿＿＿＿＿＿＿＿＿＿＿＿＿＿＿＿＿＿＿＿＿＿＿＿

   （4）我　星期天　上午　做　作业，下午　踢足球。
   　　Wǒ xīngqītiān shàngwǔ zuò zuòyè, xiàwǔ tī zúqiú.

   　　＿＿＿＿＿＿＿＿＿＿＿＿＿＿＿＿＿＿＿＿＿＿＿＿＿＿＿＿＿＿

六、选词填空　Choose the words to fill in the blanks

1. 星期六你做＿＿＿＿＿＿＿？（什么　哪）

2. 我明天打算去商店买东西，你＿＿＿＿＿＿＿？（呢　吗）

3. 我们周末_____足球。（做　踢）

4. 我_____明天下午去图书馆。（打算　做）

七、组句　Make sentences

1. 做　下午　你　什么　星期六

   _____

2. 去　他　打算　商店　十二点

   _____

3. 下午　我　银行　今天　去

   _____

4. 星期　后天　五

   _____

5. 图书馆　我　明天　看　去　书

   _____

八、完成对话　Complete the following dialogue

A：_____？

B：我明天打算去图书馆。

A：_____？

B：明天星期三。

A：_____？

B：我星期天休息，你呢？

A：_____。

九、根据实际情况回答问题　Answer the questions based on the actual situations

1. 你几点上课？

2. 明天星期几?

3. 你明天打算做什么?

4. 你周末做什么?

十、综合填空　　Cloze

明天星期六，我（1）＿＿＿＿＿＿＿去故宫。星期天我上午（2）＿＿＿＿＿＿＿东西，下午（3）＿＿＿＿＿＿＿作业。爱子周末一天（4）＿＿＿＿＿＿＿，一天（5）＿＿＿＿＿＿＿。

15 你的生日是几月几号
When Is Your Birthday

Name: _____

一、读一读，记一记 Read and memorize

月	yuè	month
今	jīn	today
昨	zuó	yesterday
祝	zhù	to wish
快	kuài	quick; fast
乐	lè	happy
年	nián	year
多	duō	how
大	dà	old; big; large
九	jiǔ	nine
岁	suì	age
属	shǔ	to be born in the year of
鸡	jī	chicken
出	chū	to go out
狗	gǒu	dog
晚	wǎn	evening
过	guò	to celebrate; to spend
主	zhǔ	main
意	yì	idea; meaning

二、写汉字，先描后写 Write the characters after tracing them

月 丿 几 月 月
月 月 月

今 丿 人 𠆢 今
今 今 今

昨 丨 冂 日 日 日' 昨 昨 昨
昨 昨 昨

祝 丶 ㇇ 礻 礻 礻 祀 祝 祝
祝 祝 祝

快 丶 丷 忄 忄 忄 快 快
快 快 快

乐 一 二 千 乐 乐
乐 乐 乐

年 丿 𠂉 匚 午 午 年
年 年 年

多 丿 ク 夕 多 多 多
多 多 多

第15课　你的生日是几月几号

大　一 ナ 大
大 大 大

九　ノ 九
九 九 九

岁　丨 山 山 屮 岁 岁
岁 岁 岁

属　フ ⺘ 尸 尸 尸 尸 屋 属 属 属
属 属 属

鸡　フ 又 ヌ′ ㄡ勹 ㄡ勺 鸡 鸡
鸡 鸡 鸡

出　⼁ ⼂ 屮 中 出 出
出 出 出

狗　ノ ⺨ 犭 犭′ 犭ク 犭句 狗 狗
狗 狗 狗

晚　丨 冂 冂 日 日′ 日″ 旷 旷 晚 晚 晚
晚 晚 晚

过 一 十 寸 寸 讨 过

主 丶 亠 二 主 主

意 丶 亠 亠 六 立 产 产 音 音 音 意 意 意

三、写生词　Write the new words

生	日
今	天
昨	天
快	乐
今	年
多	大
十	九
十	八
出	生
晚	上
	主意

第 15 课　你的生日是几月几号

四、组词　Use the characters provided to make up words or phrases

生：_____　　今：_____　　快：_____　　岁：_____

属：_____　　上：_____　　意：_____　　年：_____

五、朗读与书写　Read aloud and write

1. 朗读并抄写短语和句子

   Read aloud the phrases and sentences and copy them

   多　大　　_____
   duō dà

   多　远　　_____
   duō yuǎn

   我　属　鸡。　_____
   Wǒ shǔ jī.

   你　属　狗。　_____
   Nǐ shǔ gǒu.

   一起　学习　　_____
   yìqǐ xuéxí

   一起　游泳　　_____
   yìqǐ yóuyǒng

   一起　过　生日　_____
   yìqǐ guò shēngrì

   一起　买　东西　_____
   yìqǐ mǎi dōngxi

2. 在汉字上方标出调号，朗读并抄写句子

　　Place the tonal mark above each character. Read aloud the sentences and copy them

（1）今天 是你的 生日，祝你 生日 快乐！
　　　Jīntiān shì nǐ de shēngrì, zhù nǐ shēngrì kuàilè!

　　_____

（2）你 今年 多 大？我 今年 十九 岁。
　　　Nǐ jīnnián duō dà? Wǒ jīnnián shíjiǔ suì.

　　_____

（3）我 十八 岁，一九九四 年 出生。
　　　Wǒ shíbā suì, yī jiǔ jiǔ sì nián chūshēng.

　　_____

（4）我 属 鸡，你 属 狗。
　　　Wǒ shǔ jī, nǐ shǔ gǒu.

　　_____

（5）你的 生日 是几月几号？我的 生日 是九月二十八 号。
　　　Nǐ de shēngrì shì jǐ yuè jǐ hào? Wǒ de shēngrì shì jiǔyuè èrshíbā hào.

　　_____

（6）我们 打算 今天 晚上 一起过 生日。
　　　Wǒmen dǎsuan jīntiān wǎnshang yìqǐ guò shēngrì.

　　_____

六、填空　Fill in the blanks

1. 祝你_____快乐！

2. 我的生日是九_____十八_____。

3. 我一九九四年_____，_____狗。

4. 我们_____今天晚上一起_____生日。

七、给括号中的词语选择适当的位置 Put the words in the brackets in the right positions

1. ___A___ 老师的生日 ___B___ 是 ___C___ 十一月。（也）

2. ___A___ 下午我们 ___B___ 去 ___C___ 银行吧！（一起）

3. ___A___ 你 ___B___ 哪天 ___C___ 生日？（过）

4. 你们 ___A___ 去哪儿 ___B___ 买 ___C___ 外文书？（打算）

八、组句 Make sentences

1. 快乐　生日　你　祝

_____

2. 一九八二　日　五　十六　月　我　年　出生　，　狗　属

_____

3. 的　你　生日　是　月　日　几　几

_____

4. 下午　明天　我们　一起　打算　生日　过

_____

九、完成对话 Complete the following dialogue

A：_____？

B：我今年二十岁。

A：你的生日是哪天？

B：_____。

A：是吗？我的生日也在那个月。

B：_____。

A：好主意，我们过生日做什么？

B：_____。

十、根据实际情况回答问题 Answer the questions based on the actual situations

1. 一年有多少个月？

2. 一年有多少个星期？

3. 一年有多少天？

4. 十二月有多少天？四月有多少天？

5. 今年五月有几个星期天？

6. 你星期几没有课？

十一、综合填空 Cloze

今天（1）_____ 我的生日，我一九九四年（2）_____，（3）_____ 狗，今年十八（4）_____。今天我（5）_____ 高兴，老师和同学（tóngxué, classmate）们（6）_____ 祝我生日快乐。今天下午我（7）_____ 课，我打算下午（8）_____ 商店（9）_____ 东西，晚上跟（gēn, with）同学们（10）_____ 过生日。

16 咖啡多少钱一杯

How Much Is a Cup of Coffee

Name: _____

一、读一读，记一记 Read and memorize

咖	kā	（咖啡）coffee
啡	fēi	
钱	qián	money
杯	bēi	cup
服	fú	to serve
务	wù	affair; business
员	yuán	a person engaged in some field of activity
水	shuǐ	water
瓶	píng	bottle
块	kuài	*a unit of Chinese currency, equivalent to 10 mao*; piece
五	wǔ	five
牛	niú	cattle; ox
奶	nǎi	milk
要	yào	to want
两	liǎng	two
还	hái	also; in addition
果	guǒ	fruit
蛋	dàn	egg

81

糕	gāo	cake
共	gòng	total
给	gěi	to give
您	nín	you (*the respectful form of "你"*)

二、写汉字，先描后写　Write the characters after tracing them

咖　丨 ｜ 口 叨 叻 咖 咖
咖 咖 咖

啡　丨 ｜ 口 叮 叶 吁 때 啡 啡 啡
啡 啡 啡

钱　丿 一 ⺆ ⺆ 钅 钅 钅 钱 钱 钱
钱 钱 钱

杯　一 十 オ 木 杧 杯 杯
杯 杯 杯

服　丿 刀 月 月 刖 肌 服 服
服 服 服

务　丿 ク 夂 冬 务
务 务 务

第16课　咖啡多少钱一杯

员　丶 口 口 尸 吊 员 员
员 员 员

水　亅 刀 水 水
水 水 水

瓶　丶 丶 兰 兰 羊 并 并 瓶 瓶 瓶
瓶 瓶 瓶

块　一 十 土 țョ 圠 块 块
块 块 块

五　一 丁 五 五
五 五 五

牛　丿 匸 匚 牛
牛 牛 牛

奶　乚 乚 女 女 奶 奶
奶 奶 奶

要　一 厂 厂 冂 丙 西 要 要 要
要 要 要

两 一 ㄏ 厂 丙 丙 两 两
两 两 两

还 一 ㄐ 不 不 不 还 还
还 还 还

果 丨 冂 冂 日 旦 甲 果 果
果 果 果

蛋 フ フ ア ア 疋 疋 吞 吞 番 蛋 蛋
蛋 蛋 蛋

糕 丶 丶 丷 丬 半 米 米 米 米 米 糕 糕 糕 糕 糕
糕 糕 糕

共 一 十 卄 共 共 共
共 共 共

给 ㄥ ㄠ 纟 纟 纟 纟 纟 给 给
给 给 给

您 丿 亻 亻 伫 伫 你 你 您 您 您
您 您 您

第16课　咖啡多少钱一杯

三、写生词　Write the new words

咖	啡											
服	务	员										
服	务											
牛	奶											
水	果											
蛋	糕											
一	共											

四、组词　Use the characters provided to make up words or phrases

咖：_____　　　牛：_____　　　水：_____

蛋：_____　　　共：_____　　　服：_____

五、朗读与书写　Read aloud and write

1. 朗读并抄写句子

　　Read aloud the sentences and copy them

蛋糕　多少　钱　一　块？　_____
Dàngāo duōshao qián yí kuài?

咖啡　多少　钱　一　杯？　_____
Kāfēi duōshao qián yì bēi?

水　多少　钱　一　瓶？　_____
Shuǐ duōshao qián yì píng?

还要　什么？　_____
Hái yào shénme?

还 买 什么？
Hái mǎi shénme?

还 学 什么？
Hái xué shénme?

一共 十三 块。
Yígòng shísān kuài.

一共 八 块 四。
Yígòng bā kuài sì.

一共 二十 块 一。
Yígòng èrshí kuài yī.

2. 在汉字上方标出调号，朗读并抄写句子

   Place the tonal mark above each character. Read aloud the sentences and copy them

   （1）请问， 水 多少 钱 一 瓶？ 一 块 五 一 瓶。
   Qǐngwèn, shuǐ duōshao qián yì píng? Yí kuài wǔ yì píng.

   （2）我 要 两 瓶 水、一 杯 牛奶、一 块 水果 蛋糕。
   Wǒ yào liǎng píng shuǐ、yì bēi niúnǎi、yí kuài shuǐguǒ dàngāo.

   （3）两 瓶 水 三 块，一 杯 牛奶 三 块，一 块 蛋糕 六 块
   Liǎng píng shuǐ sān kuài, yì bēi niúnǎi sān kuài, yí kuài dàngāo liù kuài

   五，一共 十二 块 五。
   wǔ, yígòng shí'èr kuài wǔ.

   （4）这 是 十二 块 五，给 您 钱。
   Zhè shì shí'èr kuài wǔ, gěi nín qián.

六、给括号中的词语选择适当的位置　Put the words in the brackets in the right positions

1. ＿A＿咖啡＿B＿钱＿＿C＿一杯＿＿D＿？（多少）

2. ＿A＿我们＿B＿要一杯牛奶、一杯咖啡，＿C＿要三瓶水＿D＿。（还）

3. ＿A＿你买的＿B＿东西＿C＿多少钱＿D＿？（一共）

七、读一读，写一写：是"二"还是"两"？
Read and decide which character is used, "二" or "两", and then write the correct answers in the brackets

1. A：这是多少钱？

　　B：这是20879.02元。（　　）（　　）

2. 老师的电话号码是13670234082。（　　）（　　）

3. 我们那儿有3200个留学生，102个老师。（　　）（　　）

4. 你好，我要2瓶水。（　　）

5. A：你去哪儿？

　　B：我去215房间。（　　）

6. A：先生，你买几块蛋糕？

　　B：2块。（　　）

八、组句　Make sentences

1. 请问 , 牛奶 钱 杯 多少 一

_____

2. 打算 哪儿 你们 还 去

_____

3. 明天 一共 我们 四 有 课 节

_____

4. 要 我 瓶 两 水，要 还 个 水果 一 蛋糕

_____

5. 小姐，你 给 钱，十二 一共 五 块

_____

九、完成对话 Complete the following dialogue

A：_____？

B：我买水，一瓶水多少钱？

A：_____。

B：牛奶呢？

A：_____。

B：蛋糕多少钱一块？

A：_____。

B：好，我要两瓶水、一杯牛奶、一块蛋糕，_____？

A：_____。

B：_____。

十、根据实际情况回答问题 Answer the questions based on the actual situations

1. 你住哪儿？你去哪儿买东西？

2. 那儿的商店有什么东西？那儿的东西好吗？

3. 周末你买东西吗？买什么东西？

4. 商店的咖啡多少钱一杯？

5. 商店有水果蛋糕吗？

十一、综合填空　Cloze

今天我去商店（1）_____东西，那儿的牛奶、蛋糕（2）_____好，我（3）_____服务员牛奶（4）_____钱一杯，他告诉（gàosu, to tell）我三块钱一杯，我说我（5）_____一杯牛奶。服务员问我（6）_____要什么，他说水果蛋糕（7）_____很好吃（hǎochī, delicious），四块五一（8）_____。我要了一杯牛奶和两块蛋糕，（9）_____是十二块钱。我（10）_____服务员十五块，他找（zhǎo, to give back）我三块钱。

单元练习（二）（第13课～第16课）
Exercises for Unit 2 (Lesson 13 ~ Lesson 16)

Name: _____ Score: _____

一、听写句子（每句2分，共10分）

Dictate the sentences (with 2 points for each and altogether 10 points)

1. _____
   _____

2. _____
   _____

3. _____
   _____

4. _____
   _____

5. _____
   _____

二、组词（每空1分，共10分）

Use the characters provided to make up words or phrases (with 1 point for each and altogether 10 points)

午：_____   课：_____   周：_____   打：_____

学：_____   休：_____   商：_____   作：_____

水：_____   游：_____

三、给括号中的词选择适当的位置（每题1分，共10分）

Put the words in the brackets in the right positions (with 1 point for each and altogether 10 points)

1. ___A___ 图书馆 ___B___ 很多 ___C___ 外文书 ___D___ 。（有）

2. ___A___ 我 ___B___ 星期六 ___C___ 去商店 ___D___ 买东西。（上午）

3. 今天晚上 ___A___ 我们 ___B___ 一起 ___C___ 去 ___D___ 游泳。（打算）

4. ___A___ 我 ___B___ 要两瓶水、一杯牛奶，___C___ 要 ___D___ 一块水果蛋糕。（还）

5. 我的生日 ___A___ 是 ___B___ 九月二十八号，___C___ 他的生日 ___D___ 在九月。（也）

6. 我 ___A___ 一九八二年 ___B___ 十一月 ___C___ 三日 ___D___ 。（出生）

7. ___A___ 你的东西 ___B___ 五十四块 ___C___ 八 ___D___ 。（一共）

8. ___A___ 周末我 ___B___ 打算去 ___C___ 踢足球 ___D___ 。（不）

9. ___A___ 你 ___B___ 今年 ___C___ ?（多大）

10. ___A___ 牛奶 ___B___ 钱 ___C___ 一杯 ___D___ ?（多少）

四、选词填空（每空1分，共10分）

Choose the words to fill in the blanks (with 1 point for each and altogether 10 points)

1. 爱子明天下午_____有课。（不 没）

2. 他_____是留学生，他是我们的老师。（不 没）

3. 明天星期_____?（几 多少）

4. 这本（běn, a measure word for books）外文书_____钱？（几 多少）

5. 明天星期六，你打算做_____?（哪儿 什么）

6. 周末我们去_____踢足球？（哪儿 什么）

7. 咖啡多少钱一_____?（杯 块）

8. 我要水、牛奶、咖啡，_____要一块蛋糕。（也 还）

9. 你看，银行就在_____。那个红楼就是。（哪儿 那儿）

10. 我们今天晚上一起_____生日。（过 做）

单元练习（二）（第13课～第16课）

五、用括号中的词语完成句子（每句1分，共10分）

Complete the following sentences using the words in the brackets (with 1 point for each and altogether 10 points)

1. A：后天你有课吗？

   B：_____ （有）

2. A：下午我也打算去图书馆，_____，_____？ （好吗）

   B：行。

3. A：_____？ （什么）

   B：明天下午我去踢足球。

4. A：_____？ （多大）

   B：我二十二岁。

5. A：_____？ （属）

   B：我属狗。

6. A：_____？ （几）

   B：我的生日是六月二十六号。

7. A：_____？ （多少）

   B：咖啡十八块一杯。

8. A：你去哪儿？

   B：_____，_____。 （还）

9. A：我今年十八岁，_____？ （呢）

   B：我今年十九岁。

10. A：今天是我的生日。

    B：是吗？_____。 （祝）

六、组句（每句1分，共10分）

Make sentences (with 1 point for each and altogether 10 points)

1. 课 我 没有 明天 上午 ， 节 有 两 下午 课

   _____

2. 不 图书馆 那 远 个 ， 外文书 多 很 有 那儿

   _____

3. 东西 打算 我 去 星期六 买 上午

   _____

4. 星期 明天 六 ， 什么 做 你

   _____

5. 打算 一起 他们 生日 晚上 过 明天

   _____

6. 生日 我 的 今天 是 十八岁

   _____

7. 都 我们 鸡 属

   _____

8. 我 月 一九九八年 三 号 出生 二十四

   _____

9. 您 东西 八十六 的 一共 块

   _____

10. 请问 ， 钱 水 多少 瓶 一

    _____

七、完成对话（每句2分，共20分）

Complete the following dialogues (with 2 points for each and altogether 20 points)

1. A：_____？

   B：我星期五上午有两节课，下午没有课。你呢？

A：_____。

B：没有课，你打算做什么？

A：_____，你去吗？

B：去。

A：好，我们一起去吧。

2. A：爱子，你的生日是几月几号？

B：_____。

A：明天是你的生日，_____！

B：谢谢（xièxie, thanks），_____？

A：我的生日也是九月。你今年多大？

B：_____，你呢？

A：_____。

B：我打算明天晚上过生日，我们一起过生日吧。

A：好的。

3. A：你好，你要什么？

B：_____，_____？

A：一块五一瓶。

B：咖啡呢？

A：咖啡四块一杯。

B：_____？

A：有，牛奶三块钱一杯。

B：我要两瓶水、一杯咖啡、一杯牛奶。

A：_____？

B：不要了，谢谢。

八、综合填空（每空1分，共10分）
Cloze (with 1 point for each and altogether 10 points)

明天星期五，金大成上午（1）_____四节课，下午（2）_____有课。他（3）_____明天下午去图书馆，（4）_____有很多外文书。星期六金大成打算（5）_____故宫，爱子（6）_____去，他们打算九点去。星期天金大成上午（7）_____作业，下午（8）_____足球；爱子上午去商店（9）_____，下午（10）_____。

九、根据题目写一段话（10分，可任选一题，60～80字）
Write a composition (with 10 points; choose one of the topics to write a composition of 60-80 characters)

1. 我的周末　　One of My Weekends

2. 我的一天　　One Day of My Life

单元练习（二）（第13课～第16课）

60

80